Community and Catastrophe

T&T Clark Studies in Anabaptist Theology and Ethics

Series Editors:
Laura Schmidt Roberts and Paul Martens

Community and Catastrophe

An Ecclesio-Political Reading of the Schleitheim Confession

Marius van Hoogstraten

t&tclark

LONDON · NEW YORK · OXFORD · NEW DELHI · SYDNEY

T&T CLARK

Bloomsbury Publishing Plc, 50 Bedford Square, London, WC1B 3DP, UK
Bloomsbury Publishing Inc, 1359 Broadway, New York, NY 10018, USA
Bloomsbury Publishing Ireland, 29 Earlsfort Terrace, Dublin 2, D02 AY28, Ireland

BLOOMSBURY, T&T CLARK and the T&T Clark logo are trademarks of
Bloomsbury Publishing Plc

First published in Great Britain 2026
Copyright © Marius van Hoogstraten, 2026

Marius van Hoogstraten has asserted his right under the Copyright, Designs and Patents
Act, 1988, to be identified as Author of this work.

For legal purposes the Acknowledgments on pp. viii–ix constitute an extension of this
copyright page.

Cover design by Lara Himpelmann
Cover image: Abstract painting of fire with red, orange, yellow and black © Getty Images

All rights reserved. No part of this publication may be: i) reproduced or transmitted in
any form, electronic or mechanical, including photocopying, recording or by means of
any information storage or retrieval system without prior permission in writing from the
publishers; or ii) used or reproduced in any way for the training, development or operation
of artificial intelligence (AI) technologies, including generative AI technologies. The rights
holders expressly reserve this publication from the text and data mining exception as per
Article 4(3) of the Digital Single Market Directive (EU) 2019/790.

Bloomsbury Publishing Plc does not have any control over, or responsibility for, any third-
party websites referred to or in this book. All internet addresses given in this book were
correct at the time of going to press. The author and publisher regret any inconvenience
caused if addresses have changed or sites have ceased to exist, but can accept no
responsibility for any such changes.

A catalogue record for this book is available from the British Library.

Library of Congress Control Number: 2025943290

ISBN: HB: 978-0-5677-2456-4
PB: 978-0-5677-2452-6
ePDF: 978-0-5677-2453-3
eBook: 978-0-5677-2454-0

Series: T&T Clark Studies in Anabaptist Theology and Ethics

Typeset by Newgen KnowledgeWorks Pvt. Ltd., Chennai, India
Printed and bound in Great Britain

For product safety related questions contact productsafety@bloomsbury.com.

To find out more about our authors and books visit www.bloomsbury.com
and sign up for our newsletters.

CONTENTS

Acknowledgments viii

Introduction 1
   Life after Hope 1
   Gathering in Dark Times 3
   Ecclesio-Political 8

1 Beginning 13
   Introduction 13
   Decision and Ambiguity 14
   Reading 17
   The Freedom to Begin 20
   Beginning Again 24
   Conclusion 28

2 Repetition 31
   Introduction 31
   Reading 32
   Asserting the Ecclesio-Political 36
   Negotiating Ambiguity 38
   Repetition 41
   Conclusion 45

3 Presence 47
   Introduction 47
   Reading 48
   Assembled Copresence 51
   A Calling Absence 55
   A Presence without Place 59
   Conclusion 61

4 Refuge 63

Introduction 63
A Shelter for Newness 64
Reading 66
Catastrophe 68
The World and Its Evil 72
... and Other Things of That Kind 75
A Community of Refuge 78
Conclusion 79

5 Process 81

Introduction 81
Reading 82
A Kind of Care Work 84
Re-Presentation 87
A Self-Governing Flock 88
Conclusion 90

6 Authority 93

Introduction 93
An Ethic of Obedience 94
Reading 96
A Distinction between Lives 99
A Nonsovereign Messiah 103
Two Incompatible Orders 106
A Relationship of Possibility 108
Conclusion 110

7 Guarantee 113

Introduction 113
The Root of Sovereignty 114
Reading 118
Among Those Who Are Quarreling 120
Cannot Fulfill That Which We Promise 121
Yes, Yes; No, No 124
Conclusion 125

Excursus 127

Conclusion 133

Appendix: The Schleitheim Confession 140
Bibliography 149
Index 155

ACKNOWLEDGMENTS

Writing a book, even a little one, is a curious blend of solitude and relatedness. Even as you read and write and think by yourself at your desk, you also never truly do these things alone. Writing is communication; thoughts and connections and styles of reading are never simply "mine" but always emerge in a (more or less overtly) collaborative relatedness.

So in these acknowledgments, I do not claim to bring to light that full web of interdependence. Yet some names must be named here as having played a particular role in the coming together of this work.

I must here thank my partner Hannah. Shared life is interminable negotiation, I write elsewhere in this study, and parenting together is perhaps our most emotionally proximate experience of this. Since this project began, we welcomed our daughter into this world, moved house twice, started new jobs, and made new friends. I am grateful to have done these things together with you. And to my daughter Margarete: thank you for your insistent reminder that our prime belonging is not to words on computer screens but to each other.

I am further grateful to Benjamin and Rianna Isaak-Krauss. Your friendship and pastoral presence, but also comments and conversations, have significantly helped this project find its focus. The same must be said of Jamie Pitts. Your encouragement and critical comments at various stages of this project—from its earliest beginning to the near-finished manuscript—were invaluable.

Further, my gratitude belongs to Maxwell Kennel, Laura Schmidt Roberts, Kyle Gingerich Hiebert, and everyone who joined us at the *Anabaptists & Philosophy Roundtable* to make a place for philosophy and theory in Anabaptist thinking. To Joel Driedger and Wolfgang Krauss, for their enthusiastic confidence and several knowledgeable conversations. To Kees Blokland and the other board members at the Visiting Chair for Inventive Theology, Chris Doude van Troostwijk, Mirjam van Veen, and Fernando Enns, as well as Nina Schroeder-van 't Schip, Andres Pacheco Lozano, Fulco van Hulst, and the other colleagues and co-workers at the Amsterdam Mennonite Seminary, for their critical encouragement and their cordial collegiality.

To the *Luxembourg School of Religion & Society* for their kind support of the wider *Inventive Theology* project and the gatherings it allowed us to host.

And to the Mennonite congregation of Hamburg-Altona. It was with profoundly mixed feelings that, as a new and overwhelmed parent, I let go of my pastoral role to focus on my academic tasks; you accepted it valiantly and kindly. Thank you.

Finally, my gratitude belongs to God, whose blessing stands at the beginning of all things.

An earlier version of Chapter 6 was published as Marius van Hoogstraten, "Unlearning Obedience: The Ecclesiopolitical Critique of the 'Sword' in the Schleitheim Articles," *Conrad Grebel Review* 41, no. 2 (2025): 115–36.

An earlier version of Chapter 7 was published as Marius van Hoogstraten, "Without Sovereign Guarantee: Reading Schleitheim on the Oath with Giorgio Agamben," *Mennonite Quarterly Review* 97 (2023): 367–82.

Introduction

Life after Hope

How can we live together in times of crisis? As I write, still in the first part of the twenty-first century, this question seems to become increasingly fraught. Faced with ever-greater uncertainty—climate, geopolitics, democracy, machine learning—it would not be strange to seek a way out. Many grow nostalgic for communities defined by an untroubled belonging: a shared life anchored in kinship or place, guaranteed by the force of sovereign political rule. It would not be strange, and indeed it is far from uncommon, to respond to crisis and collapse with such a yearning for the (supposedly) safe boundaries of the nation, or indeed, for those who can, into the safely walled world of economic privilege. To respond to emergency with exception has a long tradition indeed.

Another tempting option, even now, remains to hope: to hope, still, for a radical turnaround, for God or technology or the spirit of humanity to come to save us from this dire situation that some have wrought on the rest of this planet's populations. Or, if not a radical turnaround, then at least the irruption of a new beginning in the midst of system collapse—an *inception*, in theologian Catherine Keller's words, into relational interdependence, still on the verge of occurring, even now, even tomorrow.[1]

But even such hope almost seems nostalgic today. Nostalgic for the unbridled optimism of modern progress, or if not that, then something not far removed, nostalgic for a time of social movements in which another world still seemed possible. Yet as begins to be increasingly clear with every election cycle and every IPCC report:[2] maybe, likely, things are not going to be alright. Possibly, maybe, likely, we will all live through a time in which

---

[1]See Catherine Keller, *Political Theology of the Earth: Our Planetary Emergency and the Struggle for a New Public* (New York: Columbia University Press, 2018).
[2]The Intergovernmental Panel on Climate Change is the United Nations body for assessing climate change on this planet. See, for example, IPCC, "Summary for Policymakers," in *Climate Change 2023: Synthesis Report. Contribution of Working Groups I, II and III to the Sixth Assessment Report of the Intergovernmental Panel on Climate Change*, ed. Hoesung Lee and José Romero (Geneva: IPCC, 2023), 1–34.

the question is not how to cherish a hope for better days but simply how to live, and live well, with faith and care and fellowship, *after* such hope has ceased. Not how to avert catastrophe but how to live together in its midst.

With this perhaps somewhat dramatic language, I certainly do not intend a wish to *hasten* the coming of such catastrophe. That would only be the reverse side of hope. I intend something more like what Donna Haraway has described as a shared life that is not oriented to a future but grows from a present.

> The task is to make kin in lines of inventive connection as a practice of learning to live and die well with each other in a thick present ... In urgent times, many of us are tempted to address trouble in terms of making an imagined future safe ... Staying with the trouble does not require such a relationship to times called the future. In fact, [it] requires learning to be truly present, not as a vanishing pivot between awful or edenic pasts and apocalyptic or salvific futures, but as mortal critters entwined in myriad unfinished configurations of places, times, matters, meanings.[3]

From such copresence, a future may grow, certainly. But it is not *oriented* to such a future in the way that modernity has taught us to think. It does not set up life in the present as an epic fight for the salvation of the future, for which the instruments of violence may well be necessary, as some philosophers and activists are now framing it.[4] Instead the operative term is "becoming-with" or *sympoiesis*: a kind of collaborative togetherness that realizes our creaturely existence requires the others in interdependent becoming. Yet what does this mean—and how can we give shape to it? Certainly, such sympoetic interdependence does not emerge fully formed from nothingness. At least now, at least in our context at the twilight of modernity, it will need to be intentionally shaped, asserted, and cared for.

In a way, these questions—how to live after hope? How to shape community amid catastrophe?—also animate the illicit gathering at the dawn of modernity with which this book will concern itself. And we may find a peculiar resonance between dawn and twilight here, a surprising relevance of the text this gathering produced—the Schleitheim Confession—to our contemporary situation.

In a sense I already write in the wake of this text. For at least a generation or two, it was seen as something of a founding document for the church in which I was baptized, served as a pastor, and of which I continue to be a member. For a significant part of the twentieth century, Schleitheim (also known as the Schleitheim "Articles") held the status of *the* defining

---

[3]Donna Haraway, *Staying with the Trouble: Making Kin in the Chthulucene* (Durham: Duke University Press, 2016), 4.
[4]For example, Mark Alizart, *The Climate Coup* (Cambridge: Polity Press, 2021); Andreas Malm, *How to Blow Up a Pipeline: Learning to Fight in a World on Fire* (London: Verso, 2021).

document for the Anabaptist movement out of which my Mennonite tradition emerged. We now know this is not accurate: Anabaptism was and continues to be more diverse and unruly than this one text can reflect. The voices that especially considered Schleitheim so foundational have similarly lost much of their appeal, their interpretations often unable to speak to the ambiguities of planetary entanglement that mark our contemporary situation.[5]

So I write in the wake of its *waning* relevance, I should say. And my intention with this study is not to reinstate it into a position of originary authority, suggesting that this really is where we find a pure, unadulterated vision of true Christian discipleship. Instead I venture that Schleitheim's loosening from such a status can allow us to return to it in a different way, with a different kind of reading, more constructive and speculative, thinking with it in ways a position of unassailable authority would never allow. So in the readings that make up the seven core chapters of this book, following Schleitheim's seven articles, I do not intend to unearth hidden truths or the true intentions of its historical authors. Instead I will approach the text with what we might call a productive anachronism; I hope to set loose a conversation with the text in which things and senses become visible that may yet illuminate our sense of life and community in catastrophic times. Behind and beneath the stark biblicism of Schleitheim's textual surface, possibilities for alternative readings may yet present themselves as we follow the trace of a kind of fellowship that is nonsovereign, unfinished, and collaborative in divine-human interaction.

Gathering in Dark Times

This will thus not be a historical study. Nevertheless, it is necessary to begin with a few words on the context and setting in which Schleitheim was composed.[6]

---

[5] See, for example, Laura Schmidt Roberts, Paul Martens, and Myron A. Penner, eds., *Recovering from the Anabaptist Vision: New Essays in Anabaptist Identity and Theological Method* (London: T&T Clark, 2020); Marius van Hoogstraten, "Das Reich Gottes Als Ver- Und Entortung: Mennonitisches Denken in Der Krise," in *Die Reich-Gottes-Botschaft in Theologie Und Politik: Jahrbuch Friedenstheologie 2023*, ed. Matthias-W. Engelke, Stefan Federbusch, Gottfried Orth, Michael Schober, and Stefan Silber (Norderstedt: Oekumenisches Institut für Friedenstheologie, 2023), 19–30.

[6] These few pages do not intend to do justice to the historical complexity of Reformation-era Europe, nor of the early Anabaptist movement within which Schleitheim takes place. For good introductions and overviews, see, for example, C. Arnold Snyder, *Anabaptist History and Theology* (Kitchener: Pandora Press, 1995); C. Arnold Snyder, "The Birth and Evolution of Swiss Anabaptism (1520–1530)," *Mennonite Quarterly Review* 80 (October 2006): 501–645; Peter Marshall, ed., *The Oxford History of the Reformation* (Oxford: Oxford University Press, 2022); John D. Roth and James M. Stayer, eds., *A Companion to Anabaptism and Spiritualism* (Leiden: Brill, 2007); Astrid von Schlachta, *Täufer: Von Der Reformation Ins 21. Jahrhundert* (Tübingen: Narr Francke Attempto, 2020).

The group that gathered in Schleitheim represented but one inflection of Anabaptism, whose unruly currents themselves took place within a more general context of reform, upheaval, rebellion, and repression shaping Reformation-era Europe. Popular imagination tends to highlight the role of Martin Luther in originating the institutional reform programs in the churches in German lands from 1517 onward. Though Luther's role as a theologian, church leader, translator, and communicator was significant, the European Reformation does not originate with one man's thoughts and intentions. Calls for religious change and renewal had been "loud and insistent" already for a century or so.[7] Reformation took up late medieval spiritualities, lay movements, and reform ideas while also repudiating much of scholastic theology and the conditions under which late medieval Christianity took place. Economic and political shifts further contributed to the conditions that made the institutional reforms of Luther, Zwingli, and Calvin possible.

For us today, the Reformation seems to mark the threshold of (early) modernity, setting the scene for much of what would follow in political, economic, and philosophical transformations. However, the dominant view among reformers was not to see themselves at the beginning of something but at an end: They believed, as the medieval generation before them, that apocalypse was imminent.[8]

It is not difficult to see why. The unmooring of a traditional world was in rapid progress. The beginning of a colonial enterprise in the Americas shook Europe's understanding of itself and raised profound new theological questions, as well as new possibilities for enormous violence and exploitation. New science challenged humanity's place in the universe, and new printing presses transformed communication across the continent. Political and economic changes began to favor cities and kings over traditional feudal landowners. As historian C. Arnold Snyder puts it, the medieval ideal of a unified social, political, and religious Christian body "had been in the process of disintegration for some time."[9]

And the continent was at war. Christian kingdoms had conquered the Iberian peninsula, leading to a flood of refugees and the birth of new kinds of religious repression. The Ottoman Empire was on the march in the East, taking Constantinople in 1453, Belgrade in 1521, and now approached Vienna, to which they would lay siege in 1529. To some radical reformers, it seemed realistic to expect these wars to destroy the regimes of European Christendom, hurrying along their apocalyptic visions.

Among those enthusiastic about religious reform, interpretation of the right way forward soon became a matter of heated debate. A crucial principle in much of the Reformation became "sola scriptura," the idea that

---

[7]Snyder, *Anabaptist History and Theology*, 15.
[8]Cf. Schlachta, *Täufer*, 16.
[9]Snyder, *Anabaptist History and Theology*, 11.

there cannot be a higher adjudicating authority to shape Christian faith and life than the words of the Bible. Yet as quickly became clear, this was not so much a clarifying principle as an invitation to proliferating disagreement. After all, the biblical text does not say anything by itself but needs to be interpreted, leading to intense disputes around the appropriate principles and authority to do so. Such unruliness was at odds with the hierarchically controlled intentions of the Reformation's most powerful figures, and soon, some currents and ideas began to be suppressed as what we now call the "radical" reformation.

As enthusiasm for reform spread through the Holy Roman Empire and Switzerland, it sparked an impatient hope with peasants, artisans, and urban citizens: they hoped it would also include economic and political change. Calls for freedom and bottom-up actions against church institutions culminated in the "largest mass movement in western Europe before the French Revolution":[10] the German Peasants' War.

Among the demands of the rebellious peasants were elected pastors, tithes that stayed in the community, an end to oppressive taxation, and access to traditionally common woods, meadows, and waters. All of these demands it considered based in the Gospels. With support from major cities, it "rejected Luther's claim that the gospel had nothing to do with altering concrete social, economic, or political realities" and also rejected "Zwingli's commitment to the role of established authorities in overseeing religious changes."[11]

The peasants' demands may not seem particularly radical to contemporary readers. Yet those in power responded with overwhelming violence. Though the rebellion briefly controlled swathes of German territory, it was soon defeated by the forces of the aristocracy, with prominent support from Martin Luther. Thousands of rebellious peasants were massacred. The radical theologian Thomas Müntzer was executed. In the words of one historian, the defeat of the peasants in 1525 "marks the beginning of an enduring differentiation between the magisterial and Radical Reformations" throughout Europe.[12]

In the wake of this loss, the spaces for more radical reform of the church were diminished. The unruly Anabaptist movement spreading out from Zurich, where radicals had broken with Zwingli in early 1525, now became the most significant radical faction. Many Anabaptists had shared in the ideals or participated in the struggle of the peasants' rebellion and were now left "precariously exposed" under the new political conditions.[13] Persecution began to increase, and Anabaptists were marginalized and exiled, as well

---

[10] Brad S. Gregory, "The Radical Reformation," in *The Oxford History of the Reformation*, ed. Peter Marshall (Oxford: Oxford University Press, 2022), 152.
[11] Ibid., 158.
[12] Ibid., 161.
[13] Ibid.

as incarcerated, tortured, and executed. Banishment and the threat of persecution forced them to relocate often, amplifying the geographic spread of the movement.

Anabaptist literally means "rebaptizer," but it is a term they themselves rejected. Anabaptists' insistence on the exclusive validity of freely chosen baptism did not lead them to "rebaptize" anyone, they held, but to offer baptism rightly and properly—that is, to confessing adults.[14] No infant could be baptized at all, they argued, and church membership should not coincide with local or national belonging but be a matter of individual free choice. This position was considered "seditious and dangerous to political stability by virtually all political authorities,"[15] Snyder remarks. Yet Anabaptism, at this point, was a disorderly affair, with much to be worked out, and the precise relation to political authority was one of many points of wild disagreement within the movement.

The gathering at Schleitheim on the margin of the Swiss confederacy in the winter of 1527 takes place under the shadow of all these things: of the many ways in which, even in the shortness of time, the tide of hope has decisively turned. The catastrophic defeat of the peasants' rebellion, the expansion of lethal persecution of Anabaptists in its wake, and the scattered nature of the movement—against the backdrop of war, economic and political disruption, and a radical questioning of humanity's place in the universe—have rapidly changed the conditions in which the movement can act. It has become definitively impossible to hope for the transformation of society as a whole or the implementation of Anabaptist reforming programs from a position of political dominance.[16] The Schleitheim group gathers in a time of crisis, catastrophe, and collapse.

---

[14]According to Snyder, the "Anabaptist movement in particular illustrates the survival of a lay piety that in some ways continued earlier forms of piety that the mainline reformers wished to repudiate ... [It] continued to resonate to the late medieval monastic ideal of 'ascetic' and 'restorationist' piety." Snyder, *Anabaptist History and Theology*, 18. For a detailed study on the continuity between (some) Anabaptists and late medieval ways of thinking and believing, see Werner O. Packull, *Mysticism and the Early South German-Austrian Anabaptist Movement, 1525-1531* (Scottsdale: Herald Press, 1977).

[15]Snyder, *Anabaptist History and Theology*, 2.

[16]Gregory thus summarizes that Schleitheim is a "reaction to the defeat of the peasants in 1525-6," and others have also highlighted this: Snyder describes it as a "post-revolt document" that "must outline directions for an uncertain future;" see C. Arnold Snyder, "The Schleitheim Articles in Light of the Revolution of the Common Man: Continuation or Departure?" *The Sixteenth Century Journal* 16, no. 4 (1985): 425; Gregory, "The Radical Reformation," 162. There has been some debate on Schleitheim's relation to the peasants' defeat, see, for example, Snyder, "Birth and Evolution," 549–64; for the contrary view, see Urs B. Leu and Christian Scheidegger, eds., *Das Schleitheimer Bekenntnis 1527* (Zug: Achius, 2004) and especially Andrea Strübind, *Eifriger Als Zwingli: Die Frühe Täuferbewegung in Der Schweiz* (Berlin: Duncker & Humblot, 2003).

It is certainly not my intention to contribute to this disagreement between (church) historians, but it seems difficult to believe that the massacre of thousands of peasants and the severe restriction of political space for Anabaptist-style reform would leave no impression at all on

A leadership role at the gathering is played by a former Benedictine prior named Michael Sattler. Sattler left his monastic community in the context of the peasants' war, but his activity as an Anabaptist leader truly began in the post-revolt context of rising persecution. Sattler himself would be captured, tortured, and executed not long after Schleitheim, and his worldview seems marked by the sharp dualism between a small, defenseless flock of Christians and the evil world that surrounds it.

Under Sattler's leadership, the group addresses a simple question: Now what? What life can there be after such a loss of hope? Under these catastrophic conditions, what possibility remains for us to live together faithfully?

In addressing these questions, Schleitheim does not simply enumerate points of broad Anabaptist consensus but represents an assertive, indeed antagonistic contribution to the debate within the movement.[17] Influential though this contribution may have been,[18] Anabaptism continues to be a diverse and unruly movement after 1527, going through at least several significant transformations in even the following generation—the election of apocalyptically minded Anabaptists into established political power at Münster and its catastrophic effects deserves special mention.

It would not be strange to expect Schleitheim, too, to approach its problems with apocalyptic expectation—to interpret the catastrophe that surrounds them as definitive indication that the end is now truly near. Yet the text shows few signs of such an apocalyptic temporality.[19] Instead, as we

---

our gathering, even if it were true that their emphases were separatist and nonviolent from the start (as Strübind argues).

[17]Snyder argues that in offering its vision as normative for the wider movement, Schleitheim also marginalized its more spiritualist or prophetic elements. This also affected the place of women, whose avenues for leadership became restricted in those parts of Anabaptism that followed Schleitheim. See Snyder, *Anabaptist History and Theology*, 253–74; Snyder, "Birth and Evolution," 594; Schlachta, *Täufer*, 86–9.

[18]There seems to be some disagreement among the historians cited earlier on the precise influence of the Articles in their historical context. Though the line of thought represented by Schleitheim seems to be an influential reference point for Swiss Anabaptism and (to differing degrees) for other currents such as the later Mennonites, it certainly does not represent the consensus of the 1527 Anabaptist movement in its unadulterated form, as it is sometimes seen. See Schlachta, *Täufer*, 10; Leu and Scheidegger, *Das Schleitheimer Bekenntnis 1527*, 16–18; Snyder, "Birth and Evolution," 587–645; see also C. Arnold Snyder, "The Influence of the Schleitheim Articles on the Anabaptist Movement: An Historical Evaluation," *Mennonite Quarterly Review* 63 (October 1989): 323–44.

[19]This is not to say no one in the gathering shared in the general apocalyptic mood of Reformation-era Europe. Sattler himself (somewhat cautiously) employs more apocalyptic language after his imprisonment, for instance—see C. Arnold Snyder, *The Life and Thought of Michael Sattler* (Scottdale: Herald Press, 1984), 169–76. Snyder holds that Schleitheim too (therefore?) must be understood as having been "drafted in expectation of Christ's imminent return, not as a constitution for a church struggling to survive long-term" (Snyder, "Birth and Evolution," 621–2), but if such a sense of expectation is present among those gathered in Schleitheim, it is remarkably absent from the text itself. See also Chapter 2 and Excursus.

will see, we find a text full of the determination to *live* amid the catastrophe[20] that is unfolding. Instead of interpreting an end, they seem more concerned with shaping a *beginning*, and indeed with shaping the regulative practices—possibly drawing on Sattler's familiarity with monastic life[21]—that allow the fellowship of believers to persist, to gather and share life in time, as week follows week, year follows year, and generation follows generation.

Ecclesio-Political

In a sense, the declaration agreed upon at Schleitheim is a confession without creed: though it lays out what it considers essential for Christian life, it is almost completely uninterested in the content of belief. Nor indeed is it concerned with ethics, at least not in the sense of the minutiae of rules that might govern the actions and life of the faithful. Instead it points toward faith as a form of life in a more collective sense, describing constitutive and regulative practices by which the church gathers and takes shape as a community. This is what it considers decisive for the existence of the church in the context of crisis and catastrophe: not *what* the faithful believe, nor even *how* they live as individuals, but the shape of their fellowship as a collective body.

Schleitheim's priorities are thus, we might say, *political*, or indeed *ecclesio-political*: it is concerned with what fundamentally institutes, shapes, and disciplines the shared life of the church as a community. Its seven articles thus each outline a performative ecclesio-political practice, from baptism and excommunication to the election of pastors and the rejection of swearing oaths. In all these, Schleitheim envisions a community that rejects the logic of sovereignty as a principle of its organization. And—though it does not use this word—one that is a place of freedom. Its membership does not rely on predetermined belonging, such as tradition, familial relatedness, or economic interest, but on the free choice of its members. These are not questions to be put aside in times of crisis, Schleitheim seems to argue, but essential to living faithfully in such times.

As we will see, the text addresses its subject matter with striking formality. The first article instructs that a candidate for baptism must be "taught" and must commit to a renewed life in the resurrection—but it does not specify *what* they should be taught or what the ethical expectations of such renewed life might be. Article II discusses the formal process by which a sinner might be disciplined—but it says nothing about what kind of sinful behavior might merit such discipline.

---

[20]For a more theoretical reading of the notions of crisis, collapse, and catastrophe, see Chapter 4.
[21]On the apparent continuities and discontinuities between Sattler's Benedictine experience and Schleitheim, see Snyder, *Life and Thought*, 33–61, 259–70.

Schleitheim's ecclesio-political assertion thus goes further than simply repeating the peasants' insistence that religion and politics cannot be separated. It is structurally similar to what some political theorists refer to as "the political" in distinction to mere "politics." If the latter refers to the everyday negotiation and administration of a collective body (the work in its state apparatus, parliamentary discussions, and so on), the political refers to the grounding constitutive depth dimension of what makes a political community. In the words of Claude Lefort, it refers to "the principles that generate society or, more accurately, different forms of society," indeed what "distinguishes one society from another ... its shaping of human coexistence."[22] It is the question of the practices and principles that institute a particular way of organizing collective life—in which "politics" can then take place.

Schleitheim is an antagonistic text, and there is perhaps always something antagonistic about drawing attention to the political (or ecclesio-political) in this way. For it means to assert that the fundamental shape of political (or ecclesial) organization is not simply fixed, the mere expression of natural (or divine) order, but can be transformed. Things could be otherwise. Church, in Schleitheim's case, could be otherwise. As political theorist Chantal Mouffe argues, the very process of political contestation can reveal a sense of contingency and possibility, as it becomes apparent that "every order is the temporary and precarious articulation of contingent practices."[23]

Schleitheim itself, as we will see, is no less precarious and contingent. Indeed the text seems deeply aware that the kind of shared life it envisions will not simply spring into place by divine fiat and is never definitively achieved. Instead, it requires interminable negotiation and attention. This is especially true for the borders of the church, which Schleitheim seems especially invested in: nearly each of its seven articles is concerned in one way or another with instituting, clarifying, and policing the distinction between inside and out. Yet, as we will see, the ambiguity of a creaturely relatedness insists at every step of the way. We could read this as an insight into tragic failure, into the irrepressible distance between ideal and reality. Yet as this study progresses, I hope another possibility will come into view: that this very unfinishedness can become a site of relatedness and belonging, indeed of good news.

The seven chapters of this book will thus follow Schleitheim's seven articles, beginning at Article I in Chapter 1 and ending with Article VII in Chapter 7. I discuss the supplementary preamble and closing lines in an Excursus.

Chapter 1 begins with baptism. Schleitheim stresses baptism, and thus membership in the church, must be freely chosen. But it is not immediately

---

[22] Claude Lefort, *Democracy and Political Theory* (Cambridge: Polity Press, 1988), 217; see also Oliver Marchart, *Post-Foundational Political Thought: Political Difference in Nancy, Lefort, Badiou and Laclau* (Edinburgh: Edinburgh University Press, 2007).
[23] Chantal Mouffe, *On the Political* (New York: Routledge, 2005), 18.

clear what kind of freedom this is and to what extent it anticipates modern individualist notions. With twentieth-century theorist Hannah Arendt, we can distinguish the modern *in*dependence of sovereign individuals deciding their own fate from the *inter*dependent freedom to make a beginning in a fellowship of equals. Read this way, baptism and the beginning it marks is perhaps not best understood as a sharp cut (as sovereign decision would suggest) but a renewal in divine-human collaboration.

In Chapter 2, I offer a reading of the way Schleitheim envisions discipline, with excommunication or the "ban" as ultimate sanction. Shaping shared life is a fragile endeavor, and even a nonsovereign community must be capable of exerting force. Yet how is this realization to be interpreted? And what does its ambivalent necessity say about the persistent unfinishedness of this community? Surprisingly, Schleitheim approaches the need for discipline with a certain casual unexcitedness: it is under no illusion that even newly baptized members will not on occasion slip and fall. In this, a certain temporality or way of being in time becomes readable: it is not from a single founding event or imminent future but from the *repetition* of its constitutive practices that this community receives its stability. Even amid catastrophic rupture, shared life is not made (nor indeed made safe) in a single stroke.

Chapter 3 discusses the gathering of the community for the breaking of bread. The text addresses at length the need to distinguish members from nonmembers, but this again raises questions suggestive of the way ambiguity insists into the dissociative clarity Schleitheim seems so invested in. The very practices instituted to produce clarity (baptism, discipline) in the same stroke seem to produce new ambiguities. Unity seems to remain in question, never simply an uncomplicated oneness, and always in need of supplementary gathering. Here, this gathering takes place not in the presence of Christ but in His memory—that is, in His absence. How can this absence be interpreted—if it is at the same time *from* that absence that a call seems to emerge?

In the fourth article, we read how Schleitheim considers the world outside the church as evil and that baptized Christians should stay as far away from it as possible. It is perhaps not an altogether strange response to the experience of collapse, crisis, and catastrophe, which can each be understood as a form of rupture and loss. Schleitheim's insistence on separation may seem to promise some immunity to that loss. Yet on closer reading, the point turns out to be less clear. Reading the text against the grain while taking its logic seriously, God's embrace turns out wider and wilder than Christians perhaps tend to imagine. A nonsovereign community, we can tentatively conclude, does not except itself out of a suffering world but takes shape as a place of refuge from its oppressive structures.

In Chapter 5, we read how Schleitheim instructs the election of pastors, whom it considers essential to the survival of the community. Yet what is the place of leadership in a nonsovereign community? On closer reading, we find the role it envisions for pastors is more one of care work than decisive authority. The pastor's tasks remain occasional, partial, and delimited—approaching what Michael Hardt and Antonio Negri describe as essential characteristics of leadership in a nonsovereign community. Times of crisis may often invite authoritarian leadership, but Schleitheim instead finds resilience in self-organization.

In its sixth article, Schleitheim opens with an enigmatic axiom: the "sword" is legitimate yet must be rejected. What does the "sword" here mean, and what can we make of such an apparently paradoxical thesis? While the sword is often taken to refer to weapons or the use of violence more generally, it quickly becomes clear it refers specifically to a kind of political authority or legal order: that is, to sovereignty. The text shows an acute sense of the ambivalence of such authority, both capable of nurturing human flourishing and giving lives up to destruction. While it may yet have a role to play in God's wish for this planet, it must be rejected as an organizing principle for the church. This rejection is more comprehensive than may at first appear: it is not simply a matter of obeying God instead but of unlearning our imagination of God as sovereign master and following an explicitly nonsovereign Messiah.

Seventh and finally, I will discuss Schleitheim's rejection of swearing oaths. This is far from an afterthought, but a recapitulation and conclusion to this very project of a nonsovereign community. With attentive reading, we come to see how the refusal to swear oaths opens into a comprehensive critique of sovereignty and a radical reenvisioning of certitude and trust in a community without such enforced guarantees. Swearing, the text seems to argue, fundamentally misunderstands the relation between words, things, God, and human beings. God does not lend Godself to the stabilization of political relations of dominion—there is no final word or guarantee, only life lived in repetition: let your words be yes, *yes*.

Finally—before recapitulating in the Conclusion—I discuss Schleitheim's preamble and closing lines in the Excursus. While not formally part of the seven articles agreed upon at the Schleitheim assembly, they make a few supplementary points, notably stressing the antagonistic character of this text and a particular interrelation of truth with community. Indeed, it almost seems as if truth *is* the interdependent becoming-with of a fellowship.

In offering these readings, I immediately admit they are constructive, sometimes even speculative interpretations. Certainly on its surface, Schleitheim seems to prescribe an uncompromising and separatist Christianity, a dour, sober, and disciplined way of being church that seems a far cry from what I am suggesting. And I certainly do not mean to suggest that the currents of Anabaptism that historically emerged from and after Schleitheim were indeed in their majority democratic fellowships of collaborative freedom. Yet upon closer reading, and perhaps in spite of its authors' intentions, the text left to us by those gathered there on that winter day on the edge of the Swiss confederacy may show itself to be marked by tensions and openings that signal a wholly different path. Reading, after all, must never simply mean seeing but always *reading*.

1

Beginning

Introduction

The first and shortest of the seven articles that make up the Schleitheim text addresses baptism. This elementary Christian rite marks the forgiveness of one's sins through Jesus Christ and incorporates the person who is baptized into the church.[1] Schleitheim argues it should only be given to those who grasp its meaning, commit to the renewed life it marks, and with such an understanding "request it of us and demand it through themselves." This implies, the text notes, that the practice of baptizing infants must end: it is an "abomination."

The emphasis on freely chosen adult baptism is the defining point for the Anabaptist movement more broadly.[2] For Schleitheim, it becomes integrally

---

[1] A concise way of describing baptism theologically is, in the words of John Burgess, that "representatives of the Church apply water to an individual to mark the beginning of his or her life in Christ and the Church." Burgess, a Presbyterian, stresses that it is God, not man, who "initiates a covenant, claiming people as God's own," and "direct[ing] him or her into the life of the Church and ask[ing] the Church to recommit itself to the covenant." The commitment of the baptized to this renewed life and to the community of faith, and their declaration of faith in God take place "in response," and the material and communal aspects and symbolic actions (e.g., the actual pouring of water) "confirm and ratify" God's promises and evocatively "dramatize" their meaning to draw the people into them. Baptism has many dimensions that play into this dramatization, from the sense of a washing clean to the restaging of the waters of birth and creation. See John P. Burgess, "Baptism," in *The Cambridge Dictionary of Christian Theology*, ed. Ian A. McFarland, David A. S. Fergusson, Karen Kilby, and Iain R. Torrance (Cambridge: Cambridge University Press, 2011), 52–4.

Mennonite theologian Thomas Finger describes baptism as one of four practices constituting the "communal dimension" of faith, in which "personal faith" is "necessarily and therefore intrinsically actualized in a communal context." It "necessarily involves conscious appropriation" and "incorporate[s] one into the church" also through "voluntary submission to … the church's authority." Finger notes modern Anabaptist theology is marked by a "relative neglect of ecclesial themes like baptism" as "most current Anabaptists approach the church in sociological, political and ethical terms largely omitting practices that make it church." See Thomas N. Finger, *A Contemporary Anabaptist Theology: Biblical, Historical, Constructive* (Downers Grove: InterVarsity Press, 2004), 157–62.

[2] In the words of historian C. Arnold Snyder, "Anabaptism became a 'church' movement when adherents insisted that the properly biblical way of forming the church was through the freely chosen baptism of adult believers." The church is "made up only of persons who had, in full

related to its effort to shape a community that is clearly bounded. Restricting baptism to those who meet its criteria, we might say, becomes a means of exerting control over ambiguity and of constituting and reinforcing the boundary between the church and the world around it.

The Anabaptist emphasis on free personal choice has been related to modern democratic freedoms, notably individual freedom of religion. This may seem like a paradox: certainly such individualist freedom is at odds with the conformism of a sharply bounded and disciplined community. Yet this paradox is appearance only. As we will see, a narrowly understood notion of individual free decision can well be made to serve both a conformist sense of control and a sense of separation from creaturely (or worldly) relationships. Yet, on closer reading, the text also suggests a different way to think about these things.

This chapter will concern itself with this relation between freedom, control over ambiguity, and community. As we will see, a closer reading of the Schleitheim text makes it difficult to simply relate the freedom of adult baptism to the individual freedoms of modernity. We find a notion of freedom that is both more embedded in shared life and more capable of embracing ambiguity with Hannah Arendt. In spite of her secular commitments, Arendt's understanding of freedom—which is intimately tied up with making a *beginning* together with others—may prove uniquely resonant with a reading of Schleitheim.

Decision and Ambiguity

One term that will return throughout this study is ambiguity. With it, I mean the kind of underlying "messiness" or unruliness that seems to insist into our existence: we are rarely only one thing, and our lives are rarely open to only one interpretation. Most of us are caught up in multiple webs of relationships, which rarely have a clear and distinct beginning and end. We get our word in English from the Latin term for moving in two directions at the same time (*ambi*, both ways, and *agere*, moving or driving), but it is really also about *being* moved in multiple directions. We are made by our relationships, by the reality around us, but that reality can be complex and complicated sometimes, and we exist in the midst of that manifold creaturely complicatedness.

Such ambiguity and messiness can seem to frustrate efforts to build a clearly bounded community. If we are all multiple things, how do we even know who "we" are? How can there be a clear border running between us and the rest when that border is crossed by various lines of creaturely interdependence? Even more so in times of crisis and collapse, such indelible

---

conscience and choice, publicly committed themselves to the Body of Christ on earth." See Snyder, *Anabaptist History and Theology*, 1.

relatedness and ambiguity can hinder the attempt to protect or insulate our communities from all that is unfolding around them.

It is therefore not surprising that so many of Schleitheim's efforts seem to be oriented toward carving out some sense of control over such ambiguity, toward making the boundaries of its community as *un*ambiguous as possible. As we will see, nearly each of its seven articles can be understood as a technique or practice to suppress ambiguity, to clarify and shore up the borders of the church, and to maintain a separation from the world around it, which (it seems) is interminably in the process of unraveling and in need of further reinforcement and reassertion.

This is exactly what the emphasis on freely chosen baptism could be said to do. In laying out the formal criteria that regulate entry into the membership of this community and marking a clear distinction between insiders and outsiders, it exerts control over the ambiguity and messiness that comes with integrating new members. It is establishing and, in a sense, policing the border of the church, regulating the practice that governs passage inward from the outside.

In a world full of ambiguities and full of crisis and catastrophe, voluntary baptism seems to offer an unambiguous point of departure. Each member has renounced their old life and the loyalties in which it existed. In passing through these waters of baptism, each member has crossed the boundary that sets the church apart from the world around it. And each has embraced the new standards this community is setting. The community is one that consists of those who have made a new beginning, we might say, and this temporal "cut" between before and after also grounds the "cut" or boundary that separates the church from what is around it.

It is only seemingly a paradox that this means of exerting control has also been identified with freedom. Specifically, it has been equated with an early instance of the modern democratic freedoms of the individual. Writing in the United States of the 1940s, influential Mennonite historian Harold Bender suggested a continuity between the "Anabaptist vision" of the sixteenth century and these modern liberal freedoms. Bender even suggests that the latter are "derived" from the former: "There can be no question," he argues, "but that the great principles of freedom of conscience, separation of church and state, and voluntarism in religion" are "for the first time clearly enunciated" in the Anabaptist movement.[3]

The implications of making church membership a matter of freedom are significant, it seems to me. Because it suggests the church is not in the first place a force of tradition or *given* belonging (such as the belonging to a family, or local origin, or economic dependence) but as a gathering of free individuals who choose to begin anew with Christ and each other. Envisioning church as a space for freedom, a place in which freedom is

---

[3]Harold Bender, "The Anabaptist Vision," *American Society of Church History* 13 (1944): 3.

practiced in the midst of a world full of unfreedom, feels both encouraging in its optimism and resolute in its ecclesio-political courage.

So it may be tempting indeed for modern individuals to read a modern individualist sense of freedom into the rejection of infant baptism. It is true, after all, that individual free decision has a central place in Schleitheim's approach to baptism. It does not merely want believers to assent or confess in response but to take the initiative to *decide*, each person, "themselves." It indeed seems to suggest a community called together from free individuals who voluntarily associate. We could even go further and note that baptism and the decision it entails also seem to make one free *from* the worldly ties that bound one.[4] If baptism is a "cut" between before and after, we could say that it also "cuts" one loose from the ties that bound one in the world.

In this light, we might well consider the practice of adult baptism here as something of a paradox—on the one hand, it is a means of control, suppressing ambiguity, and enforcing conformism, while on the other hand being an instance of profound existential freedom. Yet the paradox is only apparently so. Especially if we understand freedom as implying a compressed and singular decision, a clear and unambiguous cut, it can well become allied with conformism and control.[5] The higher the stakes of this decision, the more it is envisioned as a single momentous choice between radically different paths; the more clearly this decision also dissociates those who make it from everything else, from their life before and from the life outside. The more unambiguous and binary between *yes* and *no* this decision is conceived, the more unambiguous and clear it makes the border between *in* and *out*. So it is exactly this sense of freedom, understood as individual free decision, that cements the community's separation.

This proximity is already suggested by the very word: a de*cision* is a cut, and its Latin root *de-caedere* literally means cutting off. To decide

---

[4]This is also how Mennonite theologian Thomas Finger conceives of it, suggesting "baptism sacramentalizes ... the decisive breaking of ... allegiance to the old creation, or the 'world.'" See Finger, *A Contemporary Anabaptist Theology*, 184.

The idea that baptism is so related to freedom is not a modern invention. Already the Church Father Justin Martyr, writing in the second century CE, describes baptism as essentially related to freedom. After our bodily birth happened to us without our knowing and was thus a birth of "necessity," our second birth in baptism allows us to stop being children of necessity and become children of choice and knowledge—that is, of freedom. By baptism we are "put in the position ... determined by the conscious and voluntary choice of individuals once they have acquired ... sufficient knowledge of the order of the world in general." See Michel Foucault, *The Government of the Living: Lectures at the Collège de France, 1979–1980* (New York: Palgrave Macmillan, 2014), 105–6.

[5]An understanding of baptism as predicated on narrowly conceived rational individual decision has recently also been criticized from a disabilities studies perspective. This question is more complex than can be addressed here, but see, for example, jason greig, "No Exceptions: Baptism beyond Exclusion," *Vision: A Journal for Church and Theology* 25, no. 2 (2024): 82–90.

is to cut between two or more options or indeed to make a cut in time between before the decision and after. A decision cuts through the mess, we might say, through all the ambiguity of creaturely life, with a clear choice.

Yet this also means that once the decision has been made, freedom is over. It can only amount to a brief moment, if indeed it is possible at all. Because if freedom means individual free decision, is anyone ever free? Who could make such a choice for themselves with no other determinations, in complete freedom of the will? And even if such a choice could take place, there can certainly be no space for it *within* the shared life of a community. By any account, such radical freedom to decide in individual autonomy or independence is eminently incompatible with the shared life in community, which means not *in*dependence but *inter*dependence. Such "freedom" disappears the moment one emerges from the baptismal waters—we could even say it serves to stifle any future criticism or open deliberation in the church: you chose this. Now hush.

From a contemporary viewpoint, maybe, we might also ask whether the "cut" of baptism, cutting loose from worldly bounds, also cuts us off from the kind of *creaturely* belonging we are embedded in as living beings. Are familial relations, local ties, and our relatedness to nonhuman life repudiated as we "repent" and pass into renewed life? This would make this free decision reminiscent of modern freedoms indeed, if not as Bender perhaps intended: it would make them complicit with the exceptionalism that considers human life and organization separately from (and in dominion over) nonhuman creaturely existence.

It will not come as a surprise that the text itself says little about such ecological concerns, especially in this brief first article (but see Chapter 4). Yet even in its few lines, we may find that baptism, community, and freedom are related in ways that are more complicated and indeed more ambiguous than the equation with liberal freedom would allow. So let us take a closer look at the text.

Reading

The first of the Schleitheim Articles is brief. It begins with the instruction to "observe concerning baptism" the following. Baptism "shall [*sol*] be given to all those" who meet four criteria: (1) they have been "taught" about "repentance and amendment of life," (2) they "believe truly" that Christ has "taken away" their sins, and (3) they "wish to walk in the resurrection" of Christ. Fourth, Schleitheim gives a more comprehensive criterion, instructing that the persons to be baptized must, with these first three things in mind, "request ... and demand it" from the church "through themselves [*durch sich selbs*]."

So, we might say, the person to be baptized must know what they are doing. They must have the right intent and commitment, and they must believe they are free of their past life and its sins (presumably having not only learned about but also performed repentance). And, significantly, they must themselves approach the church with a request to which the church can only respond. Baptism is not something that happens *to* them. It is not only their understanding, their faith, or their consent that is required, but their own initiative. This approach excludes all infant baptism, Schleitheim clarifies, which is "the highest and first abomination of the Pope."[6]

The text says nothing about who can give baptism, a pastor or anyone in the church, and there seems to be no judgment or decision on the part of those giving baptism beyond these four criteria. Those who meet those criteria "shall" receive baptism.

The text proceeds with several biblical references, as "foundation and testimony of the apostles." These are merely listed, not discussed or interpreted. They include the final chapters of the Gospel of Matthew and Mark, presumably referring in particular to Mt. 28:19, "Go therefore and make disciples of all nations, baptizing them ... and teaching them to obey everything that I have commanded you," and Mk 16:16, "The one who believes and is baptized will be saved." Each suggests a particular sequence of events: baptism is to be preceded by teaching (Matthew, "make disciples") and believing (Mark) and followed by disciplined and renewed life (Matthew, "obey everything").

In its other biblical references, the text again only cites the chapter, not the verse. Its reference to Acts 2 presumably means Peter's admonition in Acts 2:38 to "repent, and be baptized" (again in this order), and its reference to Acts 8 might mean verse 12, "but when they believed Philip ... they were baptized," and Philip teaching and then baptizing the Ethiopian eunuch.

The final two citations, Acts 16 and 19, are noteworthy since they seem to go against Schleitheim's point. Acts 16 includes the baptism of Lydia "and her household" (Acts 16:15), as well as the jailer "and his entire family" (Acts 16:33), two occurrences that seem to contradict the exclusive validity of adult baptism. Perhaps Sattler and the others assume this to only include the adult members of those families; after all, it follows the instruction to

---

[6] It seems to be implied that this understanding of baptism has significance for the status of children and infants. There is no reference to baptism removing original sin; it is *sins*, plural, that are forgiven. The text does not refer to anyone who remains without baptism as being damned or lost or anything of the sort. At most, they perhaps miss out on being "resurrected with Jesus," possibly referring to eternal life. So on this logic it seems that children are not damned in any relevant sense and thus also do not need baptism. At the same time, they are not *in* the church, even if they are not simply outside either, as they obviously form part of its life. Here we see, incidentally, the first instance of how adult baptism not only controls ambiguity, but also produces new ambiguities: there now seems to be a whole class of people who are neither in nor out. This will come back to haunt us in Chapter 3.

"believe on the Lord Jesus" (16:31). With Acts 19, Schleitheim presumably refers to verses 4 and 5, where several disciples who had merely been baptized into John's "baptism of repentance" are *re*baptized "in the name of the Lord Jesus," thus apparently legitimizing the Anabaptist practice of requiring proper adult baptism for those who have received some improper baptism.[7]

Schleitheim here does not say much about how it really thinks about what goes on when someone is baptized. Some of it can be inferred: in the believer's individual life, baptism appears to mark a break and a new beginning, involving repentance, "amendment of life," and the forgiveness of previous sins. This new beginning is described (with Romans 6) as participating in the death and resurrection of Christ. Collectively, this break and new beginning also mark the passage from outside to inside the church. That one major function of baptism is to join one to the church remains implicit in this article, but the second article notes that discipline is to be applied to those "baptized into the one Body of Christ," and the third reserves communion for those "united into one Body of Christ, that is into the congregation of God, ... through baptism" (see Chapters 2 and 3). Thus baptism incorporates new members into the collective.

In general, we could say, the text here reads as an oddly abstract instruction. The criteria it lays out are purely formal: nothing is said about the content of the teaching, belief, or ethical commitment required. Perhaps this is just because it is considered obvious to the reader, a point of assumed consensus that does not need to be made explicit. Yet Schleitheim is clearly in disagreement with other Anabaptists about the content of ethics (as apparent in its preamble—see Excursus). So it seems to me more that the text operates at a different level. It lays out not the content of ethics or teaching but the formal procedures and constitutive practices by which a community can take shape, *in which* ethics and teaching then take its place. This is a point I will keep coming back to in future chapters: in its seven articles, Schleitheim is time and again interested in formal regulations and constitutive practices. More than the content of ethics or dogma, its concerns are ecclesio-political: concerned with the shaping and regulation of the collective life of the church.

"This we wish to hold simply, yet firmly and with assurance," this first article closes. This is a truth that does not assert itself but needs to be claimed, asserted, and *held to*. Being church will not simply happen. It is a task—we might say, the task of collaborative self-organization.

---

[7] As Jamie Pitts remarks, however, this passage is immediately preceded in the biblical text by the tale of Apollos, who likewise "only knew the baptism of John," yet apparently is not required to be rebaptized. See Jamie Pitts, "Baptism, Postliberal and Anabaptist Theologies, and the Ambiguity of Christian Practice," *Mennonite Quarterly Review*, no. 90 (July 2016): 333.

The Freedom to Begin

So already we can see that the text seems to have something different in mind than freedom understood merely as individual decision. Baptism is immediately a relational process: first of all, it is not simply decided individually but is preceded by a divine invitation, by the way Christ has already "taken away" the candidate's sins and indeed made this path into renewed life possible through His death and resurrection. Yet although this divine action precedes any human action, this does not preclude the space for the candidate's own collaboration and participation, even for their initiative. They do not merely respond or assent; they must actively "desire and demand" it. This demand is for "themselves"—it is a request no one can make for them.[8] They become capable of this initiative, however, not only in response to a divine invitation but also under the conditions of having been "taught." Further, after the choice has been made and initiative taken, baptism is not simply taken but "given" by a community to which one is joined. Though the community must (one presumes) perform this teaching and discern the intentions of the candidate, it does not hold arbitrary power over their admission: if the criteria are met and they "desire" it, baptism "shall" be given to them.

In this back-and-forth between God, the community, and the individual, no one acts unilaterally. Any freedom takes place in this interconnected web of relationships, in the midst of this mutual process of inviting, deciding, demanding, discerning, giving, receiving, joining, and welcoming.

So the equation of the freedom embodied in baptism with individual freedom to decide, akin to modern individualism, seems to miss a great deal. There is more ambiguity here than the singular "cut" from earlier seemed to suggest. So perhaps there is another way to understand the way this new beginning is made and to understand the relation between baptism and

---

[8]In the text this request must come *durch sich selbs*. This is generally translated as "for themselves" or simply "themselves": see, for example, John C. Wenger, "The Schleitheim Confession of Faith," *Mennonite Quarterly Review* 19, no. 4 (1945): 248; John H. Yoder, ed., *The Legacy of Michael Sattler*, Classics of the Radical Reformation (Walden: Plough, 2019), 40.

Another translation might be "on one's own initiative," which is one connotation of Heinold Fast's modern German rendition "von sich selbst aus." Literally, this means "from themselves," which suggests not only initiative but also autonomy; the request should come not (we might say) in response to family pressure or tradition or similar outside factors but really initiating with the candidate. See Michael Sattler, "Brüderliche Vereinigung Etlicher Kinder Gottes," in *Der Linke Flügel Der Reformation*, ed. Heinold Fast (Bremen: Carl Schünemann, 1962), 62.

Most of these translations elide the relationality of this process. A more faithful rendering would take note of this strange word *durch*, meaning "through," suggesting that this request and new beginning in some way pass through the convert without fully belonging to them, that they must demand baptism "*through* themselves."

On Yoder, see note 3 on p. 94–5 (Chapter 6).

freedom in this little text that gives more space to this relational back-and-forth *in* which freedom takes place.

Twentieth-century theorist Hannah Arendt might help us with this. She distinguishes two ways of understanding freedom: on the one hand, freedom understood as "sovereignty," which means the individual freedom of the will and the freedom to decide independently as master of my own self (and possibly the master of others). On the other hand, however, she suggests we might understand freedom as "virtuosity," which does not center on the individual's will but on the capacity to act in concert with others. It is the freedom to *make a beginning*, to do something that does not simply derive from what precedes it.

In modernity, Arendt argues, we have tended to think about political freedoms in terms of sovereignty. Yet this is an enormous problem.

> Politically, this identification of freedom with sovereignty is perhaps the most pernicious and dangerous consequence of the philosophical equation of freedom and free will. For it leads either to a denial of human freedom—namely, if it is realized that whatever men may be, they are never sovereign—or to the insight that the freedom of one man, or a group, or a body politic can be purchased only at the price of the freedom ... of all others.[9]

Freedom as sovereignty "has always been an illusion," Arendt maintains. It is an eminently private kind of freedom, exemplified by my capacity to decide without others interfering. To take such a notion of freedom as a basis for shared public life would mean that we are most free when we are not among equals: either when we are not in public, not among others at all, or when we are the master of those around us. For among others the sovereignty of some (at the expense of the rest) "can be maintained only by the instruments of violence ... if men wish to be free, it is precisely sovereignty they must renounce."[10]

Freedom in its proper public and political sense is better understood as virtuosity, Arendt suggests instead: the freedom embodied in self-organized action together with equals. If sovereign independence is inimical to the interdependence of a community of equals, virtuosity can only take place within such a community. It provides a "space of appearance" for it, a "realm where freedom is a worldly reality, tangible in words which can be heard, in deeds which can be seen, and in events which are talked about, remembered, and turned into stories."[11] Simply put, this is not the freedom to decide independently but the freedom to act interdependently. To be free

---

[9] Hannah Arendt, *Between Past and Future: Six Exercises in Political Thought* (New York: Viking Press, 1961), 164.
[10] Ibid., 164–5.
[11] Ibid., 154–5.

is to act, to do something, indeed to begin something new, and to do so in the presence of others who can witness it, participate, and carry it forward.

Freedom as virtuosity is best understood not as the capacity to decide but the capacity to *begin*. What, after all, is freedom, if not to act in a way not determined by what came before—in other words, to make a new beginning? To be free means to act in a way that does not simply continue processes that were already in motion but to do something, to introduce newness.

For Arendt, this sense of acting and beginning is essential to being human. Philosophers and theologians tend to define human beings as essentially mortal, indeed as beings whose wisdom, ambition, and faith may grow from facing and understanding their own finitude. Arendt opposes this sense of an essential mortality to the way human beings are essentially *born* creatures, that is, essentially marked by the way their emergence into the world marks something new, a beginning not determined by what came before. Our capacity for freedom, for shared life among equals, stems from the way we are beginners par excellence. Arendt calls this our "natality."

> The life span of man running toward death would inevitably carry everything human to ruin and destruction if it were not for the faculty of interrupting it and beginning something new, a faculty which is inherent in action like an ever-present reminder that men [sic], though they must die, are not born in order to die but in order to begin.[12]

In Schleitheim's language, we might refer to this capacity to begin as the renewal of life "in the resurrection," a new beginning par excellence. For both Schleitheim and Arendt, human beings—at least under the conditions of having been "taught"—are capable of such beginnings. For both Schleitheim and Arendt, it is this newness that counters and interrupts the rule of death and oppression. And for both, again, this newness is not merely an individual capacity but can only unfold its meaning in relational life with others.

This parallel with a deeply secular thinker may seem facile—after all, does this not lose sight of the way Schleitheim also considers a divine invitation to precede and instigate the whole process? Yet Arendt, in spite of her secular commitments, again and again returns to eminently theological material to explain the significance of such beginning. So she calls the capacity to begin in freedom "the one miracle-working faculty of man" that can "bestow upon human affairs faith and hope."[13]

> In the birth of each man [sic] this initial beginning is reaffirmed, because in each instance something new comes into an already existing world which will continue to exist after each individual's death. Because he *is*

---

[12]Hannah Arendt, *The Human Condition* (Chicago: University of Chicago Press, 2018), 246.
[13]Ibid., 246–7.

a beginning, man can begin; to be human and to be free are one and the same. God created man in order to introduce into the world the faculty of beginning: freedom.[14]

Jesus of Nazareth, Arendt notes, never instructs his followers to anything resembling sovereign freedom of the will. But he *persistently* exhorts them to action and to a new beginning. This is nowhere as clear as in his instruction to perform miracles. For what is a miracle if not an action that interrupts, with startling unexpectedness, the processes that are already in motion—what is a miracle if not an occurrence that does not simply derive from what came before it? What is a miracle, if not the introduction of newness—a new beginning indeed?

Political theorist Carl Schmitt, who has made the capacity to decide crucial to his understanding of sovereign political power (of which we will hear more in Chapter 6), reads the miracle as indicative of the unbounded independent sovereignty of God: His omnipotence exists in his capacity to perform exceptions to His own rules. But Arendt reads Jesus's exhortation to perform miracles as indicative not of an exceptional divine power but of the shared human capacity to begin, to gather and act *as beginners*.

> Every act, seen from the perspective not of the agent but of the process in whose framework it occurs and whose automatism it interrupts, is a "miracle"—that is, something which could not be expected. If it is true that action and beginning are essentially the same, it follows that a capacity for performing miracles must likewise be within the range of human faculties ... It is in the very nature of every new beginning that it breaks into the world as an "infinite improbability," and yet it is precisely this infinitely improbable which actually constitutes the very texture of everything we call real.[15]

Freedom understood in this way, as the capacity to act and to begin, is not inimical to lived community in the way that freedom as individual sovereignty was. It is not eclipsed but intensified in the presence of others. It is not limited to a narrowly defined either-or decision but takes shape in the shared life of the community as a self-organized fellowship of equals, making its own way. A community of beginners, a community called together not from free unbound individuals but from those who make a new beginning in life.

This is what it will mean to have been "taught": Arendt highlights how the influx of new generations, though it bestows faith and hope on human affairs, also requires interminable integration into the existing community. Those who have been "taught" are those who can be trusted with this

---

[14] Arendt, *Between Past and Future*, 167. Emphasis in original.
[15] Ibid., 169.

kind of freedom, who know how to take their place in a self-organized community of equals.

Beginning Again

It seems to me that this sense of a miraculous new beginning is more resonant with the life "in the resurrection" of this community than the language of sovereign decision. Though there remains a moment of existential individuality in the choice to accept God's invitation into renewed life, the process fully belongs to neither the church nor the convert, nor indeed to God, who may invoke and provoke but leaves much in the hands of human choice.[16] Though the convert must take initiative, must *begin*, this does not make them master of the process. Both their relation to forgiveness—as their sins are "taken away"—and to the wider community and tradition—as they are "taught" and baptism is "given"—are described in the passive tense. Though they must utter the request, though human beings are capable of making a new beginning in this way, this also cannot take place without the recognition that, in a very real and crucial way, it is not *simply* one's own capacity that makes this new beginning, that one is called into something greater than one's own sovereign freedom, and that in making this new beginning one is participating in the way God makes a new beginning.

---

[16]Elsewhere I have written about the way this kind of "beginning" takes place in what are described to be the very first baptisms of the Anabaptist movement in Zurich. The description of this event by sixteenth-century chronicler Caspar Braitmichel seems to acknowledge that there was something not quite proper about it. If only the church can baptize, but only the baptized can form a church, where do we begin? An improvised solution is found: Conrad Grebel first baptizes Georg Blaurock, who then turns around and baptizes the others present—including Grebel. Of course, such a mutual baptism is not the "proper" way of doing things, Braitmichel seems to admit. A congregation that does not yet exist ordains, without apparent rule or procedure, a man who is himself not yet baptized to welcome to their community a man who would, in turn, subsequently welcome them. Yet it must happen this way, Braitmichel notes, because of exceptional circumstances: "At that time there was no ordained minister." The church must begin *im*properly before it can properly begin.

Under these murky conditions, this "Anabaptist moment" fails to rise to the proud, unassailable confidence of an origin, of a true founding event to the Anabaptist traditions. Yet this improper murkiness—that is, this openness—may be especially good news: in it, we might see the conditions for a beginning *again*, a kind of beginning that does not belong exclusively to any party involved. The constructed and shaky character of all this may, paradoxically, be the conditions for divine in(ter)vention of an especially improper, destabilizing, and promising kind.

With this, we might say that the Anabaptist moment, in all its exceptional impropriety, also seems to illustrate the most common and everyday experience of being church. Beginning again, together, as we commit to, receive, and participate in a church that is still becoming, with little to go on but Scripture and the faith in our hearts and a divine invitation easily overheard or denied, that places itself into our hands as a fragile, insistent possibility. See Marius van Hoogstraten, "The Anabaptist Moment: Improper Beginnings, Ecclesiopolitical Decisions, and a Nonviolent Sovereignty," *Mennonite Quarterly Review* 95 (October 2021): 495–512.

This relational interdependence of a new beginning means it can no longer play the role of a compressed, unambiguous starting point. In the terminology of literary theorist Edward Said, this *beginning* is not an *origin*. In Said's understanding, an *origin* stands as sovereign, wholly undetermined by what precedes it and fully determining what follows from it. An origin is almost already sufficient: what follows from it is merely the enacting or unfolding of a flow of events already fixed in that original founding moment. A *beginning*, on the contrary, is merely a first step, significant though it may be, opening up what may follow instead of closing it down. In Said's words, while "origin centrally dominates what derives from it, the beginning ... encourages nonlinear development."[17]

Beginning "implies return and repetition," to which we should add that repetition is never simply the same thing again but is always to some degree also newness (see Chapter 2). That is to say, beginning does not simply stand by itself but takes up what came before it, in which it represents a change of direction. In a way beginning remains incomplete, that is to say, open—the beginning of something as yet unwritten. In this sense, Said notes, beginning is always "beginning-again."[18] A new beginning is always a *new* beginning, we might say, a renewal or reversal.

If baptism were an origin, it would both fully eclipse one's previous life and fully determine the life that follows: in a sense, it would be the only moment, the only decision that matters in one's entire life. If baptism is a beginning, however, it takes up (repents, perhaps—a change of direction indeed) one's previous life and in a sense returns it to the natality that marks human creaturely existence. Thus understood, "amendment of life" is the amendment *of* life, we might say: it itself is made new again. One's past life is not annihilated but taken up and recapitulated; this change of direction also represents a restoration and opening up of that life unto its own future "in the resurrection."

To put this differently, life "in the resurrection" does not occur *ex nihilo*, neither by force of sovereign divine decree nor by force of sovereign human decision. This is a new beginning that takes place, in the terminology of theologian Catherine Keller, *ex profundis*, from the depths. This is how Keller understands God's creative work more generally, and she especially reads the creation narrative of Genesis 1 in this light. God's creative work does not lay a unilateral origin but makes a beginning. In Keller's interpretation, God creates not as a unilateral sovereign but precisely by calling forth self-organization and newness from the waters of the Deep. Creation itself participates in its being-created; it is *co*-creation, a collaborative coproduction, as God calls and invites and creation itself

---

[17]Edward W. Said, *Beginnings: Intention and Method* (New York: Columbia University Press, 1985), 372.
[18]Said, *Beginnings*, xxiii.

responds, participating in its own beginning as it emerges from (not against) the ambiguous depths.[19]

And is there not a strange affinity between these unruly waters of creation, from which a beginning is called forth, and the waters of baptism, from which a new beginning is summoned? If this is true, it would highlight the way the waters of baptism not only safeguard against ambiguity—as per above—but also in a sense stand for the ambiguities of creaturely life. As the Deep of Genesis is eminently ambiguous, both life-giving womb and threatening chaos at the same time, so perhaps the baptismal waters also take up that ambiguity, representing after all death *and* new life at once.[20]

Seen this way, we might say that baptism does not cut us off from the creaturely interdependence that makes up our lives (as I wondered earlier) but calls us back into it. It does not eclipse our natality as born creatures but restores us to that freedom that may have gotten lost on the way.

In Greek, we can distinguish between life as *zoe*, that is, creaturely, bodily life, and *bios*, which tends to refer to professional or otherwise organized and qualified life. One might expect the renewal of life in baptism to deal in *bios*, inducting one into an organized and disciplined kind of life and separating one from unruly *zoe*. Yet the opposite seems to be the case: the "newness of life" in which the baptized are said to walk in Rom. 6:4 is precisely the *kainote[s] zoes*: the renewal of *zoe*, of creaturely, bodily *life*, not controlled and regulated *bios*. Renewed life in the resurrection, we might say, does not comprise the cutting off or excepting from this creaturely *zoe* that we share with all creation, but a renewed relationship, perhaps even a commitment to it. It does not replace one's first creaturely birth—a connotation in any case absent from the Schleitheim text—but takes up one's natality as the capacity to begin.

In this way God calls the church together: not against the murky ambiguities of creaturely existence, not cutting off from our relatedness in earthy *zoe*, but from these, in them and through them. This is not a calling that ends or disappears when one emerges from the baptismal water. The renewal marked in baptism is most true to its character as a beginning if it is not merely a singular, decisive moment but a moment of recapitulation and renewal to which the faithful return again and again. We do not decisively begin again once, but instead take on this renewal, this capacity to begin again, and carry it forward into the shared life.

This would bring us into the vicinity of contemporary Irish philosopher Richard Kearney. Kearney seeks a return to God after the disillusionment known as the "death of God" in the twentieth century. After the terrors of war and genocide, Kearney holds, it may no longer be possible to believe in

---

[19]Catherine Keller, *Face of the Deep: A Theology of Becoming* (London: Routledge, 2003).
[20]Burgess also highlights how the water of baptism evokes the watery chaos of creation, as well as "the waters of the mother's womb" and the "waters that flow through all creation ... [and] spring forth from the earth to refresh and sustain life." Burgess, "Baptism," 53.

God as a sovereign ruler. But after such atheistic disenchantment, perhaps we can return again to the biblical narrative, moved to rediscover God in a different way: not as a sovereign Lord but as a solicitous stranger who invites us into the transformation of the everyday. This is an invitation, Kearney stresses, to which we may respond in freedom, requiring our choice and participation. In an unexpected parallel to our material, he calls this return to God "anatheism," in which the *ana* of anatheism refers to this movement of retrieval: in Greek *ana-theos*, God, again. Kearney stresses that this is not achieved in a single moment: Anatheism means "repeating, recalling, returning, again and again."[21]

In a sense, the Anabaptism of Schleitheim is almost already such an anatheist venture. After all, it, too, seeks to return to God, to take up again the biblical witness, "after" (or perhaps during) the perceived failure and collapse of traditional ways of believing tied up with sovereignty.

If this new beginning thus takes place amid, not against, the interdependence of creaturely life, and if it is not a sharp disjunctive "cut" between before and after but a messier and more relational process, this also means that the cut between the inside and the outside of the church is less clear. Earlier, I noted that these two are closely related: the more unambiguous and binary the distinction between the past life of the convert and their future life in the resurrection, the more unambiguous and clear the border between the inside and the outside of the church. So, here, vice versa: if the renewal of baptism turns out to be a messier and more processual affair, marked by provocation and response, requesting and giving, this must also mean that it cannot ground the kind of unambiguous clarity Schleitheim seemed to be hoping for.

This seems to be true in a more everyday sense as well. A congregation practicing exclusively adult baptism may avoid some of the specific ambiguities related to infant baptism but will hardly thereby be able to avoid the messiness of actual existence. In a way, voluntary baptism even seems to particularly expose it to it. If we take its logic seriously, an Anabaptist community might well have *more* people in and around the church who are not, formally, "in" the church: not least children and youth, who are not formally in the church but of course will be present at gatherings and whose life shapes that of their congregant parents and other older relatives. The adult members do not enter the congregation as abstracted individuals. They pass through the waters of baptism as related and relating creatures, bringing with them much of their already formed lives: their familial relations and friendships, their profession and skills, and maybe even their interests and ways of thinking.[22]

---

[21]Richard Kearney, *Anatheism: Returning to God After God* (New York: Columbia University Press, 2011), 5.

[22]For this reason Pitts notes that although Anabaptists today often see baptism as a marker of distinction, the reality of the practice is much more ambiguous, and its effects are sometimes difficult to foresee. The "conviction that baptismal practice unambiguously distinguishes

The ambiguity I named earlier, the sheer unruliness of creaturely *zoe*, the simple indelible entanglement of our being into at least several interdependencies, is not overcome in this renewal of life but essential to the very *zoe* that is renewed. As long as we live as living creatures, we will not decisively be able to leave this behind, nor indeed does it seem to be the calling of the church to do so. Something of creaturely life will persist, even through this passage of death and resurrection, insisting into the neat clarity of ecclesial borders.

Conclusion

Baptism marks or indeed makes a new beginning. Schleitheim emphasizes it must be freely chosen. It would be tempting to read this as anticipating modern individual freedom. With Hannah Arendt, I have suggested that this freedom-as-sovereignty is not compatible with the shared life in community, nor indeed with the relational process in which Schleitheim depicts this choice to take place. In shared public life, Arendt suggests, freedom means not the freedom to decide independently of others but to act interdependently with others and to do so in ways that do not simply derive from processes already in motion but in ways that make a beginning. Time and again, Arendt returns to explicitly theological language to explain the significance of this human capacity to begin, and she finds it especially embodied in Jesus Christ's instruction to his followers to perform miracles—after all likewise an interruption of the expected.

This interruption or action in concert with others thus introduces newness to the world. But it introduces newness *to* the world in which it is acting. The renewal here does not annihilate the meaning and relationship of the life that came before but liberates it into a new beginning, indeed sets free within it the capacity to begin at all. So, in this sense, the baptismal moment is not an origin but a beginning, a renewal called forth from the waters of ambiguity.

It seems to be that the life of faith, for Schleitheim, is akin to what freedom is for Arendt: it cannot be an individual question, is not (just) a matter of the existential inner life of the singular person, but needs a realm or community where it is a tangible reality. And in turn this is the kind of freedom that, with Schleitheim, maybe we can now affirm more than the modern exceptionalism of the individual.

This freedom as self-organization (or indeed *sympoiesis*) is both an ecclesio-political task and a more general human capacity. Because, at least

---

Christians from 'the world' forecloses vulnerability." Instead, Pitts sees baptism as "relat[ing] Christians to the world," and recognizing the ambiguity of this relation allows the church to remain "open to unexpected gifts from different others." In Said's words, "nonlinear development" is essential to this new beginning and its promise. See Pitts, "Baptism," 326.

under the conditions of having been "taught," human beings appear to be capable of making such a new beginning. A person is not *so* determined by sin or human nature or their worldly upbringing that such newness would become impossible without a unilateral *ex nihilo* intervention of God. Nor indeed are human beings inversely *so* determined by the saving work of Christ, or their being part of God's good creation, or (perhaps) having been raised in an Anabaptist community that such renewal would become unnecessary. It is this in-between-state, this human ambiguity by which we are not fully determined one way or the other, in which our freedom takes place.

The incompleteness of this and every beginning, the way it never cleanly cuts apart *before* from *after* but remains a renewal within a relational process of divine-human interaction, is not as a loss or a failure, it seems to me. We might well think so, of course: the ambiguity or messiness of life often seems like a tragic failure of life in this world to ever fully live up to neat divine perfection. But maybe we would do better to see it as precisely the site and carrier of renewal. The messiness of actual existence is the place, we might say, where good news takes place.

2

Repetition

Introduction

Although baptism marks a new beginning and a commitment to a new way of life, it alone cannot guarantee the shared life of the community. Schleitheim's second article therefore discusses discipline: the practice of institutionalized mutual admonition by which problematic members can be called into account and if necessary be excommunicated or "banned."

To modern readers, church discipline may evoke associations of the oppressive enforcement of conformist norms of purity. Those churches that still practice mutual admonition and excommunication are often considered narrow-minded or oppressive in the public mind. Church discipline and the ban seem suggestive of a kind of church more invested in conformism and control than in the freedom of a new beginning of Chapter 1; more invested in the assimilation of individual members into a collective unity than a plural fellowship of equals. At its heart, discipline is a means to exert force, to assert a norm, and to impose accountability between members. The use of such a system as a heteropatriarchal instrument of shame, exclusion, and submission, employed by church leadership to cement their hierarchical control over the community, is not hard to imagine.

And yet taken by itself, it is also not difficult to imagine the necessity of *some* means of exerting force. Discipline and the ban are the closest Schleitheim gets to admitting that a nonsovereign community, even if it is in one sense a nonresistant community (see Chapter 6), must in another sense also be a *resistant* community; that, having broken with the instruments of sovereign force, it must develop some alternative means of safeguarding its members from the harmful acts of their supposed brothers or sisters. And we might well agree that membership in a voluntary community can only include the commitment to a particular way of life if there is also some way to regulate and enforce the adherence to that commitment and, if necessary, to dismiss unrepentant problematic members. Simply put, those members who prove themselves unwilling to live in a fellowship of equals with their brothers and sisters can be shown the door.

Comprehensive excommunication is certainly drastic, but it can also be seen as a way for a voluntaristic community to separate from harmful members and maintain its shared space *as* a space of freedom and plurality without relying on violent sanctions or on the disciplinary system of the state (again, more on which in Chapter 6). Unrepentant offenders are not harmed or indeed killed but merely sent on their way, their capacity to act with others suspended until they are ready to return to the fellowship. This is not, taken by itself, an oppressive or conformist notion; indeed it seems to me that an assertive and defiant nonsovereign community will barely be possible without such a system.

In this chapter, I will discuss Schleitheim's approach to discipline along three main issues. After taking a closer look at the text itself, I ask what the significance might be that such a system is required at all: what does it suggest about the nature of the church and human existence? Second, I look at Schleitheim's formulation around what seems to cause sinful behavior in baptized members at all. Perhaps surprisingly, no mention is made of an evil antagonist. Instead, members seem to fall victim to something like an inherent slipperiness to the path they are walking. Finally, I discuss how this second article illustrates the ecclesio-political community's way of being in time, as marked by a temporality, not of expectation or recollection but of repetition.

Reading

The second of the Schleitheim Articles is again fairly brief. It begins by noting that those present are "agreed" (*vereiniget worden*) on the "ban" (*Bann*). It

> shall be employed with all those who have given themselves to the Lord, to follow in His commandments, and with all those who are baptized into one body of Christ and who are called brothers or sisters, and yet who slip sometimes and fall into sin, being inadvertently overtaken.

Such problematic members are to be "admonished twice in secret," then "the third time openly disciplined or banned," as recommended in Matthew 18. "According to the regulation of the Spirit," we read, this is to take place "before the breaking of bread, so that we may break and eat one bread, with one mind and in one love, and may drink of one cup."

As before, the text is of striking formality. It regulates how problematic members may be dealt with but says nothing about what type of behavior might constitute the "sin" that warrants such sanction. It also leaves the concrete details or extent of the banning practice implicit, such as whether those banned are merely excluded from the communion ritual or also shunned from the shared life of the congregation.[1] The text is also not

---

[1] Schleitheim's contemporary and fellow Anabaptist reformer Balthasar Hubmaier insists such more general everyday exclusion must be part of the ban. For Hubmaier, interaction with

entirely clear if excommunication is an alternative to this final exhortation ("disciplined *or* banned") or perhaps a consequence of its failure (disciplined or, if that fails, banned), or if indeed "banning" here simply *means* a public exhortation as its synonym (disciplined, that is to say, banned). The second of these seems most plausible,² but the text is not definitive. These are thus not very detailed instructions, perhaps except for the remark that this final disciplining or banning should take place within the worship service and right before communion so that the breaking of bread—in which the community gathers in presence—can take place in unity.³

Perhaps not much more needs to be said:⁴ like other Anabaptists, Schleitheim affirms the need for a kind of system of discipline to hold members of the congregation to their commitments. Should a baptized congregant display sinful behavior (or perhaps heretical opinions), they should first be reproached twice privately, then openly in front of the gathered congregation, after which they may be excommunicated. By means of such

---

banned persons must strictly be limited to the bare minimum of human obligation such as giving food, water, or shelter if they have nowhere else to go. Otherwise, congregants are to have "no fellowship" with the banned: neither greet them in the street, nor eat with them, nor perform any kindnesses or mutual aid. See Balthasar Hubmaier, "On the Christian Ban," in *Balthasar Hubmaier: Theologian of Anabaptism*, ed. H. Wayne Pipkin and John H. Yoder, Classics of the Radical Reformation (Walden: Plough, 2019), 417–18.

Wenger claims that "ban" in Schleitheim means "excommunication, not the (later) Obbenite practice of shunning" but offers little to substantiate that this is indeed what is meant. See Wenger, "Schleitheim," 248n25.

Historically, fierce debates on the appropriate scope and severity of church discipline quickly became a major feature of the Anabaptist ecclesial landscape, leading to significant church splits. These include (but are not limited to) the collective excommunication of the entire Swiss Anabaptist church by the Dutch in 1559, and the Mennonite/Amish split in 1693. See, for example, Snyder, *Anabaptist History and Theology*, 339–47; John D. Roth, ed., *Letters of the Amish Division: A Sourcebook* (Goshen: Mennonite Historical Society, 1993).

On Yoder, see note note 3 on p. 94–5 (Chapter 6).
²This is also what Snyder suggests; see Snyder, *Life and Thought*, 134.
³After the words "regulation of the Spirit," Wenger adds the reference to Matthew 5, possibly intending verse 21: "So when you are offering your gift at the altar, if you remember that your brother or sister has something against you, leave your gift there before the altar and go; first be reconciled to your brother or sister, and then come and offer your gift." Yet this would suggest communion as a kind of sacrifice, an understanding with which the next article breaks. There is also no mention in Matthew 5 of a "regulation of the Spirit."
⁴One explanation for the brevity of the first three articles is given by Snyder, who notes Schleitheim's first three articles names issues "held in common with the Anabaptists who had gone before, from Hubmaier, to Grebel, to Reublin." See Snyder, *Anabaptist History and Theology*, 61.

Snyder notes three possible historical routes of provenance for the ban in the Anabaptist movement: Benedictine discipline, which also included a form of excommunication and must obviously have been well known to Sattler; Conrad Grebel's letter to Müntzer, in which it already seems to appear; and the peasants' rebellion, which likewise seemed to practice it. See Snyder, "The Schleitheim Articles," 428; Snyder, *Life and Thought*, 264.

For what it is worth, the early Anabaptist communities in Zollikon and Esslingen appear not to have practiced banning. See Snyder, "Birth and Evolution," 544, 622.

disciplining, the kind of ethical standards and collective unity ("one mind and ... one love") Schleitheim envisions for the church can be maintained.

The basis for this system is found in Matthew 18. There, Jesus gives instructions on how to respond when "your brother sins": One is to "point out the fault" privately, then, if unsuccessful, with one or two witnesses, and finally to "tell it to the church; and if the offender refuses to listen even to the church, let such a one be to you as a Gentile and a tax collector" (Mt. 18:17). This single biblical citation may seem like not very much compared to the multiple biblical sources named in Schleitheim's first article: Why should this one Gospel passage be so prominent to merit an article of its own, even the second one at that?

It seems to me that at least one reason this particular point is given such prominence is its structural necessity.[5] If baptism is not only the voluntary entry into the church but also the commitment to a particular way of life, and if at the same time people remain in principle capable of actions that go against those commitments (so if they remain free, if they are not *so* transformed by this new beginning that the human capacity to do harm is wholly excised), then some mechanism or structure is necessary by which the church can assert its way of life and to maintain its standards, to correct members when they relapse into behavior that does not fit the church's teachings, and if necessary to regulate the suspension of their membership.

The need for such a means of self-assertion is especially great, it seems, since the church is to eschew the means of sovereign state violence.[6] The contrast between church discipline and the sanctions of the "sword" is not made explicit here, but in the sixth article, the ban is more clearly framed in such a contrast: in the church, "only the ban is used for a warning and

---

[5] John Roth has therefore argued that church discipline is an "essential corollary" to voluntary baptism, required to preserve "the integrity both of the voluntary choice and the moral character of the congregation." See John D. Roth, "The Church 'Without Spot or Wrinkle' in Anabaptist Experience," in *Without Spot or Wrinkle: Reflecting Theologically on the Nature of the Church*, ed. Karl Koop and Mary H. Schertz (Eugene: Wipf, 2015), 13.

[6] Elsewhere, I have discussed the system of discipline and the ban as laid out by Schleitheim's contemporary Balthasar Hubmaier. Hubmaier has a different understanding of the church than Schleitheim, particularly of the church-state or church-world relationship, and his discussions of discipline and the ban are both more detailed and differently accented. Based on a reading of Hubmaier, I described discipline and the ban as a kind of "biopower." With this term, philosopher Michel Foucault refers to the way the exertion of power undergoes a shift in modernity: previously, sovereign power had mostly been a question of punishment or reprieve, making up the "power of life and death" in the sense that the sovereign has "the right to take life or let live." In modernity, however, the highest function of power becomes "no longer to kill, but to invest life through and through." Modern power is more about shaping, regulating, and producing a certain kind of life: "The ancient right to take life or let live was replaced by a power to foster life or disallow it to the point of death." See Michel Foucault, *The History of Sexuality: Volume 1, an Introduction* (New York: Pantheon, 1978), 136, 139, 138.

This sense of the collective shaping of a body is not entirely absent in Schleitheim but considerably stronger in Hubmaier. See Marius van Hoogstraten, "Doperse Biomacht: Balthasar Hubmaier, de Tucht En de Ban," *Doopsgezinde Bijdragen* 48 (2022): 13–30.

for the excommunication of the one who has sinned, without putting the flesh to death,—simply the warning and the command to sin no more" (see Chapter 6).

This sense of a structural necessity is amplified by the apparent mirroring between baptism and the ban: if one regulates entry into the community, the other regulates one's (enforced) exit. Schleitheim stresses that this kind of discipline is only to be applied to baptized members, suggesting the basis of the community's authority over its members is given in their voluntary commitment. If, in baptism, the ecclesio-political community marks the distinction between inside and the outside, this distinction is reasserted, it would seem, when someone is banned: the borders of the community are regulated and reinforced by the exclusion. Yet at the same time, as we will see later, this mirroring is not seamless: the banned person is not simply returned to an unbaptized state but consigned to something of a suspended position.

The orientation of this disciplinary system is, at least on the surface, explicitly collective. There is little here to suggest the main concern of admonition and excommunication is the individual character or soul of the sinning member. At stake, Schleitheim stresses, is the shared life of the community: its capacity to gather "with one mind and in one love."[7]

While this (rudimentary) system of discipline, on the one hand, seems quite clear in its structural role and orientation, it also raises at least several questions that I will address in the remainder of this chapter. These are independent of the brief character of Schleitheim's instructions (what they leave implicit) but are instead concerned with what they suggest about the character of the church and its way of being in time. For one, we might ask if this structural necessity of a disciplinary structure is not also somewhat surprising. After the new beginning marked by baptism, would it not be equally sensible to expect such disciplinary structure to have become superfluous? Yet from the very start—this is not a recognition made grudgingly after many years of Anabaptist existence—there is the tragic sense that being church is a persistent struggle, that its shared life is not once and for all given, but must interminably be asserted.

Second, we might note that it is asserted against a force that remains remarkably anonymous. How shall we read Schleitheim's suggestion of an insistent countervailing force that resists the smooth integration into a collective—what does it mean, in other words, to "slip sometimes and fall,"

---

[7] We might find it somewhat callous to speak of "one love" after a member has just been excluded. Perhaps a different reading will be possible—see below.

In historical practice the ban has often been an instrument used primarily by leaders against others, certainly not always in line with the kinds of principles of self-organization of free and equal members I am espousing in this book. Yet in the text itself, disciplinary authority appears to be a mutual authority of members over each other. Even if the text describes banning and admonishing as tasks of the shepherd (whose status as a "leader" is itself unclear—see Chapter 5), this shepherd is in turn also subject to admonition, even somewhat more harshly.

and what causes such slipperiness? Finally, a certain sense of temporality begins to emerge: how can we interpret Schleitheim's emphasis that the shared life of the church, such as it is, is not guaranteed by an unassailable foundation or imminent futurity but produced in repeated practice?

Asserting the Ecclesio-Political

From the very start, the necessity of some disciplinary procedure is clear to the Schleitheim group. There is no expectation here, not even an initial naïve optimism, that baptized Christians would be so radically remade, and that the church would be such a pure collective body, that discipline will be unnecessary. The necessity that this must, in some sense, be a resistant community, must have some means of exerting force at its disposal, is not recognized grudgingly after many years of messier-than-expected church life. From the very start, there is the realization that interminable regulating, shaping, and reasserting will be necessary for this kind of shared life to persist.

This community is not guaranteed; it is not once and for all given but remains a task and a struggle. From the very start, there is thus the realization that by itself, the new beginning of baptism remains in some sense incomplete or at least that it by itself will not suffice to maintain the life of the community in time.

At its philosophical root, we might read the Schleitheim venture as the assertion of a possibility: things could be otherwise. Even in the midst of catastrophe, human community is not simply doomed to run toward death. It is possible to make a new beginning. The current relations of power, both ecclesial and worldly, are not the inevitable and fixed product of nature or metaphysics or divine institution but are contingent and thus can be transformed.

Yet this assertion of possibility cuts both ways. The community Schleitheim envisions does not itself remain insulated from the contingency it is asserting. It itself is also not fixed, guaranteed, or inevitable. Even under the conditions of divine invitation, it is clear that the shared life of the ecclesio-political community is also—in Chantal Mouffe's words—merely "the temporary and precarious articulation of contingent practices."[8]

Perhaps Sattler and his fellows did not think about it in such terms. Perhaps they truly did consider the form of life they were enunciating as uniquely privileged and anchored to divinely revealed truth. But at least on some level, the text they have left us with seems aware of, or open to, its own fragility or weakness. In giving such prominence to the work of asserting its form of life, there is—at the very least—the recognition that the kind

---

[8] Mouffe, *On the Political*, 18.

of community it envisions will not simply fall from the sky. This becomes especially clear in the structural necessity it seems to consider discipline to have, but in a sense it is also true for the text as a whole. Each of the practices it proposes is concerned with constituting, regulating, and shaping a shared life, with the interminable work such shared life requires to persist. After all, if faithful community would simply spring into place as soon as a few believers got together, the Schleitheim Articles would be eminently unnecessary.

So it is precisely in detailing with careful rigor the practices that make and maintain the collective body of the church that Schleitheim shows a peculiar awareness that such shared life is not simply given. It does not fall from the sky whole but must be made, asserted against other possibilities, and it must be shaped, disciplined, and reasserted at every step of the way.

So there is a sense here that Schleitheim (perhaps in spite of its authors' intentions) on some level seems aware that church as a community, as an institution, remains marked by an insistent contingency or fragility. The way the life of the church takes shape is not guaranteed, even if it does gather in response to a divine call. And this, in turn, suggests something about this call: that even though it reaches the faithful from beyond themselves, even if they discern in it the weight of the eternal Creator, the call itself is as weak as a word.

It is up to the faithful to make the church real in any meaningful sense of that word. Just as Keller suggested that in creation, God calls and invites but creation itself responds, participating in its own becoming (see Chapter 1), so here it seems that while God calls and invites, the church participates in its self-organized becoming in response. It is almost—perhaps not quite—as theologian John Caputo describes it, when he states provocatively that "God does not exist; God insists, and it is our responsibility to bring about something that exists."[9] For Caputo, the life of faith and the existence of the church revolve fundamentally around this relationship between (on the one hand) God's weak but insistent, even unconditional call, claim, or promise and (on the other hand) the creaturely response which is thus empowered and tasked with making that promise real. For Caputo this is fundamentally a prayerful relationship. "In prayer, we are made strong by the insistence (or weakness) of God, and the insistence of God is made strong by our existence."[10]

So if this is the assertion of a possibility, it is not one in the style of the proud confidence of power that can do what it wishes, what Arendt described as sovereignty (see Chapter 1). Even in the best of circumstances, the text seems aware of its own weakness—especially, perhaps, in contrast to the overwhelming forces of crisis, catastrophe, and collapse that surround

---

[9]John D. Caputo, *The Insistence of God: A Theology of Perhaps* (Bloomington: Indiana University Press, 2013), 49.
[10]Ibid., 31.

it. And yet, paradoxically, it is this weakness of the divine word that leaves much in creaturely hands, that seems to also empower the faithful to a kind of freedom in which their action matters. It is their *sympoiesis* or becoming-with in persistent self-organization that makes the shared life of this persistently unfinished church real.

Negotiating Ambiguity

As the community self-organizes in response to the divine call, something resists its smooth integration into a collective body. The defense this community requires is not only aimed against influences from the outside (more on which in Chapter 4) but especially also against an apparent countervailing force at work in its inside. Even baptized and committed members, we read, are in danger of coming to "slip sometimes and fall into sin, being inadvertently overtaken."

This is an enigmatic sentence: the force against which discipline is employed, the power that causes committed members to fall into sin, remains strangely unnamed. There is no mention of any active or conscious effort that would lead or tempt anyone into sin. Not Satan, as we might well expect, nor an "old Adam,"[11] nor even the world and its tempting ways. Sin seems to just *happen*. Indeed, even less than "happen," as it does not do anything or go anywhere. In Schleitheim's formulation, it does not infest or attack the faithful; it does not even persist or hold on. Instead it is the congregant who *falls into* sin, as if sin were simply there in its own place, unconcerned with the business of the faithful, until a congregant crashes onto it.

Yet even the faithful, as they slip and fall, do not *do* anything. They do not seek out sin or choose the wrong path: they merely *are* overtaken, even "inadvertently" so, the text stresses, as if to further highlight that nobody really wanted all of this to happen in the first place. Whatever or whoever does the overtaking in any case remains anonymous.

Nobody really seems to be at fault here in any substantive sense. We must simply expect this kind of thing to happen sometimes, Schleitheim seems to be saying, with no intentional causative actor behind it. Sin is not something

---

[11]Hubmaier discusses the ongoing struggle against sin as one against human nature and the "old Adam," who actively resist their subjugation. The old Adam will "begin to raise his ears, to grumble, to buck, to snort, and to kick out before and behind" in response to disciplining. See Balthasar Hubmaier, "On Fraternal Admonition," in *Balthasar Hubmaier: Theologian of Anabaptism*, ed. H. Wayne Pipkin and John H. Yoder, Classics of the Radical Reformation (Walden: Plough, 2019), 376.

Hubmaier also uses medical metaphors that further bring the casual unexcitedness of Schleitheim into contrast. So Hubmaier argues it is sometimes necessary "completely to cut off the corrupt and stinking flesh together with the poisoned and unclean members" to prevent a whole body from being corrupted, also describing sin like a cancer or leprosy that must be excised with haste. See ibid., 374, 378.

anyone does intentionally but more a matter of ethical stumbling, a slipping or falling that simply seems to occur without a real reason. The sinner simply loses their balance or grip on the path they are walking. A path, we might thus add, that appears to be somewhat slippery simply by itself. Falling while walking on it seems to be par for the course.

So the text seems to be under no illusion that congregants can truly and definitively be prevented from slipping and falling on such a slippery path. Certainly, such occurrences require a response in order to safeguard those harmed and restore the shared life of the community. But this anonymous countervailing force, which does nothing and for which nobody is at fault, will never be definitively exorcised. It is perhaps precisely because this possibility is so ephemeral that it will continue to haunt the community as an elusive specter more than a graspable opponent.

A kind of fundamental underlying unruliness seems to haunt or inhabit things, life, and human existence, persistently undermining any attempt at shaping a pure collective. An existential messiness, we might say, or creaturely ambiguity, which occasions persistent reassertion and remaking of the ecclesio-political body.

As I noted earlier, the orientation of discipline in shoring up the community and enforcing its standards is less in the service of the individual pedagogy—helping congregants that slip and fall back to their feet—but of shaping a collective body or shared space. This orientation is especially expressed in the way discipline is to take place just before communion: that is, before the assembly or staging of the unity of the community (see Chapter 3). It must take place at this point, we read, *so that* the breaking of bread can take place "with one mind and in one love."

One way to read this would be to say that discipline is thus exerted to achieve unity in the church, indeed unity of a certain kind, the holistic oneness of a single shared body, a single shared mind, a single shared love (not, we might say, a manifold of relationships among the many members, but *one* love encompassing all). Such unity would allow for no dissent or ambiguity to stain its collective wholeness; it is thus not strange that before this collective unity is made present in communion, any such impurity must be either excised or subsumed through repentance.[12] A community of this kind would be perpetually in a bitter war with any such insistent ambiguity,

---

[12]In spite of Hubmaier's dramatic medical metaphor, he considers repentance and return the main orientation of the ban. Excommunication is intended to cause shame in the banned person, which will help lead them back. See ibid., 380; Hubmaier, "Ban," 423–4.

Repentance, apparently a highly emotionally charged event, further serves to assimilate the individual sinner into the collective body. Their emotions must both be true and appropriate: they are expected to mold their expression of grief and regret into the collective image of appropriate emotional expression, both *authentically* and *recognizably* repentant. This further shapes the force of discipline: repenting is not merely about one's own feelings and intentions; it must also be (recognizable as) submission, as the acceptance of and bending to the authority of the church. This tension can only be resolved if, for the repentant sinner, freedom

which is the constant threat of its undoing and which it cannot afford to tolerate. This seems like it would occasion stronger language than simply slipping and falling.

Yet as we will read in Chapter 3 and Chapter 5, a characteristic of this nonsovereign community is precisely that it is not *one* in this way: the shared life of the community is not a unity given by conformity and homogeneity but the process or work of gathering an irreducible plurality into relationship.[13] In this light, perhaps the "one mind and one love" can also be read slightly differently: perhaps the unity of such assembly in plurality, such as it is, exists in giving a place to discord, accountability, and the negotiation of ambiguity. Perhaps the staging and assembly of this community into copresence can only take place when the difficulties of navigating a slippery path, as well as the harm done by some members against others, are precisely not excised onto a supposed outside but given prominent place and attention in the midst of the fellowship. Only thus can a gathering take place. On such a reading, the unity of the community can, paradoxically, only be won by giving a place to its disunity.

In a sense, this is compounded by the way the ban, as the sanction of comprehensive excommunication, does not function as a simple and unambiguous excision of problematic members. If it is employed to guard and maintain the clarity of the border of the church and the purity of a holistic unity, it even seems to counteract that intention. Banned members are, after all, not simply removed from the fellowship. A banned person's membership in the church is not simply revoked but suspended—they do not need to be baptized again upon their repentance, for example. So the exclusion that is made by the ban is not simply the reversal of the motion of one's inclusion: it is not simply the undoing of baptism. Instead it produces something like a threshold state for the banned person, neither simply outside nor simply inside. If employed to safeguard the clarity of a sharp and dualistic border, it also splits or troubles the clarity of that border, which is now, it seems, at least two borders, one facing the outside world and one facing the threshold. So in its effort to safeguard a border between inside and outside, this border instead multiplies and becomes troubled.[14]

---

and submission become indistinguishable. The repentant sinner is reshaped in the collective image. See Hoogstraten, "Doperse Biomacht."

[13]This is perhaps also how the notion of *Vereinigung* in the preamble should be read; see Excursus.

[14]Hubmaier explicates the interrelation between the ban and baptism—the way they form mirror processes of entry and exit into the church—with the image of the two keys Jesus gives to the church (Mt. 16:19). One key, baptism, opens the gates and welcomes people into the church, while the other, the ban, expels unrepentant sinners and closes the gates if necessary. See Hubmaier, "Ban," 411–15.

Yet we might ask, why not *one* key and *one* gate for entry and exit alike? And indeed it appears that the two gates do not open out onto the same territories. If one is banned, one's membership is not simply *revoked*, but it is *suspended*: one is consigned to a threshold status

Far from ensuring the purity and sharp separation of the church, banning thus adds to the various groups of people that are "in" and around the church community, forming part of its life without being proper members: unbaptized coworkers, children, relatives, neighbors, and so on. For each of these, a different set of appropriate interactions will need to be in effect, thus multiplying and further confusing the clarity of inside and outside.

Repetition

In all this, what emerges is the persistent unfinishedness of this community: it is never quite achieved in any final state of being but requires persistent reassertion; this reassertion, however, not only fails to definitively achieve clarity but also itself produces new ambiguities, occasioning new negotiations. This is not a mere question of something like a dualistic tension between opposing forces or a tragic recognition that ideals are sometimes difficult to attain. It is more fundamentally exemplary of the way this community inhabits time.

This is, again, the case for the text as a whole, in which fellowship is not made once and for all but in repeated practices. But it seems especially embodied in this second article. For the ban, as "simply the warning and the command to sin no more," is a kind of sanction that especially breaks with any logic of finality. Where sovereign sanction, particularly in the form of capital punishment, offers a kind of final adjudication (at least for this particular offender), admonition and the ban are inscribed in a recurring pattern of slipping and getting back, admonition and repentance, excommunication and return. The ban does not neatly excise sinners from a pure collective body but eminently leaves things unfinished. What this second article thus begins to make clear is the way this community seems

---

neither quite inside the church nor quite outside. That the banned person is no longer "inside" the congregation, no longer simply a member, is immediately clear: they are explicitly excluded from the fellowship. Yet they are also not simply outside. Their status is explicitly distinct from the "Jews and heathen [sic]" (ibid., 419), who are simply outside the church. For one, (re)entry into the church is governed by different procedures: the banned person does not need to be baptized again to be restored to full membership but merely needs to repent. Further, there is no prohibition against greeting pagans and Jews as there is for banned persons, and interaction with simple outsiders is likewise not restricted to the "works of necessity" but must also include the "works of friendship" that were explicitly forbidden for the banned person (ibid.).

If the first key and gate thus open simply onto the outside world, from which one enters the church, the second key and gate thus appear to lead into a threshold category populated by banned persons, at the same time neither–nor and both–and. So the ban counteracts its own apparent intention, in a sense: it is employed to guard and maintain the clarity of the border (or "gate") of the church but also splits or troubles the clarity of that border, which is now, it seems, at least two borders, necessitating two keys, two gates and thresholds. In the restaging or reassertion of the border of the church, it is also displaced.

aware that its shared life takes place in what we might call the temporal mode of *repetition*.

According to Ernst Bloch, Christianity can be fundamentally understood in two ways: either from the past, as a tradition of loyalty to the Christ event, or from the future, as a community of apocalyptic or eschatological expectation. Bloch argues the Anabaptists are among the few Christian movements that genuinely seek to think Christianity as such radically transformative expectation.[15] This may be the case for other, more apocalyptically minded forms of Anabaptism. Here in Schleitheim we find something else entirely, a third category perhaps: Christianity in a thick present, as the copresence of repeated practice. Schleitheim's shared life does not gather around something imminently to come, rushing toward us to transform the world and everything in it. It seeks faithful being *in* time, in the midst of everything. It is the repetition of its constitutive practices that make this being-in-time and that make its shared life, as each time, each day, each generation, the church needs to gather again, begin again, recite, and reassert the practices by which it lives. It is thus, from the copresence of repeated collective practice, that its future, insofar as there is one, opens up.

So this is faith and shared life understood not as openness to what is coming toward us, as in an apocalyptic mode of expectation, nor indeed as the mere recollection or loyalty to a constitutive event in the past, as—according to Bloch—most of Christianity. Here, faith and shared life are centered on and made possible by a motion of beginning and repetition. It seems to me to be a particular kind of being-in-time, a particular temporality inhabiting the present as *thick* present. Not just the vanishingly thin *right now* of immediate experience but also distinct from both a futural and a recollective orientation.

This would be somewhat like what Donna Haraway is seeking when she argues for shared life as a becoming-with or *sympoiesis*. Such sympoiesis, she emphasizes, must be understood precisely as emerging from a kind of presence, a present "not as a vanishing pivot between awful or edenic pasts and apocalyptic or salvific futures" but as "a practice of learning to live and die well with each other in a thick present."[16]

In this mode, ecclesio-political existence in time is never simply there, given, guaranteed, but continually in the process of being undone and redone. It gains its stability and its capacity to exist and persist in time, such as it is, not from a singular foundation, nor from an expected point in the future, nor indeed from a metaphysical necessity or divine sovereign guarantee, but from its repeated practices, which are always in question and remain fragile enunciations. This is a community that does not repress its being the

---

[15] Ernst Bloch, *Thomas Münzer Als Theologe Der Revolution* (Frankfurt am Main: Suhrkamp, 1976); see also Catherine Keller, *Apocalypse Now and Then: A Feminist Guide to the End of the World* (Boston: Beacon Press, 1996).
[16] Haraway, *Staying with the Trouble*, 1.

"temporary and precarious articulation of contingent practices" (Mouffe) but is self-consciously so; one whose existence, such as it is, opens up or grows from its copresence, from its saying and saying-again, its persistently unfinished becoming.

Repetition, even as it breaks with a logic of futural expectation, is not identical rehearsal or the seamless return to an origin. Already in Chapter 1 we distinguished such an idea of an *origin*, which remains the blueprint to be emulated, dominating, and in a sense determining what follows from it, from a *beginning*, which sets something in motion that is not yet determined. The existence in time of the ecclesio-political community is not the rote and ultimately redundant rehearsal of an origin but one that sets out from a beginning, or indeed many beginnings, which makes possible a continuing tradition as a lively, inventive, and assertive persistence in repeated practice.

Repetition is not the restoration of the lost ideal of community but the only way community can take place. In an early John Caputo's words, it "is not the repetition of the same ... but a creative production which pushes ahead, which produces *as* it repeats, which produces *what* it repeats, which makes a life for itself in the midst of the difficulties" of factical existence.[17]

Caputo distinguishes such productive repetition from mere recollection, which "says that everything important has already been." Repetition instead "says that actuality must be continually produced, brought forth anew, again and again."[18] Metaphysics, and perhaps much of theology as well, tends to seek a way out of the difficulty and chaos of life and existence by positing a firm foundation or eternal truth out of reach of the messiness of actual existence. The logic of repetition, however, wants to make a life in its midst.

"Repetition is the exacting task of constituting the self as self" in the midst of it all, Caputo argues.[19] This requires—drawing on Kierkegaard—a particular kind of faith without guarantee. Ecclesio-political community is not a metaphysical truth to be implemented but an existential task to be performed: the task of making itself real in response to a fragile but insistent divine invitation.

This task is never finally achieved. Caputo suggests repetition moves "forward,"[20] but it is important to add that this forward motion is not, as above, oriented toward some final stasis or end as with apocalyptic expectation, nor indeed to some idea of progress or development. Its path is not predetermined.

Though it gains stability from repeated practice, the logic of repetition also makes for a structural instability or openness. Repetition is always, to

---

[17]John D. Caputo, *Radical Hermeneutics: Repetition, Deconstruction, and the Hermeneutic Project* (Bloomington: Indiana University Press, 1987), 3.
[18]Ibid., 17.
[19]Ibid., 21.
[20]Ibid., 121.

some extent, reinvention; paradoxically, "to repeat is to produce and to alter, to make and to make anew."[21] This is not just a practical concern (e.g., that we try to be faithful but just cannot seem to get it right) but a structural one. Even between iterations that are practically identical, there must logically be a distance or space. Otherwise we cannot say that anything gets "repeated"; it is just the same single iteration—which in that case also would not be an iteration but simply a one-off event. Repetition is thus only possible if there is such a space, but this space also makes for the way iterations are already not strictly speaking identical.

That is to say, in order to be the "same" as something else (in order to be recognizable as a faithful repetition), each iteration must already in some sense be *not the same*. Or, in Catherine Keller's words, "a repetition is not the same as what it repeats but is already another ... and yet performs such continuity as there is."[22] So tradition and continuity are only possible if there is also this gap or opening—which, however, also means that each iteration must, to some extent, begin again, be a reinvention of what it repeats.

The motion of repetition by which any kind of norm, practice, or identity can gain stability in time is thus "made possible only by the space between the copy and the copy. No repetition is exactly the same."[23] With the citation or application of any norm, such as here with church discipline or more broadly with societal norms, there is a slippage intrinsic to that motion. Paradoxically, the citation or application of a norm both solidifies it *and* opens it up to movement: "It is precisely this space [between iterations] that opens up the possibility for subversion and change."[24] What is stabilized, we might say, is *in the same stroke* also *de*stabilized. As Catherine Keller summarizes, "repetition grants human identity adequate stability and, at the same time, permits the destabilization of any identity."[25] In such iterative

---

[21]Ibid., 142.
[22]Catherine Keller, *Cloud of the Impossible: Negative Theology and Planetary Entanglement* (New York: Columbia University Press, 2015), 177–8.
[23]Ellen T. Armour and Susan M. St. Ville, "Judith Butler—in Theory," in *Bodily Citations: Religion and Judith Butler*, ed. Ellen T. Armour and Susan M. St. Ville (New York: Columbia University Press, 2006), 7.
[24]Ibid.
[25]Keller, *Cloud of the Impossible*, 222.

Theorist Judith Butler has famously found this logic or dynamic at work in the constitution of societal identities (such as masculinities and femininities). Identity is eminently made in repetition or recitation of a norm: it is not just a singular (founding) moment that shapes how we see "proper" or "improper" masculinity, but its repeated reinforcement and sanctioning. It is from this repetition that the norm gains its stability—we come to see it as "normal"—yet in the same stroke it also opens it up to its subversion. Drag and queer sexualities perform such subversion with particular playfulness, but this does not mean that drag is play while "regular" gender expression is simply what it is. Indeed drag is so subversive precisely as the assertion of a possibility, as it reveals that "proper" masculinities are also constituted in the logic of repetition. So "terms of ... [normative] designation are thus never settled once and for all but are constantly in the process of being remade." See Judith Butler, *Undoing Gender* (London: Routledge, 2004), 10.

application of a norm or practice, there is no "original" that gets faithfully reinstated: indeed the way we come to see some norms or terms *as* especially traditional, natural, or metaphysically necessary is simply because those terms gained stability over interminable iterations.[26]

It is in this precarious temporality that, it seems to me, the nonsovereign ecclesio-political community presses onward. Its shared life or copresence is not guaranteed, neither by an origin nor by an expected future; its shared life is made and made again by faithful, repeated practice. Church is never simply there or given; it does not offer a quick fix out of crisis and catastrophe, out of the difficulty of factical existence. It must continually be produced, brought forth anew, again and again. Repetition means that *in order* for this motion to gain stability, it must never cease or solidify. A nonsovereign community does not seek to repress this. It recognizes that its repeated practices are never simply the rote recollection of what came before but require the discerned and careful reinvention and reapplication. Its stabilizing gestures are in the same stroke what opens it up; the practices of its continuity are the occasions for its reinvention.

Conclusion

In naming church discipline as its second constitutive practice, immediately following baptism, Schleitheim seems marked by a sense of tragic realism: even after the new beginning made in baptism, it will still be possible for members to "slip and fall" into harmful behavior. This requires a response from the community, for which Schleitheim presents a basic system of admonition and, if necessary, excommunication.

Striking about this realism is that it is not grudgingly begotten after many years of church life but prominently part of the constitutive practices Schleitheim envisions for the church. From the start, it is clear that the shared life Schleitheim seeks will not come guaranteed but requires insistent and repeated assertion. The text seems aware that church in its circumstances is a fragile endeavor; paradoxically, this means it must be, in a sense, a *resistant* community—if resistant in a different mode than that of sovereignty.

The text leaves much open or implicit, but it is marked by a strange casual unexcitedness about its subject matter. There is no mention here of temptation or Satan, and the wording of its metaphor of slipping and falling suggests no one is really intentionally at fault in such an affair. The path they are walking seems to be unstable and slippery simply by itself. Within the ambiguity of creaturely existence, such things will inevitably happen.

---

[26]Perhaps the way some of us have come to see sixteenth-century Anabaptism or the early pre-Constantinian church as an original to be emulated is subject to a similar phenomenon, having gained this status as an exemplary original through its sustained recitation over theological generations.

Though they require a response—at the very least to safeguard those harmed and reassert the shared life as a space of freedom—the anonymous countervailing force, which does nothing and for which nobody is at fault, will never be definitively exorcised.

It is possible to read Schleitheim's insistence on the necessity of church discipline for the unity of the church as a desire for purity, perpetually at odds with human sin, casting out whoever is deemed too disobedient to remain in the community. Certainly, this seems to be the way it has often been read. Yet another way to approach it would be that the unity remains one in plurality and that its assembly can only take place when discord, accountability, and the negotiation of ambiguity are given space in its midst. Excommunication, in any case, even as it seems to disambiguate between proper and suspended members, produces its own ambiguities, which will require further negotiation.

What particularly emerges from this second article is the mode or temporality in which this negotiation and assertion take place. Schleitheim is, at least on my reading, marked by a temporality of repetition: its shared life and copresence do not come underlined by a fixed foundation, origin, or even by an expected apocalyptic dissolution. In times of crisis, catastrophe, and collapse, it would not be strange to understand the life of faith as a way out of those difficulties (and we will say more about a version of this in Chapter 4). Repetition, however, is the work of making life in their midst, the task of making fellowship real in response to a fragile but insistent divine invitation. Church is not simply there but must continually be produced, brought forth anew, again and again. A nonsovereign community does not seek to repress this motion but recognizes that its repeated practices require discerned and careful reinvention and reapplication.

So perhaps we can come to see this insistence of an unruly messiness into ecclesial life, frustrating the desire for purity, as not just a tragic reality to be stoically accepted but also in some sense as *good* news. As we shape a "thick co-presence" in the midst of all that unfolds in factual existence, as a community of beginners, seeking to create a space for shared life in freedom, we may find in this creaturely ambiguity also a strange and perhaps surprising ally. Its unruly insistence may undermine not only the community's efforts to shape itself in a particular identity but may also—when embraced—work to subvert and stand against totalitarian desires for purity that always threaten to eclipse the spaces for freedom so precariously won.

3

Presence

Introduction

Schleitheim's third article discusses the "breaking of bread" or, as it is also known, the ritual of communion. It is presented not as a mystical union with the transubstantiated elements but as a further step in the gathering and disambiguation of the ecclesio-political community. Already in "one faith," united by "one baptism" into "one body," the faithful are now made into "one loaf." Communion is thus framed as a moment of assembly, we might say, more than just table fellowship, in which the community is gathered into recognizable presence to itself, its unity as a collective body made apprehensible in bodily copresence.

As the community eats from one loaf, it is likewise made into one loaf. But this formulation already reveals something telling: even as it is already composed of committed members (Article I) and though it is subject to discipline (Article II), the unity or copresence of this community is still not simply achieved. In a way, it remains incomplete and in need of supplementary gathering—milling, mixing, kneading, resting, baking, the metaphor suggests. This third article thus further inscribes itself in the logic of repetition discussed in Chapter 2.

Schleitheim's main focus in this article is on the disambiguation between members and nonmembers. The text exhorts its readers to ascertain that only baptized (and, presumably, non-excommunicated) members participate— that this gathered body becomes recognizable especially in its distinctness. It is a peculiar and telling priority, also considering the restriction of communion to baptized and non-excommunicated members is mostly uncontroversial among the churches. So why stress this here? It seems to me that this emphasis on disambiguation again shows us something about the insistence of ambiguity into the shared life of the church.

The associative aspect of this gathering, or the process by which the assembly into "one loaf" takes place, thus remains largely implicit. It takes place by means of, and in response to, the memory of Christ, the text notes. Yet this, too, is telling. As the "broken body" of Christ is remembered, we read, the ecclesial "one body" is called into presence. So the *presence* of the community, we might say, seems to gather around the remembrance, that is the *absence*, of Christ. Schleitheim spends few words on this, but this is a delicate play of presence and absence that is crucial, it seems to me, to understanding the interaction between God and the church in sympoetic becoming.

This question of presence and copresence in the same bodily space, bodies digesting the same creaturely sustenance (bread), also invites the question of *place*. This is a notion that seems almost entirely irrelevant to Schleitheim's ecclesio-political venture. It constitutes and shapes community significantly by disentangling from worldly relationships, which suggests a disentangling from place as well. This is not a community for whom holy sites, local identity, or sacred lands seem to have much meaning. But at the same time, it is also not a placeless community—at least not in the sense that it would be a purely spiritual and disembodied affair. For Schleitheim, the church is eminently *immanent*, materially *taking place* in shared embodied life. To a modern reader, this ambivalence around place can seem strangely complicit with the exceptionalism that has pervaded much of modernity and its denial to mind humanity's entanglements and thus requires more attentive reading.

Reading

The practice of breaking bread and sharing wine goes back to the very beginning of Christianity. In the Reformation context, its meaning and practice had become subject to fierce debates. In this, Schleitheim's depiction of its significance as one of "remembrance" positions it with the position of Swiss reformer Huldrich Zwingli, who had argued that finite matter cannot hold the infinite and that therefore the Catholic doctrine of transubstantiation—in which the bread and wine truly in their substance (though of course not in their appearance) become the body and blood of Christ—must be rejected. We remember and expect not what is present but what is now absent: there is thus no "real presence" of Christ in the bread and wine.[1]

---

[1] Balthasar Hubmaier phrases this more clearly than Schleitheim, as he writes: "'Until he comes.' It follows that [Christ] is not present. For if he were present, then we would hold the Supper in vain and against the words of Christ and Paul. For where a person is essentially and bodily present, there a remembrance is not necessary. However, where he is not bodily present, then one celebrates his remembrance until he comes." See Balthasar Hubmaier, "A Simple Instruction," in *Balthasar Hubmaier: Theologian of Anabaptism*, ed. H. Wayne Pipkin and John H. Yoder, Classics of the Radical Reformation (Walden: Plough, 2019), 333.

Michael Sattler elsewhere argues similarly:

> That the real body of Christ the Lord is not in the sacrament, we admit: for Scripture says: Christ has ascended to heaven and sits at the right hand of His heavenly Father, whence He shall come to judge the living and the dead. It follows therefrom, since He is in heaven and not in the bread, that He cannot be eaten bodily. (Yoder, *Legacy*, 73)

In a text discussing the essential constitutive practices of the church, it is not surprising to find communion discussed. Yet it is perhaps surprising that the text seems to take its place in these Reformation debates only cursorily. Its real concern is instead to clarify who may take part: only baptized members may participate in communion. Whoever wants to break bread and "drink of one drink," we read, "shall be united beforehand in one body of Christ, that is into the community [*gemeinde*] of God whose Head is Christ, which is to say by baptism." Its reasoning consists of several different phrasings of what is in effect a single point: only those who are unambiguously followers of Christ (as marked by baptism) are called to this table of communion.

> For as Paul points out we cannot at the same time partake of the Lord's table and the table of devils; we cannot at the same time drink the cup of the Lord and the cup of the devil. That is, all those who have fellowship with the dead works of darkness have no part in the light, and all who follow the devil and the world have no part with those who are called unto God out of the world. All who lie in evil have no part in the good.

Schleitheim's argument here seems to be that there is a sharp and mutually exclusive dualism between the world and the church, whereby one can only belong to one, not both. This dualism is underwritten by a deeper metaphysical dualism: there *is* only that of God and that of the devil, with seemingly nothing in between. There is thus no space for ambiguities.

In making this argument, Schleitheim here refers to only a single Bible passage: 1 Cor. 10:21, where Paul argues against participating in the worship of idols, particularly against eating meat sacrificed to idols. In this passage, Paul had first suggested more moderate solutions to questions around eating habits in the congregation. Now, however, he seems to instruct more rigorously: one "cannot drink the cup of the Lord and the cup of demons [i.e., idols]," for doing so would "provok[e] the Lord to jealousy" (22).

Paul's argument is by no means as radical as this selective citation suggests, however. For one, he is responding to a different question than Schleitheim: Paul is addressing whether meat specifically and explicitly offered to idols can still be eaten by Christians, not the question of who may participate in the breaking of bread in the Church. Further, Paul explicitly clarifies that if one is not quite sure whether the meat in question has been sacrificed (when shopping in the market or as a guest in someone's home), one should not refuse it.

So if Paul argues Christians (who participate in the Lord's table) should not *knowingly* eat meat offered to idols, Schleitheim argues inversely that care must be taken to ensure non-baptized persons (who now *by definition* participate in the "world" and thus in the "table of devils") should not participate in communion. Paul's argument is to restrict the consumption of sacrificed meat; Schleitheim's argument is to restrict the consumption of communion.

Schleitheim thus changes and broadens the category of participation the "table of devils" far beyond Paul's narrow definition of explicit idol worship, taking it to include any person not explicitly in the church. Not only that, it also uses Paul's expression for a completely different argument.[2] In sum, Schleitheim's rigor is really at odds with Paul's much more pragmatic line. The text cites no further biblical warrant for its point here.[3]

In any case Schleitheim notes it "shall and must be thus" [*sol und mus seyn*]:

> Whoever has not been called by one God to one faith, to one baptism, to one Spirit, to one body, with all the children of God's community, cannot be made into one loaf with them, as indeed must be done if one is truly to break bread according to the command of Christ.

Here we also get the clearest sense of what happens: the congregants, who are already "one body" with all of God's church, are now made into "one loaf" (*ein Brot*) as well. It is perhaps remarkable that so little is here said of what communion actually is or does. As noted earlier, it is clear that a Zwinglian line of "remembrance" is followed,[4] but this is clearly not the

---

[2] This is heightened by reference to the devil, as it suggests all who are not baptized "follow the devil and the world." This is again a departure from Paul's text, who does not speak of the devil but of "demons" and is not referring to general non-Christian existence but specifically to non-Christian worship and sacrifice.

[3] They might well have cited, for example, Acts 2:41-42, which describes the breaking of bread as shared among those first baptized, or indeed 1 Cor. 11:27, where Paul argues "whoever … eats the bread or drinks the cup of the Lord in an unworthy manner will be answerable for the body and blood of the Lord." Implicitly referred to might be Paul's words just before the cited phrase, where he prefaces his instruction on the eating of sacrificed meat with a description how "the bread that we break, is it not a sharing in the Body of Christ? Because there is one bread, we who are many are one body, for we all partake of the one bread" (1 Cor. 10:16-17).

[4] Reflecting on the more contemporary discussion of communion among Anabaptists, Thomas Finger has noted it is often neglected or reduced in meaning to "social dimensions" as simply table fellowship, which Finger holds omits the "sacramental intersection with spiritual reality." So Finger rejects Schleitheim's, Hubmaier's, and Zwingli's "real absence" of Christ in the bread and wine. Instead, he submits it "conveys Jesus' real, communal and memorial presence as a primary manifestation of grace birthing the new creation in visible communal form." See Finger, *A Contemporary Anabaptist Theology*, 184–5, 208.

Finger's formulation is perhaps not very precise. More importantly, however, Finger's rejection of "real absence" passes up the opportunity to follow its peculiar and telling logic to its conclusion: that it is exactly in the play of absence and presence that the church is called into assembly.

For Finger, the sense of the "coming of a new creation" is essential to his understanding of communion and Anabaptist theology more generally. Yet strangely, it is exactly this dimension of expectation that is mostly absent from Schleitheim and particularly absent in its discussion of communion, which only speaks of remembrance and does not include words such as "until He comes."

main concern of the text. Further, any sense of expectation is absent, with the words "until He comes" (1 Cor. 11:26) omitted from Schleitheim's discussion.

At the same time, there are even in this brief text several peculiarities at work. For one, we may well ask a similar question as in Chapter 2: after voluntary baptism *and* discipline, how much more unity can really be necessary? Further, even if it is but cursorily mentioned in the text, the logic of this remembrance invites further questioning. If this gathering ritual indeed plays such a significant part in calling together the community into apprehensible copresence, how can we interpret this absence of Christ in its midst?

Assembled Copresence

From the text, we get the sense that communion or the breaking of bread is an extension or completion of the work baptism and discipline also performed. After the congregation is first called together and constituted, first distinguishing between inside and out (conversion and baptism), and after it is placed under a collective rule that reasserts this distinction when it becomes muddled (discipline and repentance), the community is now, we might say, staged as a visible and material whole, made present and recognizable to itself. By being gathered into the memory of Christ, the members are gathered to each other into an assembled and recognizable unity. Communion is where the church is made recognizably present, where its unity is staged in material copresence, we might say. The kind of material gathered oneness of the loaf of bread, apprehensible as a single being despite its multiple ingredients, becomes true of the church, as it is assembled in recognizable bodily copresence. In eating from the same loaf of bread and drinking from the same cup, the community, that was already in "one faith," united by "one baptism" to "one Spirit, to one body," is thus also made into "one loaf."

While this may seem, on the one hand, a very clear understanding of communion, it is less clear what is really added here besides another iteration in the repeated practice of gathering. For a fellowship that is already *one*—one faith, one Spirit, one body, we read—the supplementary unity into "one loaf" seems very little, almost nothing. If the members really are already "one body, with all the children of God's church," their calling together into the bodily copresence of "one loaf" seems, on the one hand, to be eminently unnecessary, *supplementary* truly in the sense that it is superfluous. But, on the other hand, the inverse is true as well: the necessity of such a further assembling motion or staging in recognizable copresence suggests that the unity of one faith, one Spirit, one body, is by itself incomplete, in a way that it requires further and repeated gathering—kneading, resting, baking—before it is adequately one.

In this way, the assembling motion of communion takes place in the temporality of repetition discussed in Chapter 2. Each iteration of the repeated practices that make and shape the shared life of the community confirms and gives stability to previous iterations even as it shows their incompleteness. And this unity of bodily copresence in communion is also not a definitive gathering but remains itself incomplete, dispersed as soon as it is assembled. The "one loaf," after all, is broken, distributed, to be gathered again in the future.

In discussing this supplementary gathering in bodily copresence, Schleitheim's third article has a single priority: to ensure that only baptized members participate. There can be no overlap or ambiguity, it argues, between the world and the Lord's table. In spite of its questionable biblical warrant (see earlier), this instruction is straightforward enough. Yet there is something strange, we might say, precisely about the straightforwardness of this instruction. Why should this be stressed to such an extent at all? Nothing about this demand is radical or controversial. Practically all churches limit communion to (at the very least) baptized members. So why should such an obvious and uncontroversial instruction here be the single priority?

One response could be that this focus is indicative of Schleitheim's underlying philosophical assumptions: it makes clear the way Schleitheim sees reality by a dissociative or differential logic. Existence functions by dichotomies, Schleitheim seems to believe, and it is only by the clear logic of either–or that things are distinguished from other things. So beings and collectivities and especially the church can only be what they are through their distinctness from what they are not. We saw a similar logic embodied (but also productively complicated) in the previous two articles as well.

In this logic, a collective body is most clearly defined not so much by reference to a shared *center* as by the reference to an excluded or contrasted *outside*.[5] So if we say that communion is where the church is made recognizably present, where its unity is staged in material copresence, then necessarily—by this dissociative logic—this must mean it is staged *in its distinctness*. The unity of the presented community requires, by the sheer force of structural necessity—more than any biblical literalist motivation—this reference to an excluded (or at least contrasted) other. After all, collectivities *can* only become recognizably present in their distinctness from what they are not. This is the only way communion *can* perform this staging: the unity of the

---

[5] This seems to anticipate the way some modern political theorists think about political life: that the shared life of a community necessarily takes shape around dissociation or antagonism. Depending on the line of thinking, this can be either an internal antagonism, where we might see the political as essentially a struggle between competing visions or interests (Mouffe), or it can be an external antagonism, where we might see political community defined by the distinction between friend and foe (Schmitt). See, for example, Marchart, *Post-Foundational Political Thought*, 41–4.

"one loaf" is only intelligible in its difference or even separation from other bodies, loyalties, and entanglements.

This sense of a structural necessity is compounded by the way the text frames its exhortation. The restriction of communion to baptized members is not just framed as one ethical matter among others, something the church leadership should watch out for, but as constitutive and even conditional: communion, and by extension the shared life of the church, *cannot take place* without the policing of this restriction. It is a formal requirement based on a structural necessity.[6]

The constitutive character of this restriction and its relation to something like a structural or metaphysical dualism is expressed with heightening clarity as the third article progresses. If initially, those who want to participate "shall" be baptized, it is soon stressed that there "cannot" be any ambiguity between the Lord's table and the world, indeed that those who are baptized "have no part" with those in the world—that is, not just that they *should* have no part, but that this has a structural or definitional importance. It is from this definitional necessity or underlying metaphysical reality that the normativity takes its inescapable force: it "must be" thus. There is no alternative. Things are and must be distinct from what they are not.

Yet, we may ask at this point: if it *is*—why *must* it be? There seems to be a tension between the two elements of that sentence: the normative *must be* suggests at least the possibility that it is *not* so. Otherwise, again, these extensive exhortations would be eminently unnecessary. If there were immediate clarity about the belonging and loyalty of everyone in the room, if taking part in communion were *simply impossible* for those who are not yet baptized, there would be no need for normative policing of this restriction. So it seems to me that this emphasis on disambiguation might again tell us something about the insistence of an ambiguity into the shared life of the church, which—it seems, at least—does not follow this clear logic of metaphysical dualism at all.

Because we might well ask if there is not, by now, something strange going on. Schleitheim seems to be deeply invested in the disambiguation between things that are, according to its underlying metaphysical assumptions, inherently and absolutely distinct—things that should really not be ambiguous at all, that should not require such disambiguation in the first place. Yet while the distinctness of the church is seen as rooted in metaphysical necessity ("have no part"), the text seems deeply aware that it is also, at the same time, so fragile that it needs interminable reassertion.

This community, the text seems well aware, is never simply an extension of metaphysical reality but, at least in its existence in the world, deeply fragile. Ambiguity insists into its every attempt at clear and distinct existence. And

---

[6]This is a point also noted by Snyder: the exclusion of nonmembers is a liturgical or sacramental *requirement* for communion to be possible at all; the status of the community determines the very validity of the celebration. See Snyder, *Life and Thought*, 159.

in this light, it is not only that communion *cannot be* what it is supposed to be if participation is not sharply policed. Communion also *is* that policing; it *is* the reassertion of the clarity of the borders of the church—paradoxically attesting to their insistent troubling.

As we saw in Chapter 2, such an insistent ambiguity is not simply "evil" or "the devil" but closer to an inherent characteristic of such shared life. It is the inherent slipperiness that troubles and complicates precisely those dualisms that seek rhetorical stability in reference to demons, the devil, or other absolute others. Such uncomplicated dualisms are disturbed from within by a countervailing force or unruliness, barely existing in its own right, yet conditioning what does exist.

Yet this is more than the simple realization that the world is a messy place and the church is never as distinct as we might feel it ought to be. That certainly is a widely shared insight, and it would not be inappropriate at this point: the tragic realization that even after baptism and discipline, some messiness insists and further ordering and policing is necessary. But the particular form this insistent ambiguity takes at communion is not merely a sign of the failure of the previous techniques. It here shows itself as specifically caused or occasioned by adult baptism and discipline.

Paradoxically, it is Schleitheim's approach to baptism and discipline that gives rise to the very situation this third article is addressing: one in which there is a number of individuals present during the breaking of bread who are not (yet) baptized or currently under disciplinary suspension. It is exactly the rejection of blanket compulsory infant baptism that causes this potential confusion around who is baptized and who is not because it produces a setting in which not all persons (not even all adults) in and around the congregation are baptized in the first place. And it is the disciplinary exclusion of the ban that produces the situation in which already baptized members must now again be excluded.

This is not to say that other churches do not face similar ambiguities or that they would not have their own techniques of suppressing those ambiguities and policing its borders. But it is to say that *this specific* situation is precipitated by Schleitheim's previous two constitutive practices of voluntary baptism and the ban—that is to say, its attempts to suppress ambiguity in one place *produce* further ambiguities elsewhere.[7]

So there is something curious at work here. It is not simply that baptism and discipline have *not done enough* to decisively banish this insistent ambiguity. It is not simply that they were ineffective, that they failed to perform to the desired level of precision. Paradoxically, they have done *too much*. For it is precisely their attempt to *delimit* ambiguity that seems to

---

[7]This is not a fictional problem: Schleitheim's third article may be precipitated exactly by the lack of stricture in distributing communion at the earliest Anabaptist community in Zollikon, in which apparently some not yet (re)baptized believers would already participate in communion. See Snyder, "Birth and Evolution," 543.

produce it here. It is the techniques employed to *stabilize* the distinct borders of the church that appear to, in one stroke, also *destabilize* them, producing situations that require further stabilizing and policing.

The countervailing force against which Schleitheim's efforts take aim simultaneously seems to be produced in their enactment. Contrary to Schleitheim's stated metaphysical dualism, the reality in which the church exists, insofar as it exists, is marred by an insistent unruliness or ambiguity, which eats away at structures of purity, and paradoxically is reproduced by the very techniques that seek to insulate against it. Repetition is not the interminable struggle against that incompleteness. It also produces and lives by incompleteness, as the gaps between iterations give space, perhaps in spite of themselves, for subversion and reinvention.

A Calling Absence

This dissociative emphasis might almost overshadow the way this gathering into "one loaf" is also an *as*sociative occurrence. It takes place by means of the association with the memory of Christ. The bread is broken "in remembrance of the broken body of Christ," and the drink is drunk "as a remembrance of the shed blood of Christ." The staging of the community in its material copresence takes place in, or even as, the shared orientation toward this center.

Yet there is something strange going on: this center is empty. Christ is absent. This may seem like a strange thing to write—would it not be more precise to speak of the *presence* of the Lord at His table, at least in some mystical or symbolic sense? Yet the Schleitheim text deals in no such presence, neither mystical, nor symbolic, nor indeed real. The only "body of Christ" that is *there* at this breaking of bread "is the church," and its orientation to the "broken body" of Christ is referred to as one of "remembrance." We do not gather in remembrance of one who is still with us. We remember those who are *not* with us; that is, those who are absent.[8]

So the *presence* of the community is staged and gathers around the remembrance, which means the *absence* of Christ at the center. As the "broken body" of Christ is remembered, so recalled *as absent*, the "one body of Christ" that is the church can become present. The presence of the community is rooted in the absence of Christ; paradoxically, it is not the

---

[8] See also note 1 on p. 48.

The Greek word for "remembrance" in 1 Cor. 11:24 ("do this in remembrance of me") is *anamnesis*, which some scholars note should be understood more as actualization or presenting than mere cognitive remembering. Even so, it is a presenting of something that is not *simply* present; it is a presence that must be *made present*. In any case this is not the sense given to it here. See, for example, Johannes Betz, "Eucharistie," in *Herders Theologisches Taschenlexikon*, ed. Karl Rahner, vol. 2 (Freiburg: Herder, 1972), 226–41.

real presence but the absence of Christ that calls the community together. From this absence, the text suggests a gathering call or "command" (*befelch*) proceeds.

The broken body does not exist, at least not there, not in presence, but it makes possible, calls together what does exist: the gathered body. And what does exist, the assembled body, does not *simply* exist; its unity is not simply "there"; it needs this interminable process of supplementary gathering (milling, mixing, kneading, resting, baking). This supplement is itself very little, almost nothing, never achieves or performs this unity simply by its own force, but by anchoring this staging of what is in what is not, what does not exist, at least no longer and not in the same way, which can only call and wait for the church's response. Schleitheim spends few words on this, but it seems to me this play of presence and absence encapsulates the collaborative interaction between God and the church in sympoetic becoming.

So, we might say, what does not exist, or at least what is absent, even in its brokenness, seems to give strength to what does exist and is presented, which, however, itself never "exists" in the sense that it would be finally achieved or could stand simply by itself. And vice versa, we might say: what exists and is presented, the gathered body, gives strength to, and makes real, Christ's call and command, which by itself never exists, but places itself into creaturely hands as an invitation and provocation.[9]

The broken body and the assembled body—no mention here of a resurrected body, we may note—are thus mutually dependent. It is precisely *because* one is not present that the other is called into existence and called into existence precisely around the remembrance or absence of the other. The link between these two revolves not around any mystical or metaphysical link or participation but around a call: in remembrance, the broken body of Christ calls the gathered body into assembly, provoking, invoking, convoking it into bodily, material copresence—into sympoiesis, becoming-with, collaborative self-organization.

At communion, the text thus suggests, we do not stand in the presence of the Lord at His table but instead are confronted with Christ's absence. And it is this absence, not the plenitude of transcendence, that calls us toward each other, toward the body that *is* present, toward our brothers and sisters with whom we share at this table. In so remembering, as its members are called to become present to one another, the collective body of

---

[9] Anabaptist theologian and philosopher Justin Heinzekehr has argued such a sense of absence is crucial to understanding Jesus's relation to the church. According to Heinzekehr, "The primary symbol for our analysis is the absent Christ, which begins with the physical absence of Jesus' body at the empty tomb, extends to the unavailability of Christ as an objective, transcendent authority in the development of the early church, and even now contains social, political, and ecological implications for Christian theology." This is a "dialectical movement that transitions from individual authority to communal authority to marginal authority." See Justin Heinzekehr, *The Absent Christ: An Anabaptist Theology of the Empty Tomb* (Telford: Cascadia, 2019), 18.

the church becomes the "loaf," becomes the bread. Its being stands in for the absent Jesus, whose body is *thus*, not by the elements, but by the sympoetic self-organization, made present—and in turn broken and dispersed into multitudinous plurality.

This is how the community gathers into presence: not in the fullness of the presence of Christ (mystical, symbolic, real, or otherwise) but precisely in the wake, the empty space left by Christ's broken body. If this is the ground on which the church is built, it is a ground without ground, an abyss from which nevertheless, we read, a "command" can be discerned. This is a "command" that does not resound from the height of sovereignty but sounds from its brokenness, a call barely present, barely real, and yet with unconditional significance. Christ's broken body, invoked in remembrance, does not master the congregation but invites it; inversely, its absence also means the congregation can never master it, in turn; the church does not own this broken body but exists in its wake.

I readily admit that it would be too much to say that this is really what Sattler and his comrades had in mind in any literal and historical sense when they wrote these lines. Unearthing the hidden truths in the text as they were truly intended by the authors is not the intention of this study. It is to set loose a conversation with the text, in which things and senses become visible that may yet illuminate our sense of being church.

In this speculative register, we might also notice a peculiar resonance. With its ecclesio-political venture, centered on self-organization and the break with the force of sovereignty, Schleitheim—at least on this reading—strangely anticipates the democratic political venture. Even if, of course, this is not a term Schleitheim uses, and even if (it is important to note) the practice of Anabaptist churches after Schleitheim has often been far from democratic. Yet Schleitheim's sense of an absent body at the center of a self-organized gathering seems to anticipate an insight from modern political theory: that democracy can fundamentally be understood as a form of shared life in which the place of power remains empty.

As political theorist Claude Lefort writes:

> The locus of power is an empty place, it cannot be occupied—it is such that no individual and no group can be consubstantial with it—and it cannot be represented ... We would be wrong to conclude that power now resides *in* society ... it remains the agency by virtue of which society apprehends itself in its unity and relates to itself in time and space ... [It] marks a division between the *inside* and the *outside* of the social, institutes relations between those dimensions, and is tacitly recognized as being purely symbolic.[10]

---

[10] Lefort, *Democracy and Political Theory*, 17.

Certainly, not everything here is immediately parallel to my reading of Schleitheim: at the very least, the terms "consubstantial," "represented," and "symbolic" invite further complication. Yet Lefort's stress that something happens to the place of power in democratic societies—it is not just a question of who holds power or how it is used, to what ends or in what style, but a more fundamental question of how it is considered to be located, or indeed dislocated, in relation to the self-organizing capacities of society—may yet illuminate such a democratic reading of the Schleitheim text. It is not just that power has no place but that the peculiar *emptiness* of its place, when taken seriously, enables the community to take shape in a democratic (we might say nonsovereign) way.[11]

Crucial to this is how the community becomes capable of apprehending itself: how the relation to the empty place of power enables it to appear, we might say, to itself in recognizable copresence. The kind of self-apprehension of a society gives form, Lefort notes, to society as democracy or indeed as aristocracy, monarchy, despotism, and so on. This

> implies both giving them meaning (*mise en sens*) and staging them (*mise en scène*). They are given meaning in that the social space unfolds as a space of intelligibility ... They are staged in that this space contains within it a quasi-representation of itself as being aristocratic, monarchic, despotic, democratic or totalitarian.[12]

So this, perhaps, is what a "democratic" or nonsovereign breaking of bread could be said to eminently stage, allowing the community to apprehend itself, and its members each other, as responding to a sympoetic call that always remains incomplete. With Lefort, we might see more clearly the role that this gathering around the broken body performs, in its structural necessity: communion is the ritualized disincorporation of power. In this gathering around an empty center, around a space (of remembrance) that cannot be taken up or claimed by the members, the ecclesio-political community is both staged and made intelligible exactly *as* a sympoiesis, as a particular *type* of self-organized community that gathers at a divine invitation. Lefort is fundamentally a secular thinker. Yet he, too, notes the significance of the (quasi-)theological recognition "that human society can only open on to itself by being held in an opening it did not create."[13]

If we find reason, in the text or in the universe, to complicate or question the underlying metaphysical dualism that animates Schleitheim's insistence

---

[11] For what it is worth, Lefort suggests it is "in the sixteenth century that we detect the first signs of a modern reflection upon politics and religion ... a new sensitivity to the question of the foundations of the civil order is born as a result ... of the collapse of the authority of the Church and of the struggles that accompanied the Reformation." Ibid., 213.
[12] Ibid., 11–12.
[13] Ibid., 222.

on disambiguation (a complication that will deepen in Chapter 4), we may come to see such nonsovereign self-apprehension also in a more relational light. So we might well say instead—and maybe this is all I am trying to say—that it is less the dualistic distinctness but the *relatedness* of the church to its "others," which are thus never *simply* other, that constitutes the life of the church. And that this relatedness must thus be part of the self-apprehension and staging that happens when the community assembles in bodily copresence. Schleitheim seems to recognize that the way in which this assembly is staged makes church intelligible in relevantly different ways.

A Presence without Place

This question of presence and copresence in the same bodily space, bodies digesting the same creaturely sustenance, also invites the question of *place*. This is a notion that seems to be almost entirely irrelevant to Schleitheim's ecclesio-political venture: none of its constitutive practices refer to any kind of local belonging or rootedness in a location. This is not a community for whom holy sites, local identity, or sacred lands seem to have any meaning, nor indeed the control over a city or territory. Even here, when discussing a gathering at the same physical space, Schleitheim says nothing about that space or its material conditions—walls, benches, hearth; yeast, wheat, water; vineyards, farmers, bees.

This may seem like a cursory observation—after all, a short declaration such as Schleitheim will necessarily omit more than it can address. Yet, on the other hand, the sense of a community constituted, shaped, and staged without any reference to a location, at least without (sovereign) control over a territory, seems to me essential to this venture. It is not that Schleitheim is merely disinterested in place: it envisions community as significantly achieved *by* disentangling from worldly relationships. Christians are those "called unto God out of the world." The shared life it envisions is not only one in which references to place and local belonging remain implicit—it is one that explicitly takes place without such references.

But in so loosening the connection between ecclesio-political community and locality, in so shaping a community that is not in control of a territory but also not tied to a place, it seems to me that Schleitheim has an ambivalent affinity to a different modern sense of human sovereignty: not that of control over territory or the earth, but that of separation or independence from it. Schleitheim's tendency to seek a community that is separate from the world around it can easily tip over into an understanding of a shared *human* life that denies its relatedness to the *nonhuman* life in the midst of which it finds itself: to a church that denies its ties to the planet and to place.

This has maybe been an oscillation Anabaptists have been prone to: to *either* withdraw into (territorially bounded) identitarian communities *or* feel at home in no place, understanding ourselves as sojourners only and voiding our belonging to the earthy, creaturely web of relations that sustains our bodily existence (and from which, for what it is worth, bread and wine necessarily stem).[14]

So its separatism *from* the logic of sovereignty and control can become strangely complicit with some of the most significant conditions *for* human control over and exploitation of the nonhuman world. Its separatism can fold over into the very anthropocentric exceptionalism that has pervaded much of modernity, that denies humanity's entanglements in nonhuman existence. A placeless community, which we will read is "spiritual," not carnal, and has its home in "heaven," not in this world (Chapter 6), might have difficulties conceiving of its place amid creaturely belonging.

Perhaps given the peculiar absence of any explicit reference to place (or indeed to nonhuman life) in the Schleitheim text, it needs to be reminded of the ways the fellowship it envisions is, in another sense, not a placeless community at all—at least not in the sense that it would be a purely spiritual disembodied affair. For Schleitheim, the church is eminently immanent, materially *taking place* in shared embodied life. This is not an invisible church; its shared life is not decided merely in an inward or transcendental faith. Its essential staging moment, discussed here in this third article, is a quintessentially immanent, bodily sharing: eating and drinking.

So perhaps, if we mind the ambivalence, we can yet read this placelessness as something other than simply an exceptionalism complicit in the separation of humanity from the earth and nonhuman creation. Perhaps it can be read as a sense of mindful difference: that the shaping of nonsovereign human community takes place in a particular mode that is not simply the naturally growing extension of creaturely life but requires particular care.

Hannah Arendt argues that some sense of autonomy of the political sphere is required for nonsovereign freedom to take hold. Even though she laments the alienation from the earth that she sees in late modern existence, she argues the freedom of shared life in political community requires some distance from the sheer *necessity* of creaturely survival. The shaping of political community as a space for freedom and deliberation needs to happen at some remove from those factors that would determine the shape of that community as an accomplished fact.[15] So, we might say, just as God withdraws to give space for human self-organization, so this sympoiesis needs to take place at some remove—not separation—from "nature," "national origin," economic interests, and other such matters that would

---

[14]See also Ched Myers, ed., *Watershed Discipleship: Reinhabiting Bioregional Faith and Practice* (Eugene: Cascade, 2016).
[15]See Arendt, *The Human Condition*. One of the factors making up the dangers of totalitarianism, for example, is the destruction of this distance. Totalitarian ideology introduces a notion of historical or biological necessity into the sphere of politics, leaving no space for freedom. See Hannah Arendt, *The Origins of Totalitarianism* (San Diego: Harvest Books, 1973).

foreclose the human capacity (and responsibility) to make our own story, to deliberate and act in freedom. After all, political schemata that claim a "natural order" have rarely had freedom on their mind.

For Arendt, the "necessity" that governs labor and economic life is *pre*political, not *a*political. That is to say, it is not irrelevant to the shared life of political community but gives the conditions under which it can then take place. In a similar way, we might say the webs of interdependence that make up the faithful's local and creaturely belonging are not irrelevant to the life of the church but form the conditions under which it gathers. At the same time, this gathering is not simply an extension of those belongings but takes up the contingency of human life into the shaping of a nonsovereign freedom.

This sense of a remove between creaturely relatedness and the shaping of a nonsovereign human freedom also allows for an inverse conclusion: that this gives space for a kind of letting-be. Political life does not require taking hold of the earth; the staging of its copresence does not require the control over a territory. As human freedom must take place with some independence from creaturely necessity (Arendt), so it can—perhaps—also allow for a *loosening* of the stranglehold held by human political and economic organization and the logic of sovereignty over the earth.

Maybe this is a more contemporary sense of the church being "called unto God out of the world." Its members gather at some place, certainly, but that does not signify a claim of control; they are embedded in webs of interdependence, but this does not signify a denial of the particular mode of human organization. Being "called out of the world," we might say, does not mean being called out of the planetary realm of immanence but called to break with structures of unfreedom (see Chapter 4). This call does not lead into an ascetic desert of placeless transcendence but into an existence in place without asserting control over territory.

Conclusion

At communion, the fellowship gathers around the memory of Christ's broken body—around Christ's absence. From this empty center, a call nevertheless emerges, inviting, provoking, and commanding the faithful to assemble in collaborative self-organization or sympoiesis. In so remembering, as its members are called to become present to one another, the collective body of the church becomes the "loaf," becomes the bread. But even this unity is not finally one, as it is in turn broken and dispersed into multitudinous plurality. This gathering in copresence takes place in embodied immanence, but its relation to place remains loose: this is a community that gathers, is staged, and given meaning without the claim of control over a land or territory.

Even as a community already baptized and disciplined, the unity or copresence of the community is not simply *there*. It is still incomplete, still in need of supplementary gathering—milling, mixing, kneading, resting, baking, and then breaking and dispersing again. For Schleitheim, essential to this persistent gathering is the persistent disambiguation between inside and out. Yet here, we also see that at least some of the ambiguity that insists into the desired distinctness of the church is eminently produced by its attempts at dissociative purity. Its practices and techniques that *stabilize* its unambiguous identity in one stroke also *destabilize* it.[16]

This is not to say that this is a situation that is unique to Schleitheim—indeed we may come to conclude quite the opposite, that analyzing closely these curious tensions in Schleitheim's attempt at overcoming ambiguity can tell us something about what it means to gather as a community and as a church more generally, also beyond these particular conditions. Perhaps religious communities more generally can be said to take shape through the policing and disciplining of boundaries that would otherwise be much more porous and fluid. And perhaps an unruliness insists more generally around these boundaries nevertheless, that is interminably suppressed or negotiated—perhaps we may find that collective identities rarely take shape without the suppression of ambiguity and difference.

The question of our non-isolability from creaturely existence, and its relation to Schleitheim's stated metaphysical dualism between good and "evil," is the subject of Chapter 4.

---

[16]The stark dualism that occasions Schleitheim's focus on a disambiguation between nonmembers becomes productively complicated by following this sense of ambiguity. Yet remaining in the metaphor of bodies and embodied life, perhaps it is not so strange to stress the constitutive significance of the interaction with an *outside* for the self-apprehension of a collective. We need not do it with the sense of exclusion that we get from Schleitheim to find meaning in some sense of difference to an outside. After all, our own embodied existence also becomes intelligible and capable of experiencing itself as a whole, capable of acting in concert in the experience of having an outside, of having a zone or field of interaction with what we are not. If in this moment of gathering the ecclesio-political community becomes apprehensible not just as a space in which to appear but also as a body capable of collectively acting in concert, it likewise needs the interaction with (not complete separation from) a nonself to become capable of recognizing itself as such.

Yet this interaction is always also the experience of our non-isolability, accompanied by the realization that the delimitation of self and non-self is never a sharp separation even at this corporeal limit. Just as the body of Christ that is the church, our bodies too are assemblages, tentative unities of a host of beings. The borders of a body are necessarily porous, and only thus can it relate to its outsides, can it sustain itself and grow and ultimately decompose.

4

Refuge

Introduction

Schleitheim's fourth article is as long as the first three combined. While those first three named points generally shared with other Anabaptist groups of its time, this fourth article addresses an instruction more specific to Schleitheim: the ecclesial community must be sharply separate from the world around it.[1] If a sense of separation or dissociation runs through each of Schleitheim's articles (as we have seen), here it is named more directly and comprehensively, exhorting church members to separate from the outside world in their most everyday interactions. It does this in no uncertain terms: the outside world, we read, is evil, of the devil, an abomination. Baptized Christians should stay as far away from anything worldly as they possibly can.

It seems to me that this desire for separation is essential to Schleitheim's response to the catastrophe unfolding around it. And it is not difficult to understand why the dissociation from a world filled with crisis and suffering may seem appealing when shaping community. Schleitheim suggests not simply that catastrophes and crises are events that take place in the world, currently making life difficult for the church: here, the whole world *is* catastrophic. Separation from it is the only viable path.

Yet we might ask, is this even possible? If catastrophe is so comprehensive, so universally affecting the lives of so many of God's creatures, what safety can separation offer? And on closer reading, the text of this fourth article indeed turns out to be less clear. It is quite difficult to precisely establish what this "evil and ... wickedness which the devil planted in the world" really are. And as soon as the text gives a clearer sense of what it intends, the world turns out to be a much bigger place, and the "evil" much smaller, than we might have initially thought. Relationship insists—for better or for worse.

---

[1] Anabaptist leaders who disagree with this approach include, among others, Balthasar Hubmaier. See, for example, Snyder, *Anabaptist History and Theology*, 58–63.

A Shelter for Newness

On the face of it, the desire for separation from the outside world seems sensible enough. As we have seen, the logic of dissociation runs through Schleitheim as something like an underlying assumption: things and collectivities, it seems to think, are what they are insofar as they are recognizably different from other things. It only makes sense that it would extend that logic to the most everyday interactions of congregants.[2]

Particularly in a time of crisis and catastrophe, it is not difficult to see the appeal for a community to seek to stay away from the world in crisis around it to clarify its withdrawal from those harmful structures that are now collapsing. That would seem to safeguard its sense of a *new* beginning by making sure it is disentangled from and does not repeat the *old* things it tries to get away from. After all, it is exactly those old things that are proving inadequate to the new situation we are in. Separation promises to make this community *safe*, in a way, to safeguard it precisely from the crises and troubles and inevitable collapse of the structures of the world around it. Separation seems to provide a shelter—a refuge.

The practical implementation of such separation, the precise definition of actions or groups too "worldly" for Christians to participate in, is one that has occupied much of the time and energy of Anabaptist and other alternative communities through the centuries. You could even say that for many Anabaptist traditions it has been *the* main question and in many ways continues to be to this day.[3]

Yet there is, we might say, something peculiar about this kind of dissociative logic: it is not as independent as it may seem to promise. Indeed quite the opposite, as it makes our understanding of church and world explicitly dependent on each other. And the preoccupation with defining an identity in terms of what we are *not* is often more complicated than we would prefer: there is often more happening across this supposed

---

[2] Gerald Mast has argued that this fourth article is "the framework within which" the other articles operate. There is throughout Schleitheim a sense that the shared life of the community is won by means of exclusion or dissociation; there is thus a "relation of dependence between unity and separation." Schleitheim's separation is not merely withdrawal, however, but is best understood as "antagonism." In its (catastrophic) context, it represents a "protest" against the religious and political status quo. See Gerald Biesecker-Mast, *Separation and the Sword in Anabaptist Persuasion* (Telford: Cascadia, 2006), 102–3.

[3] Schleitheim's approach to defining what the church is by reference to an outside is still quite common also outside strictly Anabaptist communities. So contemporary theologian Stanley Hauerwas, to name just one example, explicitly defines the "world" and the "church" in distinction to each other. He argues the "world" is simply that in creation that does not confess Christ as Lord and has not yet acknowledged its redemption. So he writes: "Church and world are thus relational concepts: neither is intelligible without the other." The church, as a witnessing community, gives "the world the means to see itself truthfully … as world." See Stanley Hauerwas, *The Hauerwas Reader*, ed. John Berkman and Michael Cartwright (Durham: Duke University Press, 2001), 376, 377.

border than we would like to think. If we define ourselves by reference to an opposed or excluded other, it becomes hard to think about ourselves *without* reference to that other. This decenters our sense of ourselves. In Richard Kearney's words, the other, both constitutive to a group's identity and outside its control, both "defines, and undermines, its very identity. The double which haunts and fascinates."[4] If the church is defined as those "called out of the world," it becomes impossible to understand what the church is without reference to the world. So this worldless church remains constitutively tied to the world it tries to lose. The more effort we expend on *ex*cluding something from what "we" are, the more we paradoxically *include* it into our sense of what we are. In trying to keep the world out, Schleitheim also brings it in.

And I trust I am not alone in wondering if, or to what extent, this dissociation would be desirable even if it were possible. Does it provide the refuge it seems to promise? Does it not instead merely deny and mask the way the community is, indelibly, entangled in the world around it? This includes the ways it may be caught up in structural violence and injustice but also the way it is dependent on the world around it in a more creaturely sense: eating food, breathing air, participating in a web of relationships, for better or for worse.

Especially as contemporary readers, we may well understand the desire to get away from it all—but can anyone really be safeguarded from the crises and catastrophes of the mid-twenty-first century? Or, to put this differently, those few who *will* be safeguarded from them will not be those withdrawing into nonsovereign communities but those who will succeed in leveraging the structures of worldly injustice in their favor. After all, the desire for separation from climate collapse is today mostly the purview of the ultrarich, avoiding extreme weather in their private jets and building

---

[4]Richard Kearney, *Postnationalist Ireland: Politics, Culture, Philosophy* (London: Routledge, 1997), 79.

This is a significant argument in postcolonial studies, which traces the relations between colonized societies and their (former) colonizers. These relations are often marked by ambiguities, epistemic violence, and paradoxical reversals of force. Postcolonial theorist Richard King thus paraphrases Salman Rushdie that "the trouble with the English is that their history happened overseas and so they have no idea what it means." Richard King, *Orientalism and Religion: Post-Colonial Theory, India and the Mystic East* (London: Routledge, 1999), 189.

As I have argued elsewhere,

> A closer look suggests traditions, cultures, and religions are deeply marked by their entanglement with others, and that this entanglement is ineluctable, indeed, that they cannot be understood without it. An aspect of these interchanges has been the critical examination of the element of force and domination: Discussing the "religious other" is always a discussion of an otherness defined or even produced by these ambiguous, unequal, and violent processes. The assumption, current in much of theology of religions, that this otherness is simply "there" both cements difference and masks its historical production. (Marius van Hoogstraten, *Theopoetics and Religious Difference: The Unruliness of the Interreligious. A Dialogue with Richard Kearney, John D. Caputo, and Catherine Keller* [Tübingen: Mohr Siebeck, 2020], 217)

luxurious shelters in the New Zealand bedrock.⁵ Indeed many of the crises the church must face in our day require that Christians learn to *see* their entanglement in the world—not simply state their separation from it.

So let us take a closer look at this fourth article. How can we interpret it as a response to a comprehensive situation of catastrophe? What even is the "world" and its "evil" that Schleitheim wants to keep out the door? What can it mean to be called out of it? Schleitheim calls this being called-out (which, incidentally, is what the Greek word for church means: *ek-klesia*) a "liberation"—what significance does this sense of liberation or freedom have for the ecclesio-political, and what does it have to do with the freedom we discussed in Chapter 1? And, finally, how can such a "worldless" church embrace a creaturely and planetary belonging?

Perhaps the text of Schleitheim, if we pay appropriate attention, is more open to these kinds of questions than may initially appear. As elsewhere in this study: upon close reading, the text might show itself marked by tensions and openings that may yet signal a wholly different path.

Reading

Schleitheim's fourth article begins, like other articles, by noting that they have "agreed" (or "been united") on the following. A "separation" (*Absonderung*) is to be made from the "evil and ... the wickedness which the devil planted in the world." This "simply" means that "we shall not have fellowship with them and not run with them in ... their abominations." Such separation is necessary, we read, because whoever have not entered "the obedience of faith" and "united themselves with God" are an abomination, and thus nothing but "abominable things" can issue from them.

The injunction toward separation is again rooted in something of a metaphysical dualism. There are only two classes of creatures, Schleitheim argues: "good and evil, faithful and unfaithful, darkness and light, world, and those who have come out of the world ... and none can have part with the other" (apparently a paraphrase of 2 Cor. 6:14–7:1). Whoever would be part of the category of "good" must therefore withdraw from interaction with the "evil" if they hope to avoid "the pain and suffering" that awaits earthly empires ("Babylon" and "Egypt").

After this, the text makes more concrete what is meant by this category of "evil," constituting everything "not united with our God and Christ." One might expect this to simply mean everyone and everything not explicitly baptized into the church. However, perhaps surprisingly, the list is fairly

---

⁵See, for example, Mark O'Connell, "Why Silicon Valley Billionaires Are Prepping for the Apocalypse in New Zealand," *The Guardian*, February 15, 2018, https://www.theguardian.com/news/2018/feb/15/why-silicon-valley-billionaires-are-prepping-for-the-apocalypse-in-new-zealand.

concise. Schleitheim first names participation in "popish and antipopish" church gatherings, meetings, and church attendance—presumably referring to catholic and mainline protestant services and other aspects of mainline church life.

Second, the text names drinking houses, which seems clear enough. Third, it lists the somewhat mysterious "guarantees and commitments [of] unbelief," which possibly refers to certain kinds of economic activity in bad faith, though it remains unclear.[6] Fourth, Schleitheim names "other things of that kind," that is, things that "the world regards highly and yet are carried on in flat contradiction to the command of God." Again it is not immediately clear what is meant with this broad category.

In any case, participating in such things would make even baptized and faithful Christians "hated" (!) by Jesus Christ, who, the text now notes, has "set us free from the servitude of the flesh ... through the Spirit." The avoidance of worldly matters thus seems to have something to do with liberation from servitude—though it is perhaps not immediately clear how this can be understood.

A remark on the carrying of ("unchristian, devilish") weapons concludes this article: these will "also unquestionably fall from us," as Christ has instructed, "Resist not evil." Pacifism, if we can call it that, thus almost appears as an afterthought, merely the logical consequence of the particular relation to the world Schleitheim envisions. When the "sword" is discussed at greater length in Article VI, it refers not to the carrying of weapons but specifically to the sovereign power of the state and legal order—see Chapter 6.

In addition to the more general reference to Babylon and Egypt, the main biblical reference for this fourth article appears to be 2 Corinthians 6.[7] This is, we might note, a peculiar passage in Paul's oeuvre, which uses "many words used nowhere else by Paul; the stark dualism is also uncharacteristic of him."[8] Again, we get the sense that Schleitheim does not cite biblical passages out of a (perceived) biblical literalism or simplistic biblicistic obedience but associatively, based on the ecclesio-political logic of the kind of collective body it envisions and its underlying philosophical assumptions about things and collectivities.

---

[6]See the corresponding footnote 12 in the Appendix, p. 143–4.

[7]Yoder and Fast both note the line, "He calls upon us to be separate from the evil and thus He will be our God and we shall be His sons and daughters" as specifically referring to 6:17–18. This is not incorrect, but it is really all of 6:14-7:1 that is paraphrased in this paragraph, including as it does the references to good and bad, Christ and Belial, the temple of God and idols, which appear almost identically in 6:14-16. Sattler, "Brüderliche Vereinigung," 65; Yoder, *Legacy*, 41n57.

[8]Michael D. Coogan, Marc Brettler, Carol Newsom, and Pheme Perkins, eds., *The New Oxford Annotated Bible: New Revised Standard Version with the Apocrypha: An Ecumenical Study Bible*, fully revised fourth edition (Oxford: Oxford University Press, 2010), 2032.

Yet this logical coherence or necessity also makes this article somewhat odd. It suggests after all that it is not simply obvious or a given that those baptized into new life with Christ, disciplined into a shared body, and made into one loaf should now also refrain from worshiping in mainline churches. Apparently it needs pointing out that baptized Christians should avoid attending drinking houses. So this (again) already suggests that there is something odd about Schleitheim's philosophical assumption about things and collectivities: on the one hand, it *is* the underlying truth of reality that there are only two paths, and, on the other hand, this truth must interminably be enforced and reinforced.

Catastrophe

Schleitheim's insistence on separation perhaps makes most sense when understood as a response to catastrophe. As historian Jonathon Catlin puts it,

> Catastrophes are not simply events causing death and destruction (like accidents, disasters, or calamities), but moments of "overturning" or "a subversion of the order or system of things" (Oxford English Dictionary). Catastrophe happens when concepts fail, when the trauma of history overwhelms taken-for-granted powers of experience, thought, and language ... [It] denotes the failure of conceptuality itself.[9]

Philosopher David J. Rosner, too, frames catastrophe as "when the order of things is radically and suddenly disrupted." Catastrophe represents "a dislocation which leaves individuals and sometimes even entire civilizations bereft regarding life's most basic questions."[10] In its character as an event, catastrophe is sometimes distinguished conceptually from *crisis*, which, although it also represents an uprooting of the order of things, is not sudden but stretches over a period of time. But, Rosner notes, this is a distinction that can hardly be made rigorously: some catastrophes, such as the Shoah (or indeed colonialism or the slave trade), are far from sudden and brief, yet it would not be accurate to describe them as "crises" for that reason.[11]

So while these terms I have been using throughout this book—crisis, collapse, catastrophe—cannot be taken as conceptually sharply distinct, they do have different connotations. Crisis, for one, stems from the Greek

---

[9] Jonathon Catlin, "Toward an Interdisciplinary Conceptual History of Catastrophe," *EuropeNow*, 2022, https://www.europenowjournal.org/2022/01/30/toward-an-interdisciplinary-conceptual-history-of-catastrophe/.
[10] David J. Rosner, "Introductory Essay: Catastrophe and the Limits of Understanding," in *Catastrophe and Philosophy*, ed. David J. Rosner (Lanham: Lexington, 2018), xi–xxiii, xi.
[11] Ibid., xv–xvi.

krinein, referring to a turning point, a time of distinction or decision.¹² If things had been going on relatively steadily, that order is now disturbed and different paths show themselves, none simply given, each uncertain in their own way.

Collapse, we might supplement, does not have the hint of a futural orientation that crisis retains. Etymologically it stems from the Latin *collapsus*: a fallen mass. It is not going anywhere but further down. In ecology or society, collapse can come quickly and suddenly, representing a turning point in an interdependent system in which its internal coherence begins to fail. As a term, it does not signify a path forward but merely names the breakdown of an equilibrium or relative stability, as the interdependent relationships that make up a system fail in such a way that the system can no longer reproduce itself. In the words of political scientist and climate activist Tadzio Müller, collapse names the moment "when there is no longer any matter of course."¹³ For relational subjects living in myriad complex systems such as humans, collapse is often not experienced as a single cataclysmic event but as "the sometimes abrupt, sometimes more gradual disappearance of normalities and the no-longer-simply-availability of necessary goods and services."¹⁴

What persists through the connotations of each of these terms is the sense of a rupture or breakdown in the (perceived) stability in the world and of the inadequacy of the dominant mode of thinking, understanding, and organizing that world in the face of what is happening. In philosopher Susan Neiman's words, it "threatens our sense of the sense of the world."¹⁵ Such experiences may not strictly speaking signify the end of *the* world but certainly mark the end of *a* world.¹⁶

---

¹²Dara Strolovitch has provocatively theorized crisis as "when bad things happen to privileged people." And indeed it is probably true that the execution of Mantz, the defeat of the Peasants, and the adoption of a magisterial course by many mainline reformers did not represent a "crisis" to those in positions of power in the early sixteenth century in the way that it did to the Anabaptists. See Dara Z. Strolovitch, *When Bad Things Happen to Privileged People: Race, Gender, and What Makes a Crisis in America* (Chicago: University of Chicago Press, 2024).

¹³Tadzio Müller, *Zwischen Friedlicher Sabotage Und Kollaps. Wie Ich Lernte, Die Zukunft Wieder Zu Lieben* (Wien: Mandelbaum, 2024), 296.

¹⁴Ibid. Müller argues the prospect of collapse requires us to "organize effectively, with solidarity, and openly" and envisions networks of mutual care and community, preparing for the collapse of state and economic structures. This seems not entirely far off from Schleitheim's venture.

¹⁵Susan Neiman, *Evil in Modern Thought: An Alternative History of Philosophy* (Princeton: Princeton University Press, 2015), 2.

¹⁶French "collapsology" researchers Raphael Stevens and Pablo Servigne stress that the ecological, economic, and political collapse that awaits us in the twenty-first century is "not the end of the world, nor the Apocalypse." But it is certainly also not "a simple crisis from which we can emerge unscathed." It "threatens human beings as a whole, as well as a large proportion of living species." In such a context, collapsology is to study the various interconnected crises and ruptures that await us in the next generation or so, which are (still) rarely taken up in a comprehensive view: "The climate is heating up, biodiversity is collapsing, pollution is ubiquitous and becoming persistent, the economy risks going into cardiac arrest at every moment, social and geopolitical tensions are growing, etc"—leading to the very real possibility

Schleitheim, we might say, seeks to insulate the church from this "world" in crisis, *a* world that is in the process of collapse. "Pain and suffering" are foretold for earthly empires but can be avoided by the faithful. It attempts to turn the logic of catastrophe on its head: in the face of comprehensive rupture, it seeks a path that will remain unfazed by the catastrophic nature of the surrounding world.

As part of this, it seems to view catastrophe not merely as an event or even a period but as simply the constant state of the world: it has become, and does not cease to be, wholly "evil."[17] The challenge is thus not merely to shape a shared life *after* some catastrophic destruction or crisis of meaning (that is, how to go on and to rebuild, as Catlin approaches it) nor indeed how to live with the prospect of collapse *before* us (as is Müller's focus), but how to live well together when catastrophe is all around.

This assessment is certainly sweeping. And yet with it, Schleitheim could be said to be remarkably in tune with a certain reality of the world in which it finds itself: that for countless creatures, humans and otherwise, catastrophe is not something that *might* befall them, or *has* befallen them and has now ceased to do so, but an inescapable and constant state of life. The text thus seems to anticipate a notion of "permanent catastrophe," which is developed by theorists such as Theodor Adorno and Walter Benjamin in the twentieth century.[18] Writing in the 1930s, Benjamin had noted that while catastrophe is often considered as the interruption of the status quo, in fact, the " 'status quo' *is* the catastrophe."[19] Reflecting on a sketch by Paul Klee, Benjamin sees the "Angel of History" in the picture with his

> face turned toward the past. Where we perceive a chain of events, he sees one single catastrophe, which keeps piling wreckage upon wreckage and hurls it in front of his feet. The angel would like to stay, awaken the dead, and make whole what has been smashed. But a storm is blowing from Paradise; it ... irresistibly propels him into the future to which his back is turned, while the pile of debris before him grows skyward. This storm is what we call progress.[20]

---

of "famine." See Raphael Stevens and Pablo Servigne, *How Everything Can Collapse: A Manual for Our Times* (Cambridge: Polity Press, 2020), 2–3, 6.

[17] As we learn from Neiman, "evil" is used self-evidently for suffering and disasters more broadly (such as, notably, the 1755 Lisbon earthquake) well into modernity before its use shifts to more specifically refer to human morality. See Neiman, *Evil*, 3.

[18] See especially Catlin, "Catastrophe."

[19] Walter Benjamin, *The Arcades Project*, ed. Rolf Tiedemann (Cambridge: Harvard University Press, 2002), 473.

[20] Walter Benjamin, *Illuminations: Essays and Reflections*, ed. Hannah Arendt (New York: Schocken Books, 2007), 257–8.

Devastation, suffering, and ruin are not things that happen *to* the dominant economic and political order of modernity, we might say, but an inherent feature.[21]

How indeed to live, to shape life when faced with such a terrifying reality? Adorno famously concludes it is impossible: *Es gibt kein richtiges Leben im Falschen*. There is no way to live right in a world filled with wrong. As Neiman summarizes,

> What remains is only the moral imperative not to deceive ourselves about the magnitude of the modern catastrophe. Decency demands that we refuse to feel at home in any particular structure the world provides to domesticate us.[22]

It is this kind of life that Schleitheim seems to seek, stressing its homelessness, its not-at-home-ness in this catastrophic world. The form of life it envisions for the church is not possible within the world; it must take shape outside of it. And it finds this outside not in a future in which the world would be mended or redeemed but in a particular kind of fellowship, one as much as possible isolated from this comprehensive disaster. It seeks to do what the Angel could not bring himself to do: To cut ties with the suffering and loss that make up life in the world.

In Keller's words, relationship means to be "never immune to you, or to the loss of you."[23] Schleitheim here seems to seek precisely this immunity from loss. Its separatism is born of a desire for immunization from a world whose suffering and loss would be, or is, unbearable. It allows it to (or at least this seems to be the promise) begin anew without mourning the old. As Raphael Stevens and Pablo Servigne put it, facing collapse earnestly requires us to "mourn the loss" of a vision of the future: "Accepting the possibility of a collapse means accepting the death of a future that was dear to us, a future that was reassuring, however irrational it might have been."[24]

Nothing about this world is dear to us, Schleitheim seems to say instead. It appears instead as an enemy, whose collective suffering and perdition do not even register as a loss.[25] This enemy-making move is, in its own

---

[21]In Hannah Arendt's vocabulary, the "world" has the specific meaning of a shared and durable space in which free human beings can encounter each other as equals. Conditioned by early modern destabilizing developments, including the Reformation, the advent of colonialism, and developments in natural sciences, modernity destabilizes such shared spaces in a number of ways, leading to a "loss of the world." Modern human beings are, at the same time, isolated from each other and pressed them together into a mass society—a condition for totalitarian domination. See Arendt, *Between Past and Future*, 89–90.
[22]Neiman, *Evil*, 305.
[23]Keller, *Cloud of the Impossible*, 224.
[24]Stevens and Servigne, *How Everything Can Collapse*, 6.
[25]Judith Butler has introduced a notion of "grievability," asking the question which lives register as a loss to a political community: while some lives are mourned when killed (e.g., a white

way, deeply reminiscent of the dissociative logic of sovereignty (more on which in Chapter 6), which eminently functions by distinguishing friends from enemies. In a more everyday sense, it also seems reminiscent of a perhaps very human tendency: to respond to catastrophic circumstances by withdrawing into the borders of a particular community (national or otherwise), narrowing the scope of one's solidarity. It may be that this cold separatism cannot be entirely excised from the Schleitheim text: dissociation is, after all, a theme throughout. Yet for our purposes, as we trace this line of a nonsovereign community that the text also suggests, it will need to be complicated and questioned at the very least.

And as we will see, the text itself already begins to do this work: It problematizes its own dualism, complicates its cold separatism, and—perhaps in spite of itself—opens up to a surprising relationality.

The World and Its Evil

For what precisely is this "world" and its "evil" of which Schleitheim here speaks? Already on the face of the text there is a tension. In the first part of this article, everything that is not explicitly part of the church is considered evil, even abominable. The first lines seem as unambiguous as can be: there are only two kinds of things, the church and everything else, and this second category is utterly corrupt. This would echo other parts of Schleitheim: the preamble similarly notes that the church is separated from the world in "everything," and in the previous article, there was first mention of the church being called "out of the world" and thus having "no part" with everyone else who, by not having been baptized, continue to follow "the devil and the world." So there appears to be no nuance between the world, the devil, the evil that the devil has planted in the world, and those who live in and among these three. Schleitheim here is starkly dualistic: everything not explicitly in the church is of a radically different nature, and no ambiguity or shared life is conceivable between them.

Yet there is more to be said; this stark dualism, comprehensive though it may seem in its condemnation of simply "everything" outside the church, does not foreclose further questions. In the following paragraph, the text begins to clarify what "everything" refers to more specifically. And as soon as this extremely broad category is specified, we discover it is not nearly as broad as we perhaps assumed. It only refers to a handful of quite specific types of association: going to church,to the pub, (apparently) undertaking economic activity in bad faith, and other "things of that kind."[26] Even if

---

murder victim), others are not (e.g., refugees or Black victims of police violence). See Judith Butler, *The Force of Nonviolence: An Ethico-Political Bind* (London: Verso, 2020).

[26]Mast also notes this tension, as "we discover that" the text is concerned with "a specific rejection of certain practices." Biesecker-Mast, *Separation and the Sword*, 103.

you understand this fourth item on the list in the broadest conceivable way, it will still hardly refer to things of a completely different "kind" than the first three and is again specified to mean things "highly regarded by the world and yet ... in flat contradiction to the command of God." This seems far removed from the general prohibition of "fellowship" just a few lines earlier: it is really just a small subset of quite concrete kinds of interaction one might have with those outside the church.

Even more, they are *human* kinds of interaction. Church services, drinking parties, and economic agreements are all things that take place between humans, in which nonhuman beings at most play a minor supporting role (providing the barley and fermentation for the ale, or constituting the goods being bought and sold, for example). There is no mention at all where the entirety of the nonhuman world is to be located in this dualism between "church" and "world."

So "everything which is not united with our God and Christ" turns out to not at all mean *simply* everyone and everything outside the church. It has a specific meaning: only some human activities fall in this category and are to be avoided. Everything else is of unclear status (for now) but seems to certainly not fall in the category of "abominations." Baptized Christians are not expected to withdraw or separate from buying food, we imagine, nor indeed from farming or working, nor walking in the forest or enjoying a sunset. None of these things are "evil," even if the sunset has not voluntarily repented and requested baptism.

So this troubles Schleitheim's stated dualism, it would seem: an entire category of beings—nonhuman creatures, natural phenomena, but also human friendships and everyday interactions—appears to exist in some place that is neither church *nor* "world." Schleitheim might claim broadly that "all creatures are in but two classes," but it hardly seems to think so when things get specific. The "evil" from which the church is to disentangle is really just a number of specific events and associations. These human systems and structures might proclaim their own totality and might make themselves out to be all there is, but it soon turns out that their "world" is but a small element in the universe and its teeming possibilities.

One thing we could do at this point is to simply leave it at that. Look here, we might say, life is complicated, and those gathered at Schleitheim are not blind to this. Even if we believe in the starkest of cosmic and metaphysical dualisms, life as it is actually lived is still full of messiness, full of ambiguous things and relationships that do not fit the approved mold. We can try to install techniques and practices to keep this at bay, to suppress ambiguity when it arises, but they will never definitively succeed. Ambiguity insists. This is life, at least on this plane of reality. This is a point I made in previous chapters.

But already in Chapter 2, I noted that in some sense, this ambiguity or messiness is not just a tragic reality to be stoically accepted but can be read as itself the site of a peculiar kind of good news. And the text of this fourth article also invites us to go further than such tragic recognition. If we do not discard out of hand Schleitheim's stated dualistic logic, that there really are but *two* categories of beings, the question becomes not so much "how does the emergence of a third trouble these two," but "if we find something unaccounted for, to which of these two categories does it properly belong—and how does that affect our understanding of it?"

And the answer to this question must be, it seems to me, entirely straightforward. After all, after we have identified that *one* of these categories is quite narrowly circumscribed to refer to only a certain subset of human activities and associations, then logically, everything else must belong to the other category.

That is to say, if trees and sunsets and friendships are not part of the "wickedness which the devil planted in the world," this must mean they are, in some way, somehow, "good." If the category of beings "*not* united with our God" includes only these few types of human activities, then by implication, everything else must be "united with our God." Worms and grass leaves and stars and cloud formations are, we might well say, not a disturbing third category but entirely part of this entire vast universe that Schleitheim describes as "called out of the world," part of what it calls "good." Schleitheim certainly *seems* to be saying that everything and everyone not explicitly in the church is an abomination and "evil," explicitly "planted in the world" by the "devil." But now it seems more like the inverse must be true: everything and everyone not explicitly evil and planted in the world by the devil is *in some way* "united with our God."

Of course, I hasten to add again, I really do not mean to say that this is what Sattler and the others composing and affirming this text in 1527 had in mind in a literal and historical sense. Possibly, they really did believe there were only two categories of beings, the church and "everything else," and never gave any thought to the existence of trees and cloud formations. Maybe. But it is hard to deny that the text they have left us with at least seems open to this complicative reading I have been developing. And, more importantly, it is hard to deny that the kind of dualistic logic the text endorses, if we really take it seriously, makes such a reading necessary. If there are only two kinds of things, and something is not category one, it *must* be category two. If there is only good and evil, and something is not evil, it *must* be good. Anything else would be to admit there really are not only two categories.

And is it really so strange to suggest this? Is it really so strange to suggest trees, sheep, sunsets, and friendships are, in some way, "good," not "evil"? This is certainly not such a radical proposition. What *is* a more unexpected consequence or implication is that Schleitheim seems to suggest, by force of its dualistic logic, that this *also* makes all of those things part of "God's temple," that all things not expressly "evil" are, by necessity, even if they are not in the church explicitly, *somehow* in relation with God and Christ.

The force of its own dualistic logic thus turns on its head the whole dour, narrow, and exclusivist separatism that *seemed* to mark the Schleitheim text. With it, we can now see the way God is in relation ("united") with things wherever we look. We see a universe alive with divine relationality, and we see ourselves as those who have committed to that divine, not separated out from it but pointed back into it. For this God whom we seek, who has invited us into this community we are striving to build, awaits us also "out there." And inversely, too: whenever we discern truth in the universe, we must presume it somehow to be related to God's truth; whenever we discern goodness in the universe, we must presume it somehow related to God's goodness. At least this is what Schleitheim seems to be saying: there is no *additional* category of goodness. All goodness is part (one way or another) of "God's temple."

This is not to say that all of these things are part of the explicit ecclesio-political community Schleitheim is envisioning. But it is to say that there is here an opening, even a necessity, to recognize that when this community looks out into the universe around it, it must discern there not just evil and abomination but light, goodness, and even Christ.[27]

An ambiguity insists into the effort to draw clear borders around this community. In previous chapters, we observed in the text itself how attempts at a homogeneous and pure collective body seemed to inevitably fail—sometimes because of the very techniques employed to ascertain it. The things that trouble the border between "church" and "world" are *most things*, and most of us as well. This fourth article might *seem* to propose another technique to sharpen its borders. But, at least on my reading, instead it implies the embrace of all this between-space as already in some relationship with God. The insistent, troubling ambiguity must not merely be stoically accepted but seems to point us to a universe alive with the divine. Within the category of "light," there is a veritable landscape, and the church is just one entity in that landscape, indelibly related to it. Even (perhaps especially) in times of catastrophe, our belonging to that good creation is not, and ought not be, so easily cut off.

... and Other Things of That Kind

Now that we have established that, at least in this reading, the "evil" in the world is not synonymous with simply everything outside the church—what is it?

If we look at the little list Schleitheim gives, we find quite specific events and associations: mainline church gatherings, drinking houses, (presumably)

---

[27]Stanley Hauerwas, named above as an example of a contemporary version of a church-world-separatism, is no stranger to this realization. Christ's "presence is not confined to the church. Rather, it is in the church that we learn to recognize Christ's presence outside the church." See Hauerwas, *The Hauerwas Reader*, 372.

economic activity in bad faith, and "other things of that kind." It is not immediately clear what unites these. Sure, the text adds a short explainer, suggesting these are all things held in high regard by the world (unsurprising considering we are describing the "world") but in "contradiction to the command of God." But I am not sure how that elucidates anything; it seems to go without saying that things in contradiction to the command of God are forbidden for baptized Christians. If *that* were the point here, it could have easily been handled in Article II about church discipline. And we might also find some things seemingly missing: the text here says nothing about, say, interaction with the state, which is addressed in its own article (see Chapter 6). Nor does it address the interactions among baptized Christians, even though we know from Article II that these are in danger of slipping and falling.

Perhaps we can find a first clue by taking note of the kind of point Schleitheim is making here. Going to a wine shop and making unfair business deals may seem like ethical matters, so it may seem like Schleitheim is here penning down a regulation on the kind of behavior appropriate for baptized Christians. But that is not what the text is doing. As elsewhere, Schleitheim is arguing on a different level, discussing formal and collective constitutive practices by which the church can take shape as a collective body. As before, so here as well: the text is not making an *ethical* regulation but an (ecclesio-)*political* one. Baptized Christians' participation in the world is not a matter of following the right ethical rules but one of ecclesio-political belonging.

If we take this seriously, we can also see that the text does not so much forbid *drinking* as *drinking houses*. It does not so much forbid lying or fraud or even usury as economic *agreements and commitments*. The point with mainline churches is their being "popish or antipopish," that is, being in a certain ecclesio-political constitution.

In drawing attention to the political nature of each of these, I do not mean to suggest that those gathered at Schleitheim explicitly permit drinking as such, or lying and fraud, or believing in protestant or catholic teaching positions. It is just to say that this article is not about individual behavior but about collective gathering places with what we might call a binding function. Each of the things on Schleitheim's little list is a gathering or binding operation that establishes, shapes, and maintains a certain kind of association between human beings. They are societal structures that bind people together in particular ways—ways that are at odds with Schleitheim's project. They shape communities that are opposed to the kind of community Schleitheim envisions for its followers.

So the "evil" of the world here does not mean all of heaven and earth outside the explicit church, as it seemed to in the beginning, but only certain human structures. Generalizing from the specific items on Schleitheim's list, perhaps we might say they are those structures that set themselves up as false totalities, that bind creaturely freedom, and that oppress creatures' bodies ("servitude of the flesh"). This may seem like a jump, but the evil of the world is expressly synonymous with empire, named as "Babylon and the earthly Egypt," and is explicitly named as the place of "weapons of force." And this understanding of the "world and its evil" as a question of systems of domination and exploitation seems in line with the biblical terminology: after all, the biblical Greek word for world, *kosmos*, means exactly "system." Though such systems of injustice may bring status or other benefit to some ("highly regarded"), Schleitheim reminds us they stand in "contradiction" to the kind of fellowship and relation that God invites all creatures into.

Avoiding getting caught up in these kinds of harmful societal structures, Schleitheim seems to suggest, is not a question of individual obedience to ethical rules but exactly the opposite: we should stay away from them also because we *can* stay away from them because Jesus has "set us free from the servitude of the flesh" (*entledigt hat von der Dienstbarkeit des Fleisches*), liberated us from the oppression of creaturely bodies.[28]

A community that chooses the way of relational freedom, of this beginning-again we discussed in Chapter 1, might well want to "separate" to disentangle itself from such structures. This is not a question of carefully drawing a "separatist" line between *us* and the *outside* that would make the new community safe from loss, as I discussed at the beginning of this chapter. It is simply a matter of minding the relationships a free community intends to foster and the dependencies it sees as harmful.

These structures of unfreedom will be destroyed, we read. These institutions that produce suffering are destined for suffering themselves. Even they cannot escape the unfolding catastrophe. Schleitheim seems to see the handwriting of divine agency in this impending collapse—the only mention of divine punishment for anyone, empire or not, in all of Schleitheim, we might note.[29]

---

[28]Of course, it would not be hard to defend an apparently opposite view: that for Schleitheim, the church is the place of "obedience of faith," where the members "wish to do His [God's] will," while the outside world is the place where anything goes, a place of "freedom" in the sense of libertinism. As indeed Schleitheim criticizes its Anabaptist opponents in the preamble for such apparent "freedom." But even this formulation, that Christians "*wish* to do God's will," already shows that there is something peculiar about this obedience: it is an obedience that centers on a kind of interaction or mutual relatedness of human and divine will. As we discussed extensively in Chapter 1, it is an obedience freely taken up in voluntary baptism, and it is an obedience of a completely different kind than that demanded by worldly rulers, consisting in the shared life of a community of equals. See also Chapter 6.

The type of freedom that the church should revolve around can perhaps be distinguished schematically from each of the three items on its list of evil associations or gatherings: mainline religion could be said to offer a merely internal or spiritual freedom; unlimited consumption in drinking houses seems to offer a narrow freedom of excess (perhaps not so uncommon today), and the fake camaraderie that accompanies it; economic interactions limit freedom to choice and interest. Instead, Schleitheim sees freedom more comprehensively and existentially and inseparable from self-governance in community.

[29]The precise line, "that we may not be partakers of the pain and suffering which the Lord will bring upon them," immediately follows a paraphrase of 2 Cor. 6–7. It seems an elucidation

A Community of Refuge

Even with such prophetic announcements of violence, there is a peaceful gesture here. Others might choose to continue to struggle within harmful "worldly" structures in the hopes of achieving control over them and reforming or abolishing them from such a position of power. Schleitheim hopes for none of that. It chooses instead to let them go and begin again.

It lets the evil be. Schleitheim does not want to make the world conform to its ideals but simply wants to create a space around different ideals. It does not want to destroy the mainline churches, or burn down the drinking houses, or assassinate captains of industry; it does not want to overthrow Babylon and Egypt by military conquest. But it does want to loosen the hold those systems and structures have on creatures enough so that they can take up their freedom and get away. In the midst of catastrophe, it wants to create a community of refuge for those who have made a break for it, "set free" from the oppression of their bodies by God's liberating force.

Life and future exist, Schleitheim seems to be saying, outside of these structures of exploitation that are doomed to collapse, perhaps even already have started to collapse. They make themselves up to be all there is, and they seem to last forever, but an escape remains possible. Schleitheim's gentle letting-be is thus supplemented by its rejection, its "protest"[30] to the world's structures of exploitation. Shaping community in a time of crisis may not require a sheltering separatism, but it does require disentangling from harmful, violent, and unfree structures. In our contemporary context, these may well turn out different than what Sattler and his comrades suggest—so we might see the need for church to disentangle from nationalism, petrocapitalism, sexism, and other things of that kind. This is not just a withdrawn community beginning again for itself by itself: it is a church in overt antagonism with global structures of exploitation, making spaces for those who have chosen to make a break for it.

It embraces the contingency in which it gathers, and in this contingency—in this freedom, this having been set free from what oppressed their bodies—takes up the work of reinventing, of making again, a place of fellowship. This is why, ultimately, we cannot understand the church without the "world": because gathering as church is constitutively a venture of liberation.

---

of its final line, added in to note that the people of God are commanded to come out of these empires so that the former might be saved while the latter are destroyed. This is not entirely accurate to the depiction in the Old Testament: Israel comes out of Babylon *after* its overthrow by the Persians, not before, and comes out of Egypt *after* it is visited by the plagues, not before. It is protected from some of these plagues by techniques of dissociation (notably the blood on the door that makes the angel of death pass on), but these take place while it remains *in* Egypt. What's more, the empire of Egypt, though clearly set back by the enslaved nation's escape, does not really collapse for many centuries to come.

[30]Biesecker-Mast, *Separation and the Sword*, 103.

The church needs some reference to the "world" to comprehend itself not out of a cold separatism but because it sets itself up as a community of refuge from that "world" and must not forget this central task. Church is not a fixed and homogeneous identitarian community, withdrawn from all the things outside its narrow borders, but eminently and essentially a community of solidarity, seeking God's proximity to (even being "united with") those who wish to make a break for freedom.

Conclusion

In giving shape to community in times of crisis, collapse, and catastrophe, Schleitheim *seems* to believe it requires a clear dissociation from whatever lies outside it. As catastrophe signifies a rupture or breakdown in a collective sense of the world, this is not difficult to understand: it appears as the attempt to insulate the nascent community from a loss that would be, or is, unbearable.

On closer reading, however, we found that this is only partially true. There is a veritable landscape that is already, in some way, "inside," inside God's embrace, and the church must learn to see this divine relationality and take its place among it. This, we can now say, also includes the nonimmunity to its loss: to shape community in times of catastrophe requires not cold isolation but the capacity to feel and mourn the loss of much *zoe* that was indeed "united to Christ." For the "world" here rejected is only a small part of the universe. Worms and grass leaves and friendships and cloud formations are not "evil" nor planted by "the Devil," nor even a disturbing third category, but entirely part of this vast universe that Schleitheim calls "good," even God's temple. A nonsovereign community is one that does not except itself out of *zoe*, out of a planetary togetherness or creaturely belonging, but takes shape in its midst, even in the midst of its rupture and collapse, when it mourns its loss.[31]

A zoic ambiguity troubles and expands the narrow solidarities to which we may tend in catastrophic times. Paradoxically it is exactly in this fourth article on "separation" that we find between the lines the implication of an embrace of that troubling: an embrace of the fuzziness, of all that is neither explicitly "in" nor "out," yet already inside God's embrace. In naming all of this explicitly *good*, Schleitheim seems to be making a counterintuitive

---

[31] In a sense, Schleitheim's estimation of the widespread suffering in the world *as* something akin to catastrophe could be read exactly in this light: in describing this as "evil," Schleitheim could be seen as lamenting a suffering that *registers as a loss at all*. The world is not alright; it is full of rupture and dislocation. Much that represents catastrophe to those gathered at Schleitheim will not register as such to the dominant systems of its time: the defeat of the Peasants, to name just one, will have been received more as the restoration of an order and sense to the world than its rupture.

suggestion: even amid catastrophe, life here, on this planet, amid creaturely belonging, *can be good*—which, it seems to me, is a significant claim.[32]

This may seem like an insight won against the text's more overt intentions, I admit: presented with a seeming dead end, we might say, a particular kind of reading led us to a narrow passage to squeeze through. Yet from the other side of that passage, things looked different. And also in a more straightforward sense, it seems not too much to claim that there are beings part of God's good creation yet not part of the explicit church.

This wide yet vulnerable "yes" must be accompanied by a decisive "no": not the "no" of sharp separatism, the wholesale isolation from creaturely belonging, but the "no" of protest against those structures of human organization that bind creaturely freedom and deny relationship with wider existence. The formation and shaping of community requires disentanglement, a loosening of the hold those structures of dominion and exploitation have on creatures, and a disruption of the totality they claim for themselves. In catastrophe and collapse, *a* world is perhaps lost—but not *the* world, and a new beginning may yet, insistently, be possible.

---

[32]As Bruno Latour and Dipesh Chakrabarty have put it for our contemporary situation: "A good enough planet, not the Promised Land. That's what everyone on this planet suddenly dreams of." See Bruno Latour and Dipesh Chakrabarty, "Conflicts of Planetary Proportion—a Conversation," *Journal of the Philosophy of History* 14, no. 3 (2020): 435.

5

Process

Introduction

Schleitheim's fifth article addresses the election, responsibilities, and disciplining of pastors. Noting the congregation will be "destroyed" without a pastor, the text stresses that pastors should be people of a good reputation, chosen and maintained by the community and accountable to it. It would not be surprising to find here an embrace of authority in a more comprehensive sense. In times of crisis and catastrophe, who does not yearn for someone to rally around, someone who takes control and offers clarity in confusing times?[1]

Yet this is not what we find here. C. Arnold Snyder sees in this fifth article a continuation or "direct echo"[2] of a key demand of the peasants' movement: that "pastors be elected by the community, disciplined by the community, and supported by the community."[3] Even amid the collapse of hopes of a more comprehensive reform of society, church at least should be a space in which all members participate in the election of leaders.[4] At the same time, the institution of such a proto-democratic process is also a consolidation, the apparent recognition that *some* organization, leadership, and even authority are necessary for a community to persist. It is "restricting individual action,"[5] Snyder notes, especially suppressing the leadership of prophetic women who had played a significant role up to that point.

The kind of proceduralism Schleitheim here develops thus both institutes and delimits the authority of its leaders while also both instituting and delimiting (something like) a democratic process. This may already be

---

[1] It is perhaps no wonder that in our mid-twenty-first-century context, authority and authoritarian politics are having a moment. Questions of leadership, democratic legitimacy (but also the difficulties of its process), and collective action seem like some of the most urgent political problems in a time marked by the need for collective action in the face of at least several crises. In this light, it is perhaps ironic that some of the most authoritarian political forces have embraced climatic *in*action and the sabotage of democratic process instead.
[2] Snyder, "The Schleitheim Articles," 422n9.
[3] Ibid., 422.
[4] Snyder, *Anabaptist History and Theology*, 367.
[5] Ibid., 253.

quite appealing to a modern audience, as authority and its democratic accountability have become subject to some contemporary anxiety. Yet Schleitheim goes further than this. On a closer look, the particular tasks given to the pastor fall well short of comprehensive authority. Pastors are only responsible for a limited number of specific matters, ensuring or facilitating the community is called together and its constitutive practices can take place. They are not called to control and decide but to organize and represent, or indeed to see to "the care of the body of Christ": they are caregivers to a frail yet self-governing nonsovereign collective body.

Reading

The fifth article of Schleitheim is one of its shorter ones, discussing pastors or "shepherds" in the "community of God." Except for the description of the pastor's tasks, the text consists of seemingly loose remarks, giving a single criterion for pastoral candidates and some instructions around their payment, disciplining, and replacement. Though it suggests pastors are to be elected, the precise procedure for doing so is not addressed.[6]

The first thing the text addresses is that pastors should have "a good report of those who are outside the faith." This is "as Paul has prescribed," we read, which appears to refer to 1 Timothy 3. Out of the many criteria listed there, this is perhaps a surprising choice for Schleitheim to highlight: after all, the previous article had espoused a generally negative view of the outside world, and such a good report says little about the candidate's competence or other characteristics.[7] Perhaps this is considered implied, but the text says nothing directly about whether the pastor-to-be should have discernible gifts toward any of their tasks, or if they should be married or not, or if they should be educated in some way.

The text continues by detailing the tasks of a pastor. These are

> to read, to admonish and teach, to warn, to discipline, to ban in the community, to lead out in prayer for the advancement of all the brothers and sisters, to begin to break the bread, and in all things see to the care of the body of Christ.

---

[6]C. Arnold Snyder notes at this point the ad hoc nature of the points Schleitheim makes. See Snyder, *Life and Thought*, 162.

[7]Gayle Gerber Koontz also notes that Schleitheim tellingly makes no mention of doctrine here. However, Koontz concludes that it instead envisions office chosen by "charismatic authority" and other kinds of skills or characteristics. This may be true for the historical practice of groups identified with Schleitheim, but the text itself mentions nothing of the kind. See Gayle Gerber Koontz, "Ecclesiology, Authority, and Ministry: An Anabaptist-Mennonite Perspective," in *The Heart of the Matter: Pastoral Ministry in Anabaptist Perspective*, ed. Erick Sawatzky (Telford: Cascadia, 2004), 72n10, 64.

It is not clear whether these are intended as the exclusive purview of pastors. Disciplining, at least, seems to be a more widely shared responsibility. There are also a few conspicuous absences in the list: the pastor is not tasked with officiating weddings and funerals (perhaps included in "lead[ing] out in prayer"), nor—significantly—baptisms. As we recall, in its first article, Schleitheim regulated who can receive baptism in some detail, but the question of who can give it remained, and here again remains, open.[8]

In all these tasks, the pastor's work has a dual orientation, the text continues. On the one hand, its focus is inward: pastors do their work so that "the body of Christ ... may be built up and improved." On the other hand, their focus is outward: their work (and their "good report") is to stop "the mouth of the slanderer" (which is indeed to be "*verstopfft*," stuffed).

Next, the text addresses the pastor's livelihood: they are to be "supported of the church which has elected [*erwehlt*] him [*sic*]," so that "he who serves the Gospel may live of the Gospel" (1 Cor. 9:14). The text does not go into detail how this support should take place, nor indeed the election: a consensus process, a majority vote? Do candidates put themselves forward? What is clear, however, is that pastors are chosen freely by the community they serve. They are not appointed by hierarchical church office, designated as a successor by a previous leader, or chosen by the drawing of lots. We might call this a (proto-)democratic moment and also a decentralized one: each congregation chooses their pastor for themselves, without reference to episcopal or regional institutions.

The accountability structures toward pastors are treated with slightly more detail. Disciplinary action toward them requires "two or three witnesses" and must take place publicly (thus omitting the first steps of the regular discipline process) "in order that the others may fear" (1 Tim. 5:20). It is not clear whether this implies the end of their role as a pastor. The text mentions nothing about fixed terms or reelection but notes that when a pastor dies or is displaced (an altogether likely scenario under conditions of persecution), another should be chosen promptly "so that God's little people and flock may not be destroyed." The pastor is thus both essential and replaceable, and each of these two adds to the resilience of the community.

The biblical references in this article are limited in scope and marked by surprising absences. There is no reference to the choosing and installing of leaders in Acts, for example. Instead, the text refers to only three passages: 1 Timothy 3, 1 Timothy 5, and 1 Corinthians 9.

1 Timothy 3 lays out a comprehensive list of criteria for leaders in the church. Its recommendations are differentiated between bishops and deacons and detail the specific types of virtues and character traits someone aspiring to such a role should have. Remarkably, Schleitheim only takes on verse 7 (on bishops): "Moreover, he must be well thought of by outsiders."

---

[8] See also Hoogstraten, "The Anabaptist Moment."

1 Tim. 5:19-20 discusses the disciplining of leaders, instructing to "never accept any accusation against an elder except on the evidence of two or three witnesses. As for those who persist in sin, rebuke them in the presence of all, so that the rest also may stand in fear."

The instruction that pastors should be maintained in their material needs by the congregation could also have come from 1 Timothy (indeed immediately preceding the passage just cited: 1 Tim. 5:17-18). Instead, Schleitheim uses words from 1 Cor. 9:14. This is a peculiar choice, as Paul is here actually defending himself for *not* being supported by the congregation, which apparently was cause for suspicion. Paul frames it instead as a right he is not making use of; Schleitheim cites only the line establishing this right.

In all this, Schleitheim's focus is again strikingly formal. It leaves out most of 1 Timothy's specific character requirements of pastors and says nothing about the content of the teaching they are responsible for, the skills they should have, or the theological relation between God, Jesus, the church, its pastors, and the Holy Spirit. Yet also the formal aspects of leadership are not elaborately laid out—there is no mention of elders or deacons, whether there are more pastors called for a single congregation, or whether there should be regional overseers or bishops. And it is left open how a pastor should be elected and what happens to their function if they are disciplined.

A Kind of Care Work

To get a better sense of what kind of role this is, let us take a closer look at the tasks given to pastors. We read the pastor is tasked, broadly, with four categories of responsibilities: first, what we might call liturgical presiding (reading, leading prayer, beginning to break the bread); second, preaching and teaching (*vermanen und leren*); third, overseeing or perhaps executing disciplinary action (though clearly not exclusively as the pastor can also himself become subject to it); and finally "in all things see to the care of the body of Christ."

Of these four categories, none include the kind of discerning wisdom, visionary strategizing, or deciding authority that we might associate with leadership in a modern sense. In this light, Snyder remarks on the contrast between a Benedictine abbot—Sattler's context prior to his Anabaptist life—and the way the pastor is presented here. While the abbot is also elected, which might suggest a parallel, his authority is "virtually absolute," and he can only be removed in "extreme cases by persons outside the community." By contrast, the shepherd "remains one of the congregation."[9]

---

[9] Snyder, *Life and Thought*, 266.

The pastor's tasks and responsibilities are clearly circumscribed. The first category of tasks, liturgical presiding, is phrased in clearly limited terms: to *begin* to break the bread (*anheben zu brechen*), to lead *in prayer* (*vorbeten*), to *read* (*lesen*), so to present texts that already exist. Of course, there is power in these tasks: reading, for one, is never simply *reading* but always also selection and emphasis. But this power is clearly circumscribed, its extent is mostly procedural, and, importantly, it is occasional, limited to a worship setting.

The second grouping comes closer to what we might today understand as leadership but again seems limited to the context of the worship service: preaching and teaching. The extent to which these imply significant power is not immediately clear: does it refer to a kind of teaching authority, laying out a binding interpretation of the biblical text? Or merely to someone who is expected to repeat the (supposedly) clear and obvious truths found in the biblical text? Or, again differently, someone who encourages and empowers? That, too, is teaching, after all, and seems closer to the orientation of "teaching" back in Chapter 1: there, the condition of being "taught" enabled the freedom of an authentic choice. In any case, it seems to me that although preaching and teaching certainly connote influence, they still fall well short of comprehensive decision-making authority.

The third category of tasks, concerned with the implementation of discipline, seems to include a kind of executive power at least. But it is unclear if the pastor also judges whether a ban might be appropriate or if they merely pronounce the conclusion that has been reached through some other process—we might note that the instructions on mutual admonition in Article II do not give any explicit judicial power to pastors. Further, the concrete implementation of the sanction (the exclusion from congregational life) is certainly not something they can enact or enforce without the cooperation of the collective. So perhaps their role is again mostly procedural: to proclaim and make official the exhortation, call to repentance, and excommunication.

The fourth grouping is simply summarized as seeing to "the care of the body of Christ" (*in allen dingen des Leibs Christi acht haben*). The English translation suggests an aspect that remains implicit in the German *acht haben*: the pastor's responsibilities are a kind of *care* work. The pastor does not so much represent Christ's authority on Earth by proxy as *tend* to Christ's frightened, fragile body on this Earth, a body and presence that cannot exist without such care.

So although each of these tasks certainly involves power, this power is immediately delimited and made accountable. It is occasional and partial, better understood as a kind of facilitative care work than a position of comprehensive authority. Of course (need I say it), in highlighting this sense in the Schleitheim text, I do not mean to suggest that this is how authority and leadership have historically been understood in Anabaptist communities that have followed Schleitheim. I merely mean to suggest that this reading is at least also possible; that the text the Schleitheim group has left us with (if not historical practice) seems remarkably open to an understanding of leadership that is facilitative, occasional, and delimited.

The particular focus of the pastor seems to be a formal one: they are entrusted with the care for the constitutive practices through which the community is gathered into copresence and negotiates its creaturely ambiguities. And *this is why*, we might say, the pastor is so essential; this is why without a pastor, the community will be "destroyed": not because it would be without *authority*, but because it could no longer perform its constitutive collective practices. The pastor is not so much the leader of this body but tasked with ascertaining that there can be a body at all—*in which* strategic and discerning leadership can then take place in a more decentralized and dispersed manner, perhaps. This reading would certainly explain why a pastor is both so essential *and* so replaceable, can be replaced "in the same hour": because pastoring, for Schleitheim, does not imply some kind of deeply held charismatic leadership but a set of partial, occasional, and delimited facilitative tasks.[10]

The pastor's care for the collective body is mirrored by the care of the collective for the body of the pastor. In spite of its brevity, this fifth article stresses the community's responsibility in caring for the material needs of the pastor. The text thus seems aware of the material, embodied aspect of this work; care work requires time and resources. The pastor is not expected to be so independently wealthy and free of other (care) responsibilities that they can simply devote all their time to congregational matters while their families or servants pick up the slack.

This heightens the way this kind of facilitative care work is distinct from a position of comprehensive authority. Authority must be exclusive and unilateral (and, we might add, tends to be patriarchal), but care work can be shared and mutual. As the pastor cares for the fragile body of Christ, that body in turn cares for them, recognizing the precarious economic position their caring role might put them in. As they care for the life of the church, they remain embedded in a web of creaturely needs and responsibilities, as one creature among others. Much as life "in the resurrection" is transformed, it is not excepted from its creaturely *zoe*. Their body and the bodies of their families still need sustenance.[11]

---

[10] This thus goes further than Koontz' conclusion that the formal authority of office is "temporary." See Koontz, "Ecclesiology, Authority, and Ministry," 69.

[11] This attentiveness to embodied (and economic) existence is the entire extent of any remarks on the economic in Schleitheim. Certainly all the other congregants also have needs that must be cared for—yet the text does not consider such mutual aid a constitutive practice in the sense of its seven main Articles. This is not to say the authors of Schleitheim do not consider it a task for the church: a "congregational order" from the same period is sometimes seen as a companion text to Schleitheim, which speaks of a common fund. See, for example, Yoder, *Legacy*, 45–6.

Re-Presentation

But the pastor is not only tasked with caring for the collective practices of the community: they are also tasked with representing it to the outside world. It is perhaps for this reason that they should be well thought of by those "outside the faith." In Chapter 4, I already questioned whether Schleitheim's underlying dualism does not also paradoxically trouble its apparent condemnation of what lies outside the church. If this still seemed a speculative reading there, here it is confirmed: clearly the relations to the outside world are not simply severed by the force of metaphysical antagonism, nor are they set in stone in a cosmic dualism. The enmity between church and outside world can be softened, and the pastor plays a role in this.[12]

Such representation has a dual orientation: as we see ourselves represented to the outside world, so our representative also represents our collectivity back to us, the members, as we see ourselves acting and speaking in them. This is also an aspect of the pastor's more explicitly inward-focused tasks: in their formal function of chair or facilitator, they call the congregation together and in a sense stand formally for its assembled unity. Beginning to break bread, leading out in prayer, and pronouncing judgment, they act not on their own accord but as representative of the gathered wholeness of the community.[13] Everyone in the congregation speaks and prays for themselves, we might say; when the pastor speaks in their formal role, they do so for the whole. This is again distinct from simple authority: it is not a sense of unity that flows down from the authority at the top, but one which takes

---

[12]There seems to be a connection here to the preamble: there, Sattler and his comrades are worried about the lack of internal discipline and moral uprightness leading to a delegitimization of the Anabaptist project.

It is not so strange to want our representatives to be respected or indeed respectable. In this light, "respectability politics"—a notion that first emerges in Black communities of the United States—is hotly debated in some social movements. The question here is whether (for example) queer activists should downplay all of the "bad" aspects of queer identities that make heterosexuals uncomfortable (e.g., to do with sexual practice, gender roles, or the relation to economic life and class), presenting an image of queer people as generally "respectable." Doing this, goes the reasoning, will make a case for social change as requiring only minimal readjustment of society's normative value system. It thus increases the chances of success. The downside, it is argued, is that this wins the liberation of the most privileged members of that community at the expense of their assimilation to dominant norms and the continued marginalization of the other members. See, for example, Dara Z. Strolovitch and Chaya Y. Crowder, "Respectability, Anti-Respectability, and Intersectionally Responsible Representation," *PS: Political Science & Politics* 51, no. 2 (2018): 340–4.

[13]Koontz also highlights this formal representative function: pastors "represent the congregation to its members, to the wider church, and to the world" while at the same time also representing the wider church and God (though not exclusively). See Koontz, "Ecclesiology, Authority, and Ministry," 67–8.

place in the gathering of the assembly and is taken up by the pastor in their occasional, partial, and delimited formal function.

In Chapter 3, I discussed a strange play between presence and absence in the breaking of the bread: the absent remembered body calls the body of the church into copresence. In its own way, the representative function of a pastor suggests a similar dynamic. After all, only what is not simply *present* needs to be *re-presented*. The unity of the congregation, as it sees itself represented in the pastor, in the same stroke is shown to be not simply *there*, simply present. It becomes recognizable as a body but as one whose unity is not the simply *given* unity of conformity or homogeneity. It needs to be called together and gathered.[14] And without someone to care for these processes of gathering, assembly, and representation, the community will be "destroyed," we read. So it seems even the assembled, present body of the church is not by itself simply *a body*, without in turn needing to be *re*-presented and assembled to be able to act and speak collectively. Its copresence is not seamless self-identity; its shared life is not uniform oneness.

A Self-Governing Flock

Pastors are not tasked with leading, discerning, and deciding but with safeguarding the spaces in which leadership, discernment, and decision can emerge. And it is not without leaders that this nascent community will be "destroyed" but without the capacity to delegate and act, to speak and to assemble. Pastors are not so much entrusted with *authority*, we might say, as with the work of *organization*.

If in Chapter 1 I described the capacity to decide with uninterrupted authority as sovereignty, we might well call Schleitheim's effort here the search for *organization without sovereignty*, a kind of facilitative and occasional leadership embedded in the ecclesio-political work of creating a nonsovereign community. With this, Schleitheim seems to resonate with the more contemporary search for "nonsovereign forms of organization and institution,"[15] as discussed by philosophers Michael Hardt and Antonio Negri. Hardt and Negri are looking for a logic of organization by which a movement or collective can act together without suppressing their multiplicity into a homogeneous "one." The logic of sovereignty, they argue, is ultimately the logic of the one: be it one ruler, one party, or even one class or one nation. The domination and suppression of the "multitude" that comprises actual social life by some such "one" is the hallmark of all forms of hierarchy and authority. All political visions that do not actively and

---

[14]It is in this sense that the notion of *Vereinigung*, so central to Schleitheim's preamble (and returning in nearly each article), must be understood: not as a preexisting oneness but as the process of gathering. See Excursus.

[15]Michael Hardt and Antonio Negri, *Assembly* (Oxford: Oxford University Press, 2017), 14.

intentionally break with the logic of sovereignty ultimately revolve around the domination of the many by the one in some form or other.[16]

Breaking with this logic of sovereignty requires posing the question of how such a multitude can shape public life and exert power without simply "reversing the relationship of domination, ruling over others ... merely changing who sits at the controls."[17] It requires a "political articulation that weaves together the different forms of resistance and struggles for liberation in society," indicating "a path of freedom and equality" and democratic self-governance.[18] For this, Hardt and Negri argue, movements cannot rely on spontaneous gathering and initiative. Institutions are necessary. But it is crucial that these be *nonsovereign* institutions, that is, "not institutions to rule over us but institutions to foster continuity and organization, institutions to help organize our practices, manage our relationships, and together make decisions."[19]

So, echoing Schleitheim, they argue that while organization is crucial for social movements and the democratic management of society, leadership must be "occasional, partial, and variable."[20] Major strategic political discernment should never be the task of "the one" but always of "the many."[21] Nonsovereign institutions must be rooted in the already-plural social life of the multitude, and leadership "must be completely subordinated to and submerged in the multitude."[22] This does not make communities and movements leaderless. More often than not, under these conditions they can be leader*ful*, but only if structures of shared discernment and assembly are cared for.

To be sure, Hardt and Negri's observations are embedded in a different kind of political project than Schleitheim's, perhaps more reminiscent of the peasants' revolutionary goals of transforming society as a whole. And, for these secular left thinkers, the place of power in the political is certainly not left empty by an absent-present God, nor does the community gather in response to a divine invitation. For them, "a lasting political framework does not need a transcendent power standing above or behind social life, that is, that political organization ... [does] not require sovereignty."[23]

Perhaps for secular thinkers it is difficult to imagine God as anything other than the height of sovereign force. And yet they recognize "various forms of congregation in religious communities" as also revealing the power of "assembly," that is, "the power of coming together and acting politically

---

[16] Even representative parliamentary politics in democratic societies are "necessarily founded on a relationship of unequal power of political decision-making," Hardt and Negri hold. Ibid., 27.
[17] Ibid., 39.
[18] Ibid., xxi.
[19] Ibid., 38.
[20] Ibid., 19.
[21] Ibid., 25.
[22] Ibid., 20.
[23] Ibid., 14.

in concert," and as embodying "new democratic political possibilities."[24] Perhaps we can therefore supplement Hardt and Negri's observation that political organization does not "require [divine] sovereignty" with the suggestion that God's collaborative call to self-organization is vehemently misunderstood when apprehended as a transcendent sovereign power standing above or behind social life to guarantee it.

God empowers the community and its pastor precisely by *not* empowering them with the force of transcendent sovereign authority. Instead, God yields the space to the authentic discernment of a community of free and equal believers. The task of the pastor in this is likewise not to represent God in a way that would short-circuit this discernment in the play of presence and absence. This is a church that makes itself, whose unity is not simply given but consists in its assembly, its "coming together and acting ... in concert." God acts as a provocation and invocation, calling it into self-organization. The pastor is tasked with caring for this self-organization, which never simply emerges or happens but needs to be intended and asserted, and without which it will be inevitably "destroyed." This tension between God, the congregation, and the pastor is not resolved but remains in process.

Conclusion

In this chapter, I have suggested that the type of function and procedure Schleitheim envisions for pastors in the church is embedded in its effort to break with the logic of sovereignty: its pastors are less authority figures and more facilitative care workers who remain "submerged" (Hardt and Negri) in the community. They tend to the fragile existence of the fellowship, calling it into presence to itself and its others, including the world around it.

I have been framing Schleitheim's ecclesio-political venture as a response to the question of how to build community in a time of crisis. It would not have been strange to expect authority to play a role in this: in times of crisis, it is not uncommon to rally around "strong" authoritarian figures. Yet instead, we find a care for organization, or we might say for *process*, and for the resources that process requires in order for the community to assemble and act together. So the answer, here, is not so much that building community needs leaders, or needs someone in charge, but that building community, and maintaining the things without which community cannot exist, is work and requires resources from the people performing that work.

---

[24]Hardt and Negri, *Assembly*, xxi.

Someone needs to tend the whole, even if that is a relationship of mutuality; someone needs to call the community together and speak in its name—even if that role is strictly occasional, partial, and delimited. Because the shared life of the community is not simply *there*, its unity is not simply *given* by conformity and homogeneity. With Hardt and Negri, we might say that a nonsovereign community is not *one*, and this irreducible plurality must be central to its self-apprehension and action in the world.

6

Authority

Introduction

In its sixth article, Schleitheim makes an argument that has become one of the most well-known points of definition for Anabaptist faith: it discusses the relation of the church to what it calls the "sword." It opens with an enigmatic axiom: the sword is "ordained of God outside of the perfection of Christ."

This is Schleitheim's longest and most elaborately argued passage, seemingly befitting the central importance its subject matter would soon take on among Anabaptists. Both historical and contemporary Anabaptists have often held to the rejection of the "sword" in some way, in many cases resulting in a version of nonresistance or pacifism and the reluctance to participate in affairs of the state. This is far from universal, however. Anabaptists today act in broader society as activists, teachers, and social workers but also serve in police and military forces, as civil servants, and even hold political office. They act in these roles with a wide variety of motivations, from starkly conservative to radically progressive, and with a wide variety of political imaginaries.

One way to respond to this situation would be to simply argue that today's Anabaptists no longer strictly hold to Schleitheim's stipulation, if they ever did. But in this chapter, I hope to show that Schleitheim's argument itself is also more complex and more subtle than a simple call for political separatism. The church is called to be a nonsovereign fellowship, distinct from the political logic of the "sword." But even within the logic of the text, the relation between these two is deeply ambiguous, remaining underdetermined and requiring multiple clarifications.

Again, Schleitheim's argument is more ecclesio-political than ethical, by which I mean it is more concerned with the kind of political logic by which the church should be organized than with establishing rules individual Christians are to obey. This may seem counterintuitive, as this article (and Schleitheim in general) is often related precisely to an ethic of obedience, following Christ's command to "resist not an evildoer"[1] and thus considered

---

[1] John Richard Burkholder, "Historic Nonresistance," in *Mennonite Peace Theology: A Panorama of Types*, ed. John Richard Burkholder and Barbara Nelson Gingerich (Elkhart: AMBS/IMS, 2024), 11–18.

exemplary for Anabaptist theological ethics centered on such obedience to God's authority.

Yet such words are entirely absent from Schleitheim's sixth article. Indeed, as we will see, it is precisely authority and obedience that are rejected as categories for the way God relates to the church.

Indeed on closer reading it quickly becomes clear that the "sword" Schleitheim here rejects does not refer to violence in general but specifically to a particular logic of political domination. It is a kind of political order or legal authority that—seemingly anticipating modern discussions of sovereignty—makes a distinction between lives: the "wicked" and the "good," those that are to be protected and those lives given up to death. Although the text stresses that such authority can be legitimate, the shared life of the church should operate according to a different logic, shaping communities that are nonsovereign, in emulation of Christ's nonsovereign character.

Read in this way, Schleitheim seems to envision the church as a place of collaborative sympoiesis, where the theopolitical image of God as one who "ordains" can be unlearned. On it surface, Schleitheim seems to insist that Christians should withdraw from sovereign structures as much as possible, but on closer reading the text also suggests the relation between the nonsovereign community and its political others is more complex than might initially be assumed, marked by incompatibility more than simple withdrawal or antagonism.

That Schleitheim thus suggests something like a "two-kingdom" theology, as this is often referred to,[2] on the one hand, seems beyond discussion: it indeed distinguishes between two orders or political logics. Yet, on the other hand, calling this two "kingdoms" risks eliding the strange peculiarity of the ways the text considers these two to relate to each other, or indeed fail to relate to each other. If two normal kingdoms might reach a détente around a shared border, the relation between the "sword" and "non-sword" orders remains one of underdetermined incompatibility, giving rise to a wide spectrum of possible interactions and interminable negotiation.

An Ethic of Obedience

It has often been argued that obedience is essential to Schleitheim, Sattler's thought more broadly, and indeed the historical Anabaptist venture in general. John Howard Yoder, for instance, writes that "Sattler's known writings emphasize literal obedience to Christ's words and actions,"[3]

---
[2]Ibid., 12.
[3]Yoder, *Legacy*, 7. Yoder, a perpetrator of sexual violence and abuser of his own position of power, emphasizes obedience as a central ethical task for Christians. This jarring fact may particularly encourage us to revise the place of obedience in our thinking.

and C. Arnold Snyder frames the Schleitheim Confession as calling for "separat[ion] from the world in ... careful obedience to God."[4] He describes the sixth article in particular as an application "of the general principle that true Christians must obey the commands of Scripture."[5] More generally, both Ben Ollenburger and Stuart Murray have described the historical Anabaptist approach to Scripture as "hermeneutics of obedience."[6] Ollenburger, writing in the 1970s, argues this makes for Anabaptism's enduring relevance: modern Christians also "must read the Bible as obedient people, followers of Christ first and foremost."[7]

So it would not be strange to expect Schleitheim's argument against the sword to similarly revolve around the notion that God has given rules that Christians simply are to follow out of obedience to God as sovereign lawgiver. Christians, we might say, must simply obey God's command to "resist not an evildoer" (Mt. 5:39) or that "thou shalt not kill" (Exod. 20:13).[8] We might call this an obedient or "strong" pacifism, one whose nonviolence is rooted in the unwavering sovereign providential rule of the Almighty. The church is called to nonviolence, we might say, because it is called to fully

---

Reception of Schleitheim and Swiss/South German Anabaptism of the sixteenth century more broadly has been closely bound up with Yoder's translations and interpretations. Though this was most significant in the twentieth century, to some extent, it remains so today. Since knowledge of Yoder's abuse and institutions' complicity or silence in response to it has become more widespread, Yoder's status within Anabaptist thought has rightly suffered. I hope that this book can be part of an alternative approach, reading Schleitheim against, or better still without, Yoder and his dubious theology. See, for example, Roberts, Martens, and Penner, *Recovering*; Isaac Samuel Villegas, "The Ecclesial Ethics of John Howard Yoder's Abuse," *Modern Theology* 37, no. 1 (January 2021): 191–214; and especially Rachel Waltner Goossen, "'Defanging the Beast': Mennonite Responses to John Howard Yoder's Sexual Abuse," *Mennonite Quarterly Review* 89 (January 2015): 7–80.

[4]Snyder, *Life and Thought*, 156.

[5]Ibid., 163.

[6] Ben C. Ollenburger, "The Hermeneutics of Obedience: A Study of Anabaptist Hermeneutics," *Direction* 6, no. 2 (1977): 19–31; Stuart Murray, *Biblical Interpretation in the Anabaptist Tradition* (Thunder Bay: Pandora Press, 2000), 186.

[7]Ollenburger, "The Hermeneutics of Obedience," 30. Eloquent critiques of such obedience from (among others) a feminist perspective include Hilary Jerome Scarsella and Stephanie Krehbiel, "Sexual Violence: Christian Theological Legacies," *Religion Compass* 13 (2019): 1–13; Kimberly L. Penner, "Mennonite Peace Theology and Violence against Women," *Conrad Grebel Review* 35, no. 3 (2017): 280–92; Dorothee Soelle, *Beyond Mere Obedience* (Cleveland: Pilgrim Press, 1982); Traci C. West, *Wounds of the Spirit: Black Women, Violence, and Resistance Ethics* (New York: New York University Press, 1999).

In spite of these, the suggestion that Anabaptism revolves around obedience continues to be difficult to shake. The North American *Confession of Faith in a Mennonite Perspective* names Christ's "obedience" as one of His most relevant characteristics and describes how "the Holy Spirit nurtures the obedience of faith to Jesus Christ" through the Bible. It also understands sin explicitly as disobedience and salvation as essentially tied to obedience. See Mennonite Church Canada and Mennonite Church U.S.A., *Confession of Faith in a Mennonite Perspective*, 1995, https://www.mennoniteusa.org/wp-content/uploads/2024/02/Confession-of-Faith-In-a-Mennonite-Perspective.pdf.

[8]For example, Burkholder, "Historic Nonresistance," 11.

trust in this rule instead of in human weapons and machinations. It would not be strange to expect such a notion here, and it is not difficult to see why such an approach would be attractive after the failure of violent revolution and under the weight of increasing persecution. It seems to offer a clear explanation of events and an unambiguous path forward.

In this light it may come as a surprise that the notion of obedience to a sovereign Lord is entirely absent from Schleitheim's sixth article and that it nowhere cites such commandments to "resist not an evildoer" or "thou shalt not kill."[9] In making its argument against the sword, it points not to the sovereign character of God as a lawgiver but to the nonsovereign character of Christ as an example for the kind of collaborative fellowship the church is called to be.

So let us take a closer look.

Reading

Schleitheim's sixth article begins with a succinct axiom on which the gathered assembly has agreed: the sword is "ordained of God outside the perfection of Christ [*ein Gottesordnung ausserhalb der volkomenheit Christi*]." So, we could say, God seems to have instituted the use of the sword for the world at large, but within the "perfection of Christ" (presumably referring to the church), different principles apply. This already says a good deal: Schleitheim is not simply positing a general critique of the sword but one deeply related to the kind of fellowship the church is called to be. There may be other ways than this, and God may be at work in those ways as well, Schleitheim affirms—but for the church, the sword must be rejected.

It is important to note that the "sword" here does not seem to refer simply to the use of violence (as if violence were generally legitimate outside the church) but to something more specific. The term *Gottesordnung* is already suggestive of this: the "sword" is a distinct kind of order or political logic. This becomes more explicit in the following sentences. We read the sword has something of a dual orientation: on the one hand, "for the punishment of the wicked and for their death," while on the other hand, it "guards and protects the good" (a reference to Romans 13). It is with this dual orientation that the sword is explicitly "ordained to be used by the worldly magistrates," and it is the "same" one that God ordained in the Old Testament Mosaic Law. If, for the people of Israel, God institutes the Law as an enforceable legal order (i.e, one with violent sanctions, even if not a "state" in any modern sense of that word), Schleitheim suggests, God has ordained the legitimacy of an enforceable legal order and (now) state authority in the same way.

---

[9] As also noted by Snyder, *Life and Thought*, 165.

So, the sword seems to refer to a kind of political order or legal authority that is marked especially by the capacity for violent sanction. It is not so much the question of violence in general that is addressed, then, but the question of violent sanction as part of a political system of authority. On the one hand, the church must recognize such power as legitimate, at least for certain purposes. On the other hand, the church must itself be a community without such violent sanction. That is not to say it is left without means to assert disciplinary force or to call problematic members to account, merely that the means it can employ must follow a different logic: it can use "only the ban," which explicitly does not kill but is oriented to rehabilitating the sinner for the community as "the warning and the command to sin no more." Not all readers will immediately be convinced by Schleitheim's optimism around the supposed nonsovereign character of the ban, it seems to me, and its contrast with the sword order will also allow us to say more about its ambivalences now than I did in Chapter 2.

The rest of Schleitheim's sixth article is concerned with the precise relationship between the sword order and the "non-sword" order of the church. This is peculiar: surely the initial axiom, defining two incompatible political logics or orders, is clear enough? But the text immediately seems to admit that its schema fails to achieve the kind of clarity perhaps desired, that many questions around the relationship and possible interaction between the two orders are still open. Further stipulations are required. Schleitheim provides three such stipulations in response to three questions "asked by many who do not recognize [this as] the will of Christ for us."

The first question is the following: if Christians recognize the legitimacy of a legal order, then "may or should" they not also "employ the sword" themselves for such legitimate functions? The text responds in the negative. Christ "teaches and commands us to learn of Him," and we should particularly follow Christ's character, which is "meek and lowly in heart" (Mt. 11:29). More specifically, it cites John 8, where Jesus is asked about a case of capital punishment of a woman apparently caught in adultery. The text argues He operates exactly according to Schleitheim's dual logic: He does not doubt the legitimacy of the Mosaic Law ("ordained of God") but also instructs "not that one should stone her ... but in mercy and forgiveness and warning to sin no more" sends her on her way ("the perfection of Christ"). So Christ does not cancel or abolish the Law so much as suspend its application in this case.

Second, the text similarly asks if Christians may act as judges in cases between non-Christians, for whom such judicial proceedings are, after all, divinely instituted. The answer is again no, and again by means of Christ's example: "Christ did not wish to ... pass judgment between brothers ... but refused to do so [a reference to Luke 12]. Therefore we should do likewise."

The third question is whether a Christian may act as a magistrate (*Oberkeit*), a representative of state authority. The answer is again by analogy with Jesus: "They wished to make Christ king, but He fled ... Thus we shall do as He did." The way of Jesus, in sum, is one that refuses sovereign power, and the church is to emulate Christ in this refusal. "He Himself forbids ... the authority of the sword saying, the worldly princes lord it over them ... but not so shall it be with you."

The text supplements these biblical arguments by reiterating and elaborating on the more fundamental incompatibility between the logic of the sword and that of the church community, noting they are oriented in fundamentally different ways.

> The government order is according to the flesh, but the Christians' is according to the Spirit; their houses and dwelling are bodily in this world, but the Christians' are in heaven; their citizenship is in this world, but the Christians' citizenship is in heaven; the weapons of their conflict and war are carnal and against the flesh only, but the Christians' weapons are spiritual, against the fortification of the devil. The worldlings are armed with steel and iron, but the Christians are armed with the armor of God, with truth, justice, peace, faith, salvation and the Word of God.

In many ways, Schleitheim seems to be saying, the sword simply operates by a different logic than that by which the church grounds its fellowship. It understands the world and its creatures differently; it has different tools, which in turn shape the way it approaches its problems. Most importantly, it is beholden to the structures of exploitation in the "world" in a way inimical to what the church is intended to be. Though these structures of exploitation are not synonymous with the sword (which, after all, has a legitimacy, while the "world" is "abomination" [Article IV]), they do seem to have a structural affinity or belonging: working as a magistrate seems to thicken one's entanglement ("homes and dwelling" and "citizenship") in worldly exploitation.

Schleitheim closes by summarizing its fundamental point: the church should emulate Christ's rejection of political authority and follow Him in forming a community that breaks with the sovereign logic of the sword. "As is the mind of Christ toward us, so shall the mind of the members of the body of Christ be through Him in all things," the text argues. "Since Christ is as it is written of Him, His members must also be the same."

So already we can say a few things: first, the "sword" that is both affirmed and rejected here refers to a certain kind of political authority or legal order, not simply to violence in general (nor indeed to government in general, at least not in the sense of a collective administration). By extension, the church is called not simply to reject violence (nor indeed public life) but to reject the political logic the sword stands for and to give shape to a community rooted in the break with that logic. Second, in doing so, it does not simply obey the command of a sovereign lawgiver—which would, after all, continue to follow the logic of sovereign rule—but it emulates the nonsovereign character of Jesus, who himself rejects authority, suspends the application of the sword, and refuses the position of lawgiver or judge. Third, the relationship between the order of the sword and the ecclesio-political logic of the church is not one of simple antagonism but of incompatibility, as they are fundamentally oriented in different ways. Nevertheless, fourth, the appropriate kinds of interaction between these two orders do not simply follow from their incompatibility but require supplementary negotiation and interpretation (given here in the form of three questions).

A Distinction between Lives

As we have seen, the "sword" here seems to refer to a particular kind of political rule or legal order and not generally to the use of violence. This is clear both from the way it is defined—the capacity for violent sanction—and from Schleitheim's focus in its discussion and examples, which lie entirely with questions around government and political authority.[10] Ethical issues related to the use of violence more broadly, such as the legitimacy of self-defense on the road, violent revolution (we recall the very recent peasants' war), or domestic violence, are absent entirely. This is not to say that Sattler and the others at Schleitheim do not affirm pacifism in a more general ethical sense (a rejection of "the unchristian, devilish weapons of force—such as sword, armor and the like" is found at the end of Article IV). It is merely to say that here, in Schleitheim's longest article, its focus lies elsewhere, and its argument is more political than ethical.

Yet to say the sword simply refers to what we today understand as the state or government would also be inaccurate. For one, the crystallization of the Western system of sovereign states with defined territorial borders is still over a century in Schleitheim's future, taking shape as it does with the Peace of Westphalia in 1648. But the incipient state structures of Schleitheim's early modern context also do not seem to be what the "sword" is specifically referring to: after all, it names the Torah as the divinely ordained "sword" order par excellence, and although this is an enforceable legal order, it is not a state or government in any modern or even premodern sense of that word. So, what is rejected with the sword is at once more and less specific than simply the state or government, and it certainly does not appear to refer to the kinds of collective administration and organization that we often consider essential for modern states.

---

[10]This in and of itself is not controversial among commentators of Schleitheim: John Howard Yoder states that "in this entire discussion 'sword' refers to the judicial and police powers of the state" (glossing over the way the non-state legal order of the Law is also a "sword" order), and Snyder also notes that "the detailed sixth article on the sword deals explicitly only with the 'sword of government' rather than with the 'sword of war.'" See Yoder, *Legacy*, 42n74; Snyder, *Life and Thought*, 163.

The sword order in Schleitheim's understanding seems to be definitionally marked by a certain dual orientation or capacity: on the one hand, it has a destructive capability, which it brings to bear "against the wicked," whom it can "put to death" and "punish." But, on the other hand, it also has a nurturing or protective capability: it sets itself up "for the defense and protection of the good," whom it can "protect" and "guard." So, the sword is not merely defined by its capacity for killing and destroying but also paradoxically by its capacity to nurture, to create spaces for human flourishing. We could say that the essence of the sword order lies in this dual orientation, in the way it causes and governs over death and life. And essential to this dual orientation is a more fundamental capacity: the sword is the kind of order that makes a difference between the "wicked" and the "good" in the first place. The essence of a sword order seems to lie in the way it distinguishes between lives worthy of protection and those worthy of death—between lives that matter and lives given up to destruction.

It is by making this distinction that the political logic of the sword enforces an order. According to Schleitheim, it is the practice of producing this distinction between lives that is held in common by the early modern political entities of Schleitheim's direct context—from free cities to feudal lordships and papal domains—as well as the Old Testament legal order (and, we might add, with the modern sovereign state). This essential operation lies at the root of the functioning of all of these. Again, I do not intend to say that philosophical critique of the logic of the sovereign order was front of mind for those gathered at Schleitheim in a historical sense. Perhaps their words and selection of biblical references were more guided by the ambivalence of their own experiences with the state order than with theoretical analysis. And yet the text they have left us seems to be remarkably attuned to the ambiguity of what it is discussing, offering—despite its sweeping scope—already a somewhat nuanced understanding and critique of political power that goes beyond its immediate historical context.

In doing so, Schleitheim in a way anticipates a modern understanding of what is known in political philosophy as sovereignty. In Chapter 1, this term appeared in our discussion of freedom. Hannah Arendt had contrasted freedom understood as sovereignty with freedom understood as "virtuosity." If the former named the freedom to *will* and to decide as an individual, one who is their own master and unconstrained by others (and possibly the master *of* those others), the latter refers to a kind of freedom we can only experience in public life where we are among equals. It is virtuosity, not sovereignty, Arendt argued, that should inform our sense of freedom in a political sense, as the capacity to shape public life together. The political consequence of freedom-as-sovereignty, however, is "tyranny," as it "can be maintained only by the instruments of violence."[11]

---

[11] Arendt, *Between Past and Future*, 164.

Only one, at most, can be truly sovereign. This is not far removed from the definition given by one of the most prominent theorists of sovereignty, legal scholar (and prominent fascist sympathizer) Carl Schmitt. Schmitt argues like Arendt that sovereignty is quintessentially the capacity to decide. Moreover, sovereign power is the capacity to decide on the exception: that is, to have the final word in a way that surpasses the regulations or procedures of the legal order.[12] Paradoxically, the establishment of a political and legal order can only exist if it is grounded in such an exceptional power (e.g., that the Torah receives its normative force in a similar way from being given by a Lawgiver who is Himself not a subject among others). Significantly for our purposes here, Schmitt argues that the distinction between friend and foe, that is, between those belonging to my own community and those we may have to face and kill, is the irreducible beginning point of the political.[13]

Philosopher Michel Foucault draws attention to the way the modern sovereign has the "power of life and death" in the sense of a dual orientation, noting—remarkably similar to Schleitheim's discussion—that the sovereign has "the right to take life or let live," noting that its "symbol, after all, was the sword."[14] Foucault notes a transformation as the West proceeds through modernity so that the expression of power comes to lie less in the instruments of sovereign violence and more in shaping, regulating, and producing a certain kind of life. Foucault calls this biopower or biopolitics (after Greek *bios*, life). In spite of this transformation, however, the way power fundamentally takes shape as the capacity to produce a distinction in life or between lives did not disappear. "One might say," Foucault writes, "that the ancient right to *take* life or *let* live was replaced by a power to *foster* life or *disallow* it to the point of death."[15] Achille Mbembe has in turn questioned Foucault's perspective here, arguing that modern political authority has by no means given up its capacity, nor its propensity, for taking life, for example, in colonial ventures (a sentiment Schleitheim would perhaps share).[16]

Italian philosopher Giorgio Agamben picks up on a similar insight—that the essence of sovereign power lies exactly in this more fundamental capacity to produce a distinction between lives worth protecting and lives given up to death. For Agamben, however, this does not need to mean actively killing or executing, and he notes the oldest forms of sovereign sanction are types of banishment and exile: the production of lives that are outside of protection and that may be killed without consequence. Echoing Schleitheim, Agamben

---

[12]Carl Schmitt, *Political Theology: Four Chapters on the Concept of Sovereignty* (Chicago: University of Chicago Press, 2005).
[13]Carl Schmitt, *The Concept of the Political* (Chicago: University of Chicago Press, 2007), 26–7.
[14]Foucault, *History of Sexuality 1*, 136.
[15]Ibid.
[16]Achille Mbembe, "Necropolitics," in *Biopolitics: A Reader*, ed. Timothy Campbell and Adam Sitze (Durham: Duke University Press, 2013), 161–92.

argues the "fundamental activity of sovereign power"[17] is more fundamental than overt killing, embodied in making the distinction between life that matters and life devoid of significance. For Agamben, this is ultimately what all legal orders in the West, even ones that are not explicitly headed by a single "sovereign" ruler—from the ancient Roman kingdom to modern democracies—have in common: in their essence, they always operate by distinguishing between the lives they protect and the lives they condemn, between citizens and noncitizens, insiders and outsiders. Or, as Schleitheim puts it, between the "good" and the "wicked."

The ambivalence around this analysis, that the power of the sword can both destroy and foster life, that the protection to the "good" offered by the sovereign order always depends on its production of some others as "wicked," is central to Schleitheim's argument and seems to also give rise to its ambivalent axiom.

Yet sovereign rule is also, less ambivalently, "a relationship of power and domination," as Hardt and Negri stress:

> The sovereign always stands in relation to subjects, above them, with the ultimate power to make political decisions ... the concept of sovereignty that functioned in early modern Europe was also a pillar of the ideological justification of conquest and colonization.[18]

Schleitheim spends little of its explicit argument on this aspect of domination. It does not argue for the equality of all humans and the unjustifiability that some hold power over others, for example. And yet in rejecting sovereign power of the sword, it is (perhaps more implicitly) looking for a kind of ecclesio-political community that is nonsovereign, in which no ruler "lords it over" (Mt. 20:25) their subjects, in which the force of violent and final sanction is broken. The church is to be a kind of shared life not grounded in the capacity for violence nor in the power of some over others. This becomes clearer in its discussion of the way Jesus's rejection of the power of the sword stands as an example for the church.

---

[17] Giorgio Agamben, *Homo Sacer: Sovereign Power and Bare Life* (Stanford: Stanford University Press, 1998), 181.

In contrast to Schleitheim, Agamben's critique of sovereign power does not seem to be embedded in any effort to construct an alternative community. This makes it nearly impossible for Agamben to envision any kind of collective action as legitimate. This limitation especially came to the fore in early 2020 when Agamben published a series of apparently ad hoc writings attacking the Italian government's emergency measures during the coronavirus pandemic (which he considered an indefensible exertion of sovereign power). These texts display a callous disregard for creaturely vulnerability in the face of disease, which I do not mean to endorse (nor trivialize) here. For a careful but by no means apologetic interpretation, see Adam Kotsko, "What Happened to Giorgio Agamben?" *Slate*, 2022, https://slate.com/human-interest/2022/02/giorgio-agamben-covid-holocaust-comparison-right-wing-protest.html.

[18] Hardt and Negri, *Assembly*, 25.

A Nonsovereign Messiah

Schmitt considers his understanding of political sovereignty a matter of "political theology": it ultimately reflects a secularized version of the idea of an omnipotent God who can perform miracles (that is, exceptions) at will. Indeed, Schmitt argues that "all significant concepts of the modern theory of the state are secularized theological concepts."[19] Catherine Keller has argued this realization of a certain continuity between political and theological imagination has potential: it also invites us to consider the political cognates of less authoritarian theologies. Perhaps imagining God not as sovereign Lord but as gentle provocation or encompassing embrace may thereby inspire and invigorate more democratic political ventures as well.[20]

This is, in a way, exactly what Schleitheim does in this sixth article, as it considers the ecclesio-political consequences of following a nonsovereign Messiah.

After establishing the kind of order the sword refers to, Schleitheim addresses three particular questions around Christians' interaction with it. In addressing these three questions, in each case, the text illuminates its point by drawing the comparison with Jesus. It refers to biblical narratives in a way it does not do elsewhere, showing Jesus refusing to exert judicial and executive power in several instances. In so doing, the text not only answers the question directly at hand but also develops the general point it is making: that the church should reject sovereign power, not out of simple obedience to a rule, but because, in this way, it emulates Jesus's own rejection of sovereign power. This is the argument throughout this article: Christ "teaches and commands us to learn of Him"; "he who wishes to come after me, let him deny himself and take up his cross and follow me" (Mt. 16:24); "whom God did foreknow He also instructed to be conformed to the image of His Son" (Rom. 8:30); "Christ has suffered, not ruled, and left us an example, that you should follow His steps" (1 Pet. 2:21).

This distinction between obeying God as sovereign ruler and following Christ as one who rejects sovereign rule may seem largely academic. And perhaps for some readers, the emulation of Christ's character is not so different from just another rule to be followed. But that would miss the way this emulation reorients the relationship between God and God's church. The text does not call for ethical obedience to God as a lawgiver but for following Christ's example as *explicitly not* a lawgiver, as a figure who refuses the position demanding obedience and who suspends the working of the Law. At the heart of Schleitheim's argument is not the discontinuity or categorical difference between a God who commands and a church that obeys but exactly a continuity or relationality between the two.

---

[19]Schmitt, *Political Theology*, 36.
[20]Catherine Keller, *Intercarnations* (New York: Fordham University Press, 2017), 174–92.

In framing its political theology in this way, Schleitheim is also making an argument about the nature of God. In giving shape to a nonsovereign community, the church is embodying a continuity with the nonsovereign character of God as revealed in Christ. God, the text seems to suggest, is ultimately, in God's most authentic expression (for this is, after all, what Christianity teaches Christ to be), not a sovereign Lord demanding obedience but a nonsovereign Messiah inviting fellow creatures into fellowship. Jesus calls this fellowship the Kingdom of God, but on closer look, it is perhaps best understood as a non-kingdom,[21] in which God is encountered as one who does not command but issues a collaborative call.

In a way, all of Schleitheim can be understood as a response to this call, which invites creaturely community into cooperative self-organization in ways not indebted to structures of exploitation and domination. After all, it envisions the church as a community of free persons, each of whom has responded to God's invitation "through themselves," a freedom nevertheless essentially entangled in community as baptism is asked and given and enters one into a shared life among equals (Article I). It calls this path the "obedience of faith" (Article IV), certainly, but this "obedience" is nothing like the obedience demanded by sovereign authority; it is essentially described as an escape from the grasp of empire, of being "set free" (Article IV). Its leaders are elected (Article V), and their tasks are clearly circumscribed, appearing more as facilitators or care workers than leaders. In sum, it is more a community of refuge than a kingdom in any recognizable sense of that word.

Embedded in this understanding of God's call as a nonsovereign invitation is Schleitheim's insistent awareness that the kind of community it envisions does not come guaranteed. No institutions, not even divine ordinance, can be relied upon to simply make nonsovereign community happen. It does not simply gather in obedience to a sovereign ruler but self-organizes in response to a collaborative call, which means it needs to be made and asserted. If earlier we discussed a "strong" pacifism, anchored in God's final authority, here we have the outlines of a "weak" or nonsovereign pacifism, which does not have such metaphysical backing.

Paradoxically, it is exactly for this reason that the church must be capable of exerting force. As we have seen in Chapter 2, Schleitheim has no illusions that the church could do without such a capacity, that it could do without claiming the space for its shared life against the forces that would subdue it. It is in this light that it suggests the ban as an alternative means of sanction.

The need for some way to assert the community's standards and maintain a space for its form of life seems clear. What is not immediately clear, however, is why comprehensive excommunication—if this is indeed how the ban is to be understood in Schleitheim—would really be structurally different from

---

[21]See also Maki Ashe van Steenwyk, *The Unkingdom of God: Embracing the Subversive Power of Repentance* (Downers Grove: InterVarsity Press, 2013).

sovereign sanctions, especially in light of Agamben's argument mentioned in the previous section that the most originary sovereign sanctions are also kinds of exile and banishment. Does not the ban function similarly by making a distinction between lives, specifically by producing some lives as exiled from the community? These ambivalences come into starker relief here than in Article II, where the explicit contrast with the sanctions of the sword order was less of a theme. And it seems to me these ambivalences are difficult to dispel definitively, as indeed the history of the ban's application shows.

A clue to how we might read these ambivalences might be found, however, precisely in this juxtaposition between ban and sword-type punishment—that is, in the way the text frames the ban as embedded in the break with the logic of sovereignty. This break is perhaps most clearly embodied in its nonfinal character. While a perpetrator may need to be excluded from the community, the "warning" to "sin no more" also shows that this exclusion is oriented toward their (for lack of a better word) rehabilitation: that it takes place in the temporality of repetition. This means, in a way, that the community is never definitively made safe from those that come under the ban's sanctioning force (explicitly not *wicked*, we might note, merely "slipping and falling"): their disciplining is oriented to their return. So perhaps we can make a distinction between a sovereign temporality of finality and the temporality of repetition that marks nonsovereign practices. The sovereign's decision (Schmitt) is not up for discussion; the sword punishes for the "death" (Schleitheim) of the "wicked." But nonsovereign practice is never so final. It is in this light, it seems to me, that the nonsovereign character of the ban must also be read—or, we might say, *insofar as* it embodies this nonfinal temporality of repetition can the ban be deemed a nonsovereign instrument.[22]

The force exerted by this nonsovereign community does not take place in the register of finality but of repetition. Anyone who is disciplined may be welcomed back; anyone who is welcomed back may again "slip and fall" (Article II). Nothing is final; there is only the interminable process of reassertion in which each iteration at once stabilizes and destabilizes the identity of the community. If the logic of sovereignty is exemplified by the capacity to kill, to make a final decision on life and death, the logic of the nonsovereign community is exemplified by repetition, which has no recourse to such final guarantees but must be risked.

---

[22]We might note at this point that Agamben himself also makes a clear distinction between the sovereign ban and ecclesial practices of excommunication, at least in the Benedictine (!) monastic rule. There, excommunication does not have an "afflictive character" but "an essentially moral and amendatory meaning, comparable to therapy prescribed by a doctor." The excommunicated brother is not left to die but becomes the subject of "particular care" by the abbot. Indeed, Agamben concludes, this monastic "rule" is not a kind of legal order in the style of sovereignty at all, and indeed the "obedience" it calls for is nothing like that demanded by sovereign rule. See Giorgio Agamben, *The Highest Poverty: Monastic Rules and Form-of-Life* (Stanford: Stanford University Press, 2013), 31.

Two Incompatible Orders

In the latter part of this fourth article, Schleitheim stresses the conceptual or intrinsic incompatibility between the political logic of the sword and ecclesial nonsovereignty. They are oriented in fundamentally different ways, we read: one is "according to the flesh," the other "according to the Spirit;" one is entangled in the structures of exploitation that make up the "world," while the other has its citizenship in "heaven." They have distinct "weapons," we read, one "carnal and against the flesh," made up of "steel and iron," the other "spiritual, against the fortification of the devil" and consisting of the "armor of God."

The point, it seems to me, is not just that the church *should* not use the instruments of sovereign power. More significantly, what the church is oriented toward cannot be achieved with such instruments. By their very logic, they work in a different way. The sword may be able to "protect" the church—this is a question Schleitheim leaves open—but it cannot ascertain the kind of community it is called to be.[23]

Again, if this is how these lines are to be interpreted, they seem to anticipate a more modern discussion. We recall Hannah Arendt's argument that freedom as sovereignty is entirely incompatible with democratic freedom in a community of equals. Elsewhere, she broadens this insight: there is a general incompatibility between the realm of the political (properly understood as a sphere of freedom) and violence. Political interaction, after all, is rooted in communication, that is, in speech. But "where violence rules, … everything and everybody must fall silent." One cannot ascertain the other; each has its own distinct logic. This is a mutual incompatibility: "The point here is that violence itself is incapable of speech, and not merely that speech is helpless when confronted with violence."[24] For Arendt, this does not mean that democratic polities must be incapable of waging war (or indeed of enforcing its laws), to be sure. But it does mean that "in so far as violence plays a predominant role in wars and revolutions, both occur outside the political realm."[25]

Along this line, Arendt likewise distinguishes violence from the potential that emerges when human beings act together, which she refers to as "power." It is this potential, by definition both nonviolent and nonsovereign

---

[23]Another way to put this would be to say that the "downstream" ethical question of violence or nonviolence is in a way already decided by the "upstream" political (or ecclesio-political) question of the kind of logic and authority structure that shapes the collective life of the church. The question is not so much an ethical prohibition keeping Christians from working with the state but more fundamentally whether the political logic by which the church is organized already constitutes a break with the structures of exploitation and authority of the sword order and whether it continues to found its togetherness in a logic of some holding power over others.
[24]Hannah Arendt, *On Revolution* (London: Penguin Classic, 2006), 9.
[25]Ibid.

but also fragile and transient, that "keeps the public realm, the potential space of appearance between acting and speaking men, in existence."[26] The relation between power and violence is complex: "While violence can destroy power, it can never become a substitute for it."[27] And although violence can destroy power, the latter can be "almost irresistible ... in the face of vastly superior forces."[28]

Arendt's sense of an incompatibility between proper political freedom and violence is embedded in her larger argument on human capabilities and the human condition, which I will not get into here. Nevertheless, it seems to name something remarkably similar to Schleitheim's sense of an incompatibility, more than a mere antagonism, between sovereignty and the non-sword order of the church. It is not so much that the former would be evil and must be destroyed but that it represents a particular logic or type of order that is distinct from (and under certain conditions inimical to) the kind of togetherness that allows for human freedom and shared action.

In the Schleitheim text, a significant aspect of this incompatibility seems to be the way these two orders are structured by different imaginaries. The way they are equipped with different tools and techniques ("weapons of their conflict") shapes the way they understand the world and its creatures ("against the flesh only"), causing them to envision fundamentally different kinds of political projects ("against the fortification of the devil"). This is why, perhaps, it is so important to Schleitheim that Christians limit their interaction with the sword order: if we spend too much time in the operative logic of sovereignty, we might say, we start to think and imagine like it and risk losing sight of the kinds of ecclesio-political projects to which the church is called.

But the logics of sovereignty and nonsovereignty do not merely shape the political imagination. The text suggests they also shape the theological imagination: God is encountered in radically different ways under the sword and in the church. It is important to notice that Schleitheim clearly affirms that God is authentically encountered and in active relationship with creatures "outside the perfection of Christ." States are clearly not necessarily part of the "wickedness which the devil planted in the world," referred to in Article IV. But even so, God appears radically different there from the nonsovereign Messiah of the church. Under the rule of sovereignty, God is encountered as one who "ordains"—that is, He (*sic?*) very much still seems to be a sovereign Lord.

---

[26]Arendt, *The Human Condition*, 200.
[27]Ibid., 202.
[28]Ibid., 200–1.

On its own, however, power is—perhaps not unlike the church—in danger of being perverted into a kind of conformism, Arendt fears. She sees such conformism in the modern emergence of "society," consumerism, and the nation, all of which endanger power's public quality (the plurality of human beings acting together) and its relation to artifice, scholarship, and art, which it requires to flourish.

Again, I do not wish to suggest that those gathered at Schleitheim intended to make a point about the way our theological imagination is shaped by our political structures in any historical or literal way. But the words they have left us with seem remarkably open to this conclusion. And is it not altogether plausible that life under the rule of the sword, under political authority that derives from a capacity for violence and for making a distinction between lives that matter and those that do not, would also shape the way we envision God? That living under sovereign kings and rulers, we also come to imagine God as a king or ruler, master over life and death? If we live in a world marked by obedience and authority, we will inevitably come to see God in this way as well, the text seems to suggest. Under the conditions of sovereign power, the image of God is constricted into merely a greater or stronger version of sovereignty. Inversely, the church is tasked with being a fellowship in which God is encountered differently, a space that nourishes and shapes a nonsovereign imagination of God. It is a place where we can unlearn, we might say, the image of God as sovereign ruler. By living together collaboratively as equals, we might learn also about the way God could be said to interact collaboratively with God's creation. Paradoxically, God's will seems to be achieved most successfully where God does not "ordain" but invites. Yet part of shaping such spaces is to affirm that God is still at work outside them; that even in the constricted imagination of God in the image of worldly power, God can still be affirmed as acting.

A Relationship of Possibility

Gerald Mast has noted that there are really two different ways the relation between these two incompatible orders is envisioned in this sixth article. In its opening axiom, Schleitheim takes a position of "dualism" or "legitimate difference,"[29] Mast argues, according to which the sword has a legitimate place alongside the church. This position already signals a recognition of "ambiguity and instability," as it "destabilizes the binary oppositions established in the doctrine of separation" in Article IV.[30] But then in the latter part of the article, the text reverts "back to a clear and simple opposition between the Christians and world and thus between the spiritual rule of Christians and carnal rule of magistrates."[31] So on the one hand the church recognizes the limited legitimacy of the sovereign order and simply stays out of its affairs, while on the other hand it is not willing to give up on its more radical claim that it is a profound evil.

Mast concludes this is a "profound instance of rhetorical movement within a confessional text," as it displays an "unstable rhetorical stance," indicative

---

[29]Biesecker-Mast, *Separation and the Sword*, 106.
[30]Ibid., 105–6; this differs somewhat from my reading of Article IV.
[31]Ibid., 106.

of "the contradictory space inhabited by these early Anabaptists."[32] It shows that a doctrine of separation based on simple binary oppositions is quickly, even immediately, recognized to be practically impossible—a recognition and an instability that Mast then finds throughout the Anabaptist textual tradition.

C. Arnold Snyder formulates the ambivalence in Schleitheim on this point thus: Its "teaching on authority is ... the result of a dialectical process" indebted especially to the failure of the peasants' revolt. It asserts a worldview in which worldly political rule is on the one hand "ordained by God" (for now) but on the other hand also "evil," and the Christian may well have "a duty to disobey."[33] Mast calls the opening axiom of this article a "formula for containing this ambiguity,"[34] but as the text continues, it quickly becomes clear that it, too, seems to leave many questions unanswered.

In spite of the apparent clarity of the disjunction between these two entirely different logics of sword and non-sword orders, the precise nature of their relationship seems to require supplementary negotiation and interpretation. This at least is what the text seems to suggest as it poses three questions (and we could certainly imagine countless more) to which it provides three answers. These take up a significant amount of text in this sixth article and further contribute to establishing the appropriate kinds of interaction (or rather non-interaction) between the two incompatible orders. As previously established, Schleitheim stipulates a restrictive approach in each of these cases: Christians should not employ the sword nor act as judges or magistrates.

It is telling that these supplementary stipulations are necessary at all. Should the appropriate interaction not simply follow from the initial axiom that the church and the state follow discrete logics? Apparently, it does not—and perhaps more than one kind of answer would have been possible to these questions, and different questions entirely might have given rise to different answers, too.[35] Apparently, the separatist or quietist approach for which Schleitheim is renowned only represents one possible set of conclusions from its basic axiom. It is not simply and obviously implied but itself needs to be made and negotiated.

This sense of possibility, or at least of uncertainty and complexity, is also implicit in the way Schleitheim frames the incompatibility between church and sword. Mast here identifies a closing down of the possibility and ambiguity of the text, a return to a clear and simple opposition. But the terms the text

---

[32]Ibid.
[33]Snyder, "The Schleitheim Articles," 429.
[34]Biesecker-Mast, *Separation and the Sword*, 105.
[35]In any case, Schleitheim's answers are not overwhelmingly clear, either. For one, in John 8 Jesus interrupts an execution taking place between people who are not (perhaps not yet) His followers. In which realm does this take place: the realm of the Law, and thus the sword, or of the "perfection of Christ"? By extension, would the conclusion that Christians ought to interrupt executions—not merely abstain from them—not be at least as plausible?

uses to depict the two orders come in strange pairs, which do not simply map onto an opposition: magistrates have their houses "in this world," while the Christians' houses are "in heaven." This is already a strange thing to write—certainly, Christians still live in material houses, not in "heaven." But the opposition between "world" and "heaven" is also odd: should it not be between the world and the *church* or between *earth* and heaven?

This opposition, if it is one, is rephrased in the same paragraph as being between flesh and spirit: the church has a "spiritual" orientation, while the sword a "carnal" one. That the sword is oriented to the "flesh"—so to the material and bodily conditions of life, which it fosters or destroys—seems clear enough. But the meaning of this "spiritual" orientation of the church is peculiar. "Spiritual" here certainly does not signify anything like an inward or transcendental faith: Schleitheim is entirely uninterested in inward contemplative concerns or transcendent truths. It considers the relevance of faith to take place in concrete, embodied practices. So, this is a spiritual and heavenly orientation that is, for all intents and purposes, not spiritual or heavenly at all; it is entirely negotiated in the immanent sphere of ecclesio-political contestation, among the "flesh."

So, this quasi-opposition between flesh and spirit, or between world and heaven, certainly does not seem to imply that the church order might sit quietly alongside the worldly order, one responsible for the faithful's bodies, the other for their souls, existing in different spheres of life, or days of the week, one untroubled by the other. But it is also not a difference between two basically similar kinds of things that could coexist by taking up separate places or territories, like two states might come to a détente by drawing a territorial border between them. There is, we could say, a logical underdetermination in the way these heterogeneous orders might relate to each other.

It is because this relationship is so underdetermined, because it takes shape neither simply as an opposition nor as a complementary relation, that it requires supplementary stipulation and negotiation, and that, in turn, Schleitheim's quietism is but one of many different conceivable expressions. There is no one set of relations between the church and the sword order that is necessary or implied. Their incompatibility does not imply spatial separation, quietist withdrawal, or (for that matter) active citizenship. Each of these is just one of many possibilities. And this underdetermined incompatibility makes for a potential dynamism in this relationship, allowing it to be reinvented and renegotiated in different times and contexts—as Anabaptists have indeed done, the world over.

Conclusion

Instead of calling for nonviolence out of obedience to a sovereign lawgiver, Schleitheim's sixth article formulates a critique of political authority and a call for nonsovereignty. The "sword," which it both recognizes and rejects, seems to refer to a kind of authority or order that is rooted in its capacity for violence and, more specifically, its capacity to distinguish between lives worthy of protection and those worthy of death. In spite of its legitimacy, this kind of order is incompatible with the kind of nonsovereign political project the church is called to be in emulation of its nonsovereign Messiah.

The church is not called to be a place of obedience but a community where we can unlearn obedience and unlearn our imagination of God as a sovereign master. Schleitheim's sixth article seeks to regulate the relationship between these two heterogeneous orders, but in so doing, it shows that this relationship is not simply given. Even if the church must recognize that God is in some way at work outside of the "perfection of Christ" and so must recognize the (conditional) legitimacy of states and governments, the relationship between the two is not fixed but subject to negotiation and transformation. It is this tensive, underdetermined relationship between incompatible orders—not simply different sets of laws for different domains but truly different kinds of (ecclesio-)political logic—that an overly simple understanding of church and sovereign rule as "two kingdoms" is in danger of eliding, at least insofar as it misses that one of these kingdoms is a non-kingdom, and the relationship between these is far from clear.

Insofar as Schleitheim's critique of the sword is relevant for the church today, this relevance does not lie primarily in the question of whether Anabaptist Christians are permitted to work for the state as judges or public school teachers or social workers, it seems to me. Nor indeed in whether it is appropriate for them to rely on public institutions—be it in everyday life or for crisis response. Indeed, in many of these questions, Schleitheim's strange axiom may turn out to be quite sensible. It allows us to recognize the ways legitimate sovereign order and legal systems may yet play a role in God's wish for this planet and its creatures while accompanying that affirmation with the level-headed realization that sovereignty can only imagine and work toward political projects that are in line with its own logic. This will always be in some sense heterogeneous to the kind of political imagination the church is called to.

Yet the major significance of Schleitheim's ecclesio-political critique is in its identification of this different path—in the call for building nonsovereign community. It asks to what extent our communities continue to participate in this distinction between lives that matter and lives that are given up to insignificance. The enduring force of its critique of sovereign power is in its contention that the church is called to work by a different logic to become a space in which a nonsovereign fellowship can be learned and practiced. Even in times of crisis and catastrophe, the formation of a shared life in a fellowship of equals remains possible, even crucial.

7

Guarantee

Introduction

Schleitheim's seventh and final article instructs baptized Christians to abstain from swearing oaths. It is sometimes seen as an archaic afterthought to its other points, difficult to relate to questions facing the church in our day. After all, oath-swearing no longer plays the role it once did in our societies. In its sixteenth-century context, oath refusal is generally interpreted as a matter of political separatism: oath-swearing played a significant role in political and legal life, and to refuse to take part in such a practice would cement the outsider status of the Anabaptists, and further clarify their singular obedience to God alone and their break with worldly authorities.

On that interpretation, this final article seems to offer little in the way of response to our recurring question—how to build a community in times of crisis—that we have not read already in other articles: ascertain your separateness from the structures of the world, let there be no ambiguity around your absolute obedience to God. In more contemporary terms, maybe we could render it as something like: be mindful of the practices you participate in that bind you to anything other than God and the Church. So Schleitheim's final article may seem to do what Schleitheim has seemed to do at every step: attempting to still the ambiguity that inevitably emerges between the outside world and the community it seeks to shape. An afterthought indeed, perhaps even somewhat redundant—have the previous articles not done enough to mark the separateness of this community?

Throughout this study, however, I have been claiming that both Schleitheim's emphasis on separation and its apparent call to obedience need to be questioned. And the same is true in this case: in my interpretation, Schleitheim's instruction to refuse oaths is far from an afterthought but a recapitulation and conclusion to this very project of a nonsovereign community. With attentive reading, we may come to see how its refusal to swear oaths opens into a comprehensive critique of sovereignty and a radical reenvisioning of certitude and trust in a community without such enforced guarantees. Not the suppression of ambiguity but shared life within it, seeking ecclesio-political structures that break with the logic of sovereign binding. Here, there is no final word or guarantee; there is only life lived in repetition: *let your words be yes, yes.*

In a surprisingly sophisticated argument, Schleitheim argues that oath-swearing, though a common practice in the political and legal life of its day, does not do what it claims. For one, it produces perjury rather than eliminating it. But there is also a more significant and theological problem with swearing: it lays a claim over the world, attempting to bring it under the dominion of one's words in a way not appropriate for human beings. So overcoming the oath, and more generally this sense of a claim over the world through language, is an essential component of a nonsovereign community.

Of course I must stress again that I do not mean to say that for those gathered at Schleitheim, formulating a philosophical critique was a main concern in any literal or historical sense. But (need I say it) the text they have left us with nevertheless seems open to such a reading, and as I enter into conversation with it, what I will finally argue is perhaps not at all so far removed from what they also sought: the possibility of trust and shared life in a persistently ambiguous world, and of church as a kind of collective body that is never definitively achieved or guaranteed but must be restaged interminably.

The Root of Sovereignty

Because the historical significance of swearing is so far removed from contemporary practice, let us briefly discuss oath-swearing more generally. Of course, the ways in which societies have sworn oaths vary across times and places. But if we generalize, we can say that an oath is a solemnly given and in some sense institutionalized guarantee for a statement or promise by appeal to a divine or sacred force.[1] What this means is that by swearing, the swearer is thought to give some kind of special assurance for their words. Maybe what they are reporting cannot be otherwise verified, or the promise they are making (such as loyalty to a king) is considered especially important. The oath binds the swearer to what they are saying or promising. And it does this not just by its own force but by some external appeal, in many cases God or a god, who is called upon to stand for the truth of what is being sworn to.

Historians have noted the way swearing seems to stake something—a particular possession but more frequently one's very life—in the face of this divine or sacred force. In many cultures, the original form of oath-swearing was a conditional self-curse: the swearer asks for the wrath of the gods, or some other negative consequence, if they commit perjury or fail to live up to their sworn commitment. If I am lying, may God strike me down, we might

---

[1] Émile Benveniste, *Dictionary of Indo-European Concepts and Society* (Chicago: Hau Books, 2016), 440.

say.² Historians have also noted that by swearing, the declaration itself becomes in some way sacred. Oaths are thought to carry some special force.

This special kind of sacred and guaranteeing function has made oaths crucial to European political life for centuries. Historian Paolo Prodi especially remarks on the way an oath binds the swearer not just to what they are saying specifically but also more generally to the collective body in which the oath takes place. Your loyalty to your king or country is not just one of many things; you stake your life to it, grounding your belonging to the collective body.³ Oath swearing is thus a "junction of the relation of politics and the sphere of the sacred."⁴ In this function, the oath comes to anchor political and legal order throughout Western history. This is true both for vertical relations of obedience (such as feudal loyalties) and for more lateral civil orders (such as in free cities or the Swiss commonwealth), which are likewise constituted by collective oaths.⁵ Prodi thus describes the role of oath-swearing in medieval Europe as "the basis of every authority and normative force, the metapolitical root of law, the connecting point between the invisible and human worlds."⁶ Historian Edmund Pries similarly describes oath-swearing in medieval and early modern Europe as the "button that fastened together the various social and political structures."⁷

In modernity, Prodi notes that oath-swearing transforms, becoming more oriented toward the nation, to which the pledging of one's life is now demanded. In the twentieth century, however, oath-swearing falls into decline. For Prodi, this decline is deeply troubling: "We are the first generation" to live without the constitutive and comprehensive bond provided by the oath. Without noticing it, we are thereby experiencing "a crisis that has seized the human being itself as a zoon politikon, ... [and] which threatens the entire development of the western political system."⁸

Perhaps not all readers will quite share Prodi's sense of the severity of this crisis. Yet given the function of oath swearing as a constitutive political and legal practice, it is not hard to understand why Prodi considers the Anabaptist refusal to swear a comprehensive "rebellion against the state order" that seeks to "attack the heart of power in its sacrality."⁹ For centuries, perhaps even millennia, and in a variety of Western political and legal cultures, oath-swearing functioned as an anchoring point for truth, forming both the metapolitical and

---

²See, for example, Helen Silving, "The Oath: i," *Yale Law Journal* 68, no. 7 (1959): 1329–90.
³Paolo Prodi, "Der Eid in Der Europäischen Verfassungsgeschichte: Zur Einführung," in *Glaube Und Eid*, ed. Paolo Prodi and Elisabeth Müller-Luckner (Munich: R. Oldenbourg, 1993), VII–XXIX, VIII.
⁴Ibid., XXVIII.
⁵Ibid., XV–XVI.
⁶Ibid., XII.
⁷A formulation that comes from Heinrich Bullinger; Edmund Pries, *Anabaptist Oath Refusal: Basel, Bern, and Strasbourg, 1525–1538* (Thunder Bay: Pandora Press, 2023), 1.
⁸Prodi, "Eid," VII.
⁹Ibid., XIX.

metaphysical root of sovereignty. In attacking the legitimacy of oath-swearing, the Anabaptists were therefore not just formulating nonparticipation in one practice among others but in one of the constitutive institutions in the legal, economic, and political systems of their time.[10]

Edmund Pries, whose seminal study on Anabaptist oath refusal in the early sixteenth century has recently become more widely available, seems to agree: "The Anabaptist refusal to swear oaths was the most radical political act that could have been undertaken by anyone ... short of declaring war against one's overlords."[11] From the perspective of the authorities, "oath refusal made society ungovernable; the means of exercising control ... had been sabotaged."[12] In an important sense, refusing to swear oaths meant refusing the control of the authorities, which significantly functioned by means of various kinds of oaths; Pries thus described the Anabaptists (at least in some cases) as "religiously-anarchistic."[13] At the same time, "more than any other action," oath refusal signified the separation of nascent Anabaptist communities from the social and political structures around them and their commitment to constructing alternative communities with alternative loyalties. Pries particularly notes the significance of baptism, in some Anabaptist arguments, as a comprehensive covenant and commitment that "replaced the civil oath ceremony."[14] In baptism, Christians are already "sworn," we might say, and no other loyalty may bind them. The alternative communities they formed, Pries argues, were "not places for withdrawal" but "activist conventicles."[15]

Snyder is more cautious in his assessment. At least in the case of the Anabaptists of Schleitheim, a détente with the state order was quite conceivable, he argues. He notes Schleitheim's historical authors were less interested in rebellion than in withdrawal, more in building alternative structures of community than in overthrowing or attacking state power.[16] This is not to say such a détente with worldly rule was immediately realistic in Schleitheim's historical context: Snyder describes the effects of the refusal to swear as "catastrophic ... Those who refused to swear any and all oaths were placing themselves outside the margins of acceptable civil society."[17]

---

[10]This is not to say that oath refusal as such originates with the Anabaptist movement; Silving notes that in the early church "acceptance of the oath in Christianity was achieved only after a considerable struggle, and even then the acceptance was not unqualified." Prodi likewise discusses the "radical change of opinion" in the church in its first centuries, from initial rejection to its integration into the Christian worldview. See Silving, "The Oath," 1344; Prodi, "Eid," XI; see also Pries, *Anabaptist Oath Refusal*, 5–33.
[11]Ibid., 385.
[12]Ibid., 386.
[13]Ibid., 164.
[14]Ibid., 3.
[15]Ibid., 4.
[16]Snyder, "The Schleitheim Articles."
[17]Snyder, *Anabaptist History and Theology*, 186.

So this metapolitical significance of swearing gives rise to quite a plausible interpretation of Schleitheim's oath refusal. Though historians disagree on the precise modality in which oath refusal engages with, rebels against, or withdraws from the political and civil order, they still seem to agree that the refusal to swear is best understood in its political and civil significance. It is the refusal to give allegiance, we might say. Oath refusal appears to be a principled and fundamental kind of nonparticipation: an anti- or metapolitical assertion of the primacy of the Christian's allegiance to Christ and the church community, contesting the validity of worldly sovereignty precisely at this "junction" between political rule and the sacred.

Even if worldly government might in some way be part of God's ordained plan (for now), calling on God to guarantee one's obedience to it, as swearing does, is wholly inappropriate for baptized Christians. So in this reading, oath refusal sharpens the way Anabaptism and the Schleitheim group seek to dissociate themselves from worldly political rule while underlining their exclusive belonging to Jesus Christ. In response to the question I have been asking—how to build community in times of crisis—Schleitheim seems to be saying, clarify your allegiance. Do not divide your loyalty. Do not participate in political practices that would compromise your exclusive and direct obedience to God.

But something about this reading remains unsatisfying. Not that it would be inaccurate—oath refusal as principled political nonparticipation seems entirely plausible, especially for a community engaged in ecclesio-political contestation and the formation of an alternative community in a context where oath-swearing is crucial to the worldly political order. But to just read the refusal to swear as the refusal to swear allegiance to this particular worldly order seems a little limited. That would make the meaning of oath refusal a matter of content and degree: as mostly an instruction to refuse *those* oaths that bind you to a political allegiance. Given that Christians are bound by an "oath" (baptism), the question is just *which* oath and *which* obedience takes precedence. But this would fail to take into account the way God's sovereignty is *non*sovereignty and the *kind* of loyalty the church owes to God's (un)Kingdom is fundamentally different than that of a vassal to their lord.

It would also seem to make the seventh article somewhat redundant. Have the preceding articles not done more than enough to establish nonparticipation in worldly political life as a norm for the church?[18] The

---

[18] Any civil authority that would accept voluntary baptism and the refusal to bear arms will presumably also be willing to make some accommodation concerning oath-swearing, as indeed Michael Driedger details: as long as they operated as particular exceptions and privileges, the Dutch Republic was unfazed by the supposed revolutionary potential of any of these points. See Michael Driedger, "Anabaptists and the Early Modern State: A Long-Term View," in *A Companion to Anabaptism and Spiritualism, 1521–1700*, ed. John D. Roth and James M. Stayer (Leiden: Brill, 2007), 507–44.

previous article has discussed the relation to the state in some detail. Is the seventh article truly no more than a continuation of the sixth? If that is all oath-swearing means, it would make the seventh article an afterthought indeed. It would just be another implication or concrete (and for us mostly archaic and obsolete) case of its general axiom. Or, inversely, this interpretation would make the *sixth* article redundant: surely anyone refusing to swear oaths is already disqualified as a magistrate or judge.

And indeed the text itself goes much further. It does not merely ask *which* oath and *which* sovereignty may be binding to baptized Christians but whether the world and human existence structurally allow for the kinds of guarantees oath-swearing claims to provide. The sixth article clearly speaks about participation in, and legitimacy of, political authority. In this seventh article, Schleitheim fundamentally calls into question the logic by which the sovereign guarantees of oath-swearing function. The reasoning is not just political but (anti-)metaphysical, fundamentally questioning the relation of human beings, their words, God, and reality embodied in the oath.

So let us take a closer look.

Reading

Schleitheim's seventh and final article is one of its longer ones. Nevertheless, it addresses its subject matter strictly and radically. It begins by briefly characterizing oath-swearing, which it says is "a confirmation among those who are quarreling or making promises." Though the text notes that in the "Law," so in the Old Testament, swearing is "commanded" and only false oaths are forbidden, for Christians, all swearing is formally forbidden.

> Christ, who teaches the perfection of the Law, prohibits all swearing to His [followers], whether true or false,—neither by heaven, nor by the earth, nor by Jerusalem, nor by our head,—and that for the reason which He shortly thereafter gives, for you are not able to make one hair white or black. So you see it is for this reason that all swearing is forbidden: we cannot fulfill that which we promise when we swear, for we cannot change [even] the very least thing on us.

After this, the text discusses several counterarguments, such as Old Testament instances of God swearing an oath to Abraham. God's swearing, the text argues, is mostly for pedagogical purposes ("that ... we might have a strong consolation," Heb. 6:18), but in any case not an argument at all: "Everything is possible for Him ... therefore He can keep His oath. But we can do nothing ... to keep or perform: therefore we shall swear nothing." I will say more about this later; for now, we can already note that the argument is not about fealty so much as about capacity: humans do not know what the future holds, and we do not have the capacity to ascertain that we will not have committed perjury or break our word. God's case is different: "No one can withstand nor thwart His will."

After rejecting the literalistic argument that only swearing by those specific things listed in Mt. 5:34 would be forbidden, the text moves on to the apparent swearing in the New Testament by "the apostles Peter and Paul."[19] Their cases are not precisely swearing, merely "testifying," the text concludes, as they themselves "promise nothing," but merely refer to God's promise.[20] They thus do not affect the general ban on swearing. In closing, Schleitheim returns to Matthew 5:

> Christ also taught us along the same line when He said, let your speech be yes, yes; and no, no; for whatsoever is more than these comes of evil ... Christ is simply yes and no, and all those who seek Him simply will understand His Word. Amen.

As in previous articles, it is clear that this injunction against swearing oaths must be read as a formal regulation. This is not just an ethical instruction or one element of Christian morality among others. It must be understood in its ecclesio-political significance as a practice (or non-practice) by which the constitution of the church, its incompatibility with worldly sovereignty, and the negotiation of its borders with the outside world are played out. Given

---

[19] For Paul, this may refer to Gal. 1:20, 2 Cor. 1:23, and Rom. 1:9, which contain phrases such as "God is my witness that." For Peter, it is not clear, but it does not appear to refer to Peter's panicked and false swearing in Mt. 26:74 ("I do not know the man!"). Perhaps Hebrews 6 is intended, in which the author does not refer to (or seem aware of?) a prohibition on swearing.

[20] Pries considers this passage especially significant, as it seems to make a distinction between assertory oaths, which swear to a truth in the past or present (such as by a witness in a judicial proceeding), and promissory oaths, which swear to uphold a certain promise (as a vassal might swear fealty to their lord). And indeed the text seems to argue that Peter and Paul's apparent oaths do not fall under the general prohibition because they attest to the past instead of swearing to future events. Pries may be right that this seems to imply that assertory oaths are permitted or perhaps not considered to be oaths at all (*pace* Calvin), in Schleitheim's logic. However, this remark is embedded in a particular discussion of apparently biblical cases of swearing, not as a self-contained point, so its status seems unclear. Either way, it seems doubtful that this would be the crucial question in understanding the logic of Schleitheim's argument. See Pries, *Anabaptist Oath Refusal*, 168–80.

Silving in any case suggests that the distinction may not be so elementary. At least in the premodern contexts she discusses, supposedly assertory oaths were sworn not to establish truth in "accordance with objective facts" but to bind the swearer to *a* truth, that is, to one of the disputing parties. At least in these contexts, Silving concludes, oaths were "not means of establishing a fact but expressions of solidarity with the group which the oath taker wished to prevail." The ability to keep one's word, to not become a perjurer, was here not primarily a matter of fact but one of virtue and strength—and so not at all so different from promissory oaths. See Silving, "The Oath," 1334.

Giorgio Agamben (more from whom in the second half of this chapter) also notes that the "difference concerns, in fact, not the act of the oath, which is identical in the two cases, but the semantic content of the *dictum*." Giorgio Agamben, *The Sacrament of Language: An Archaeology of the Oath* (Stanford: Stanford University Press, 2010), 6.

the constitutive role of oath-swearing for worldly political and legal systems I discussed earlier, this ecclesio-political significance is only heightened. By this refusal to swear, fundamental questions of allegiance and sovereignty are decided.

But to make this argument, the text does not discuss allegiance and sovereignty directly. The sense that the loyalty given to Christ in baptism would supersede any sworn oaths—as was stressed by Pries—is entirely absent. Instead, Schleitheim argues a more fundamental point. It does this in two steps: first, by noting that oaths are sworn "among those who are quarreling." So, instead of ascertaining trust, swearing is eminently done by those who are *un*trustworthy. And second, by noting that the reason swearing is forbidden is that "we cannot fulfill that which we promise." Oath-swearing is not only unnecessary or ethically forbidden but structurally *impossible*: human beings simply cannot offer the kind of certitude, the kind of assurance that they claim while swearing. So Schleitheim's critique of the guarantees given in oath-swearing, and the political structures of allegiance anchored by such oaths, is rooted in a much more fundamental questioning of the human capacity to make promises and give guarantees at all. It has something to do with the way oaths attempt to bind together words, things, human beings, and God in a way not appropriate to the ambiguity of human existence.

Among Those Who Are Quarreling

The first thing Schleitheim remarks on is that an oath is an assurance given "among those who are quarreling and making promises." This may seem like a throwaway line, simply establishing what oaths even are. But for all its brevity, there is already a somewhat refined argument here. The oath, in seeking to guarantee the truth of an expression, presupposes that truth is already in question. In seeking to solidify and ascertain a statement or promise, it presupposes discord, presupposes (and so admits) the possibility that this promise may *not* be kept or that the swearer is in fact lying. *In* swearing to truth, one admits the possibility of perjury. You could even say there is no perjury outside of oaths, that swearing produces the possibility of perjury—so swearing an oath can never decidedly banish it.

So these few words already say a good deal: the oath does not guarantee anything because it is sworn precisely when there is *no* (other) guarantee, where the truth or reliability of the swearer is not clear and cannot be ascertained other than by swearing. Paradoxically, this means it is exactly the oath that casts doubt on what is sworn to: if it were clearly, transparently, and verifiably true, an oath would be eminently unnecessary. Oaths do not still the ambiguity of human existence; they heighten it. Baptized Christians, Schleitheim seems to be saying, have no need of such additional and counteractive guarantees. The relationality and trust of the ecclesio-political community should function by other means.

This sentiment that oaths are ineffective almost by definition takes up and echoes a much older problem. Historians note that the oldest discussions of oath-swearing already include the sense that people generally swear oaths in vain. There never seems to have been a time when oaths really had the guaranteeing effect they claim to have. To swear has always been a means to *at once* stress the veracity of one's statement *and* to raise profound suspicions about that veracity. To swear does not so much give knowledge about the truth of a statement or honesty of an intention—quite the opposite, it seems to imply that we will never know the truth independently.

So Benveniste notes that the Greek etymology of the words for oath and perjury already indicates how disastrously ineffective oaths were at ensuring truth. While the Greek word for oath is *horkos*, the word for perjury, already found in the oldest texts, is *epiorkos*. Taken literally, this means "to add (to one's statement) an oath." Paradoxically, to "add an oath" *is* "to perjure oneself."[21] This is less strange than it might seem, as we see in the Schleitheim formulation, where this sense is still clearly present: oaths are sworn by those "making promises." We do not even need to add anything to make clear that these are *vain* promises. Making promises, swearing oaths, stressing that one is telling the truth—none of it can really relate the claimed trustworthiness. And this already shows something that Schleitheim then goes on to elaborate: the way such binding operations are, at their root, a claim of control over an ambiguous world.

Cannot Fulfill That Which We Promise

Schleitheim makes its second argument after referring to the Gospel passage in which Jesus rejects all swearing. Jesus had instructed to "not swear at all, … for you cannot make one hair white or black" (Mt. 5:34). Schleitheim summarizes: "So you see it is for this reason that all swearing is forbidden: we cannot fulfill that which we promise when we swear, for we cannot change [even] the very least thing on us." First, it was suggested the oath is not *necessary* (for those who are trustworthy) and not *effective* (for those who are untrustworthy). Now, Schleitheim seems to more profoundly claim that the oath, as a guarantee for one's words, is structurally *impossible*.

---

[21] As Benveniste comments, this "throws light on a fact of morals; it shows that all too lightly support was given by an oath to a promise which one had no intention of keeping or a statement which one knew to be false." It seems to indicate that there was never a time when oaths were generally effective. In Agamben's words, "Already in the archaic epoch … the oath seems to constitutively imply the possibility of perjury … As a guarantee of an oral contract or a promise, the oath appeared, according to all the evidence, from the very beginning to be completely inadequate to the task." See Benveniste, *Dictionary*, 445; Agamben, *Sacrament*, 7.

Independently of one's intentions, even "we" (baptized Christians, presumably) "cannot fulfill that which we promise when we swear."

So this seems to radicalize the first argument: one runs the risk of perjury even if one *is* trustworthy because the risk is there in spite of oneself. Whether a promise is kept, or whether the truth is spoken, is not under the control of the swearer. Human beings simply cannot offer the kind of certitude, the kind of assurance that they say they are giving when swearing. Not because humans are dishonest and untrustworthy but because they live in a world structurally not under the dominion of their words. We cannot change even the very least thing on us.

And what this means is that swearing does not so much try to verify or ascertain truth or honesty as try to perform a kind of *binding operation* between the words spoken, the speaker, God, and the outside world. There is, we could say, a violence in it: oath-swearing is an attempt to bring the world under the dominion of one's words.

This intuition is shared by Giorgio Agamben in his "archaeology" of the oath.[22] Oath-swearing, Agamben suggests, is foundational to the mode in which we have become human exactly *as* such a claim of control, setting our shared life on a particular track from the very beginning. As soon as living human beings begin to speak, Agamben suggests, they are faced with the problem of truthfulness: "that is, of what can guarantee the original connection between names and things, and between the subject who has become a speaker—and, thus capable of asserting and promising—and his [*sic*] actions."[23] This is not just because of the moral character of the speaker but "a weakness pertaining to language itself."[24] The sheer fact that lying or vain promises are possible at all already raises this question. The bond between human beings, words, and things is not immediately clear: a kind of *binding operation* is required.

As such, oath-swearing as we find it in history is the "historical testimony"[25] of exactly this binding operation at the dawn of humanity and its capacity to speak and act together. It stands for this very original moment of taking responsibility for one's words, of binding and even staking oneself and one's life—a broken oath invites a curse, after all—to one's claim or promise. This is done by making a distinction between truth and lie or in other words between blessing (an oath kept) and curse (an oath broken).[26]

---

[22]The point of such an "archaeology" is not so much to find out what historically happened at a certain point in time but to trace the first principle (or *arche*) of such a practice, the underlying structure that persists, while also fading from view, over the centuries. It especially hopes to bring into viewpoints at which another road might have been taken.
[23]Agamben, *Sacrament*, 68.
[24]Ibid., 8.
[25]Ibid., 66.
[26]Ibid., 56. It is also for this reason, Agamben notes, that oaths are so bad at eliminating perjury: after all, perjury and the curse it implies are part of the operation by which oath-swearing performs its work.

Agamben sees this arche-oath, the original binding operation that oaths recall and rely on, as grounding the entire Western structure of sovereignty. The distinction made in oath-swearing between blessing and curse sets the scene for the way a sovereign legal order operates throughout history, always working by distinguishing between the lives it protects and the lives it condemns, between citizens and noncitizens, insiders and outsiders, between those lives that are protected (blessed) and those that are insignificant (cursed).

So this distinction between truth and perjury made by oath-swearing, Agamben argues, is far from an innocent or even commendable attempt to instill trust into the shared life of human beings. There is a deeply violent moment in it that underlies the analogous violence of the sovereign order. Swearing stands for the way language, in the register of sovereignty, lays a total claim on the world, declaring anything that escapes that claim as cursed. This, in turn, enables the political to lay a similar claim over life.

As theologian Adam Kotsko elucidates, this

> means that all of Western society is structured by the logic of the curse. All of Western society follows the model found in the human claim to make language correspond to reality—and to subject what escapes this claim to destruction.[27]

Sovereignty, be it democratic or otherwise, is impossible without this binding operation between human beings, language, and the world that is asserted in oath-swearing. In Kotsko's words, "The oath is not simply parallel to the operation of the machinery of sovereignty but provides its ground."[28]

Agamben's argument is certainly sweeping. And yet the way it links oath-swearing to the functioning of sovereignty strangely echoes and elucidates Schleitheim: it, too, seems peculiarly aware of an interdependence between the dominion of one's words over the world claimed in oath-swearing and the kinds of sovereign dominion such oath-swearing in turn guarantees. As we saw in the previous chapter, Schleitheim seems to consider a "sword" order to function in almost exactly the same way as in Agamben's analysis, by its capacity to both "protect" *and* "put to death," so by distinguishing between lives protected (the "good") and those condemned (the "wicked"). The *political* significance of oaths, as a question of allegiance, Schleitheim and Agamben both suggest, is deeply related to the more fundamental question of humanity's relation to language and the world and to its promises and claims as themselves claims of dominion.

Oaths try to overcome a fundamental weakness in language, Schleitheim seems to be saying, by enlisting God in claiming a position of power over

---

[27]Colby Dickinson and Adam Kotsko, *Agamben's Coming Philosophy: Finding a New Use for Theology* (London: Rowman & Littlefield, 2015), 223.
[28]Ibid.

the world. In seeking to guarantee the truth of one's words or the outcome of one's promise by swearing, the text seems to argue, one is reaching for a kind of divinely guaranteed fixedness or certainty, indeed mastery and control, that fundamentally misunderstands the relationship between God, human beings, words, and things. What is at stake in swearing oaths is not just the *particular* obedience to which one is sworn, nor merely the risk of perjury or the superfluity of institutionalized guarantees for quintessentially trustworthy Christians but humanity's relationship to the world through language and the place for God in that relationship.

Fundamentally, human beings should not swear because they live in a world not under their control, because they cannot "perform" what they promise, because (we might say) they live an existence indelibly marked by ambiguity and uncertainty.

Yes, Yes; No, No

So perhaps we have, after all, unearthed something of the radicality of this sixteenth-century text that would have remained hidden if we had only understood it to refer to an ethical instruction inspired by biblical literalism. In its brief text, Schleitheim notes the interrelation of oath and perjury and the way oath-swearing reaches for a kind of dominion or mastery over the world, seeking to control its ambiguity. If oaths come to anchor the political order, they do so exactly by bringing to bear such mastery onto the sphere of human community.

Rejecting oath-swearing means that the truth of my statement, the trustworthiness of my promise, cannot be given or guaranteed by linguistic ritual performatives. It can only be verified in time and relationship. In a way, Schleitheim's refusal of the oath thus reads as exemplary for a more comprehensive reorientation of this relation between God, human beings, words, and things and of the kind of community that relation enables. With Schleitheim, we might see human beings invited into a fundamentally different kind of relation: one not marked by sovereign guarantees of obedience but by the simple everyday practice of community. In this light, Schleitheim's seventh article is far from an afterthought but the condition upon which the entire text takes its relevance, as a text singularly concerned with the construction of such a community without sovereignty in the midst of an ambiguous world.

One of the main marks of a nonsovereign community is thus here again its break with structures of a *final* word or *final* promise, its relinquishing of exactly these binding operations. Instead of the sovereign sword of control, we can see ourselves invited into a community "bound," such as it is, by repetition. Schleitheim's critique of the oath is embedded in this effort to construct and shape the life of the ecclesio-political community, and it envisions its alternative to the sovereign guarantees of oath-swearing eminently in the *repeated* practices of that community.

Certainly, Schleitheim's vision of a disciplined and somewhat sober community is not one all contemporary readers will find appealing, and maybe the real potential of Schleitheim for the church today will need to be claimed in this creative tension (as I hope this book has so far done). Yet in envisioning a collective life apart from the structures of sovereignty, it shows how it really is a *confession without creed*: describing not the propositional content of belief but pointing toward faith as a form of life, seeing its truth manifested in the relationships shaped by its repeated practice. This is a togetherness that cannot be ascertained or guaranteed, is never finally given or achieved, but must interminably be restaged and reasserted.

Assurance and trust, for Schleitheim, are not given in linguistic performatives or binding operations but in repetition: in the interminable process of gathering, which is never quite decisively achieved, in which each negotiation with ambiguity invites further restaging and reshaping. It is never *achieved*, never finds a final word, but remains in process. And do we not find this sense of repetition oddly illustrated in these words of Jesus that Schleitheim cites in the closing lines of this final article? "Let your speech be yes, *yes*; no, *no*" (Mt. 5:37). We might notice a strange affinity between this "yes, yes" and the kind of repeated practices that Schleitheim proposes as the basis of assurance and trust without sovereign guarantees. Yes, *yes*: if you say yes, once will not be enough. Faith as practice must be affirmed and reaffirmed. This originary yes, not beholden to the oath structure, does not guarantee or seek to seize or dominate a relation to the world but admits to its own incompleteness: another *yes* will always be required. Likewise, no, *no*: if you say no, once will not be enough. Resistance must be reasserted interminably. Let your words, Jesus seems to be saying, not gather into themselves but open up into the future, for you live in a world structurally not under their dominion.

Conclusion

What is it to live together in times of catastrophe? At the beginning of this chapter, it seemed as though Schleitheim would approach this question as it seemed to do elsewhere: by pointing to a practice of political nonparticipation that shores up the distinction between the church community and the outside world. Oath-swearing is rejected, we seemed to read, because it functions to politically and legally organize that outside world. On more careful reading, however, we found a more subtle and more radical argument. In this reading, Schleitheim rejects oath-swearing because it attempts to subdue the ambiguity of human existence. Oath-swearing roots the structures of shared life in a claim of mastery that fundamentally misunderstands the relation between God, human beings, words, and things.

What is at stake in swearing oaths is not just the *particular* obedience to which one is sworn, nor merely the risk of perjury or the superfluity of institutionalized guarantees for quintessentially trustworthy Christians but humanity's relationship to the world through language and the place for God in that relationship. In the temporality of repetition, a community gains its stability and its capacity to exist and persist in time, such as it is not from divine sovereign guarantee or linguistic performative but from its repeated practices, which are always in question and remain fragile enunciations.

Schleitheim's rejection of the oath can encourage us to embrace the ambiguity of life amid unruly zoe. In times of crisis and catastrophe, this may not sound especially appealing, I admit: indeed, in such times, a desire for guarantees may be felt with particular urgency. As a society's way of thinking and sense of itself are ruptured, we may well yearn for something in the midst of it all that we can rely on: undisputable truths, unshakable political loyalties, indubitable economic realities. Yet Schleitheim seems to warn us of this desire, imploring us to be wary of whatever and whoever promises certainty and guarantees in such times. Indeed it is especially the experience of rupture in catastrophe and collapse that should make us wary of the proud confidence of sovereignty and of worldly structures of exploitation: they, too, cannot fulfill what they promise.

Oath refusal is thus far from an afterthought, let alone an archaic and obsolete point of biblical literalism. It goes to the heart of the way the ecclesio-political community grounds itself in a temporality of repetition, the way we might find trust and fellowship in an ambiguous world. Shared life cannot be guaranteed or made safe in the way the oath promises (yet inevitably also fails) to do. It must be risked, interminably, in shared repeated practice. In this mode, God is present not as a fixture, called upon to guarantee the power of some over others, but as a force that sets loose an existence in time and relationship. The absence of a guarantor opens up into the existence in time of the community. Repetition, yes, yes—the only thing I can do to stand for my word and my promise is to stand by it in the days, months, and years in which this fellowship will live.

Excursus

In most editions, Schleitheim's seven articles are framed by two further textual elements: a preamble and a few concluding closing paragraphs or postscript.[1] Both the preamble and the postscript are about as long as Schleitheim's longer articles. They do not seem to be part of the articles proper as agreed upon at the Schleitheim meeting. Nevertheless, these introductory and closing remarks give a sense of the rhetorical situation of the articles themselves and make a few supplementary points.

The preamble opens with a trinitarian greeting formula, wishing "joy, peace and mercy" to all who "love God," who are "the children of the light," and who are, while "scattered everywhere," at the same time "assembled together in one God." To these addressees, the author reports the results of their assembly in Schleitheim, recorded in "points and articles." Those participating in the assembly were "of one mind to abide in the Lord as God's obedient children, [His] sons and daughters, we who have been and shall be separated from the world in everything, [and] completely at peace."

The text notes the unity or consensus experienced at this assembly suggests (or perhaps constitutes) a particular divine presence: "In this we have perceived the oneness of the Spirit of our Father and of our common Christ with us. For the Lord is the Lord of peace and not of quarreling, as Paul points out."

The preamble is mostly silent on the material or historic conditions under which this assembly takes place. That it would say nothing about the peasants' rebellion or about Felix Mantz' recent execution is perhaps wise enough. Yet it does make it difficult to infer (at least from the text itself) what is intended with formulations such as that a "very great offense has been introduced by certain false brethren among us." Under the mentioned historic conditions, this supposed offense seems to be the direct or at least stated inciting incident for this assembly. Yet it is only named obliquely.

---

[1] Yoder calls them a "cover letter" and notes the Articles "circulated most often without [them]." Yoder, *Legacy*, 44, 40n44.

Who are these false brethren? What is the great offense?[2] It seems to be of an ethical nature, as Schleitheim condemns the way "they think faith and love may do and permit everything." Faith in Christ should not take the form of individualistic anything-goes freedom, the text argues. "It does not produce and result in such things as these false brethren and sisters do and teach."

"But you are not that way," the preamble continues, addressing again its intended readers. Those who belong to Christ have "crucified the flesh along with its passions and lusts." Though the intended readers' conscience was too "previously confused," they are now invited to return to the fellowship of the "true implanted members of Christ." To do this, they need to separate from those others ("you understand me well and [know] the brethren whom we mean," the text notes perhaps too confidently), for they are "verkehrt," wrong.

So there seems to be a distinction here: on the one hand, there are "false brethren," whose sense of individualistic freedom is condemned by the text. Then, there are the addressees of the text, who were wrong but might yet return. And third, there are those gathered at Schleitheim. But *even they* have been previously "turned ... aside" by the "devil."

It is perhaps surprising to find here such a reference to the devil, after we had noted in Chapter 2 that the devil seems not to be held responsible for the harmful behavior of congregants. Yet the devil plays a more significant role here: the named false brethren, we read, "do not serve our Father, but their father, the devil." So this is already somewhat confusing. We might expect to find here a simple schema distinguishing those who are right from those who are wrong. But instead we find various groups, each of which has been wrong, but in different ways and with varying effect on their potential participation in the ecclesio-political community Schleitheim is envisioning. The devil plays a role in the irredeemable status of the false brethren but also played a role in the altogether redeemable (indeed already redeemed) error of those assembled in Schleitheim.

The postscript, appearing after the seventh article, begins by noting again that we have just read "the articles of certain brethren who had heretofore been in error," whose disagreement caused confusion in "weaker consciences" and was thus a "slander" to the Name of God. This is why it was so important that they be agreed or indeed united (*vereynigt*) as they are now. Thus the "will of God" has been made known "by us," and it is up to the reader to "achieve [it] perseveringly [*harriglich ... vollnbringen*]."

---

[2] Snyder summarizes that "some scholars conclude that the Articles were directed against other Anabaptists of a more spiritualistic persuasion ... other scholars ... conclude that the Articles were directed against the broader Reformation movement." Snyder himself concludes that it must be understood as internal to the Anabaptist movement, perhaps especially related to the kind of unruly prophetic events around Spirit-oriented female Anabaptist leaders. See Snyder, *Life and Thought*, 137; Snyder, "Birth and Evolution," 594.

Things might look bad for those who fail to do so: the text suggests a dire "recompense" for those who knowingly continue to live in harmful ways. Everything done before or without such knowledge, however, will be forgiven through faithful prayer in assembly, through the blood of Jesus Christ.

The text then again instructs to "keep watch [*habent acht*]" on those who do not "walk according to the simplicity of the divine truth," that is, who do not wish to be part of shared life or community as laid out in the preceding articles, so that "henceforth the entry of false brethren and sisters among us may be prevented."[3] The reader is to separate (*sondert ab*) from what is evil, the text reiterates.

The postscript closes with a reference to Tit. 2:11-14, which instructs "in the present [world] to live lives that are self-controlled, upright, and godly"[4] and to continue to "wait for that blessed hope" and appearance of the glory of Christ, who redeems from "iniquity" [Schleitheim: *Ungerechtigkeit*, injustice] to "purify for himself a people of his own who are zealous for good deeds."

The reader is told to "think on this" but also to "exercise yourselves therein"; in so doing, "the God of peace will be with you."

May the Name of God be hallowed eternally and highly praised, Amen.
May the Lord give you His peace, Amen.
The Acts of Schleitheim on the Margin, on Matthias' [Day], Anno MDXXVII.

Perhaps not much can be said about these words that has not been already said about the articles that make up the core body of the text. It is simply an accompanying introductory and concluding note, stressing the significance of the core text and its intended normative status for all Anabaptist Christians. It implores the reader to take it seriously and makes a few supplementary remarks about truth, sin, and forgiveness.

Yet a few remarks can be made here. For one, from reading this preamble and postscript, it immediately becomes clear that while the agreement of those at the Schleitheim meeting is considered to be enormously important, it is not a consensus document for the broader movement. Those *vereynigt* at the meeting are under no illusion that others will simply come to the same conclusions through a level-headed reading of the biblical text. This is an assertive, combative, indeed antagonistic contribution to a broader

---

[3]We may note here again that even after seven articles, the borders between proper and improper Christians are still not so clearly established. New members remain unpredictable; the possibility of an impurity in the collective body has in any case not yet definitively been excised.

[4]Here cited from the New Revised Standard Version. The NRSV translates the Greek "aioni" as "age," rendered by Schleitheim as "Welt," world. See later.

ecclesio-political debate, suggestive of an understanding of the ecclesio-political as itself the space of a battle between conflicting possibilities of what church could be.⁵

This is not diminished by the way the articles are here given the status of divinely revealed truth. Snyder remarks on the "astounding" confidence of the author in this regard, identifying the articles with "a revelation of the divine will of God" and "the divinely revealed key to the understanding of Scripture."⁶ Yet Snyder also notes that there is something peculiar going on with this truth: its status is attested most significantly not by biblical warrant but by the character or quality of the discourse and ultimately agreement at the meeting. So Snyder points to the repeated use of the term *vereynigt* in this regard: "The clear implication is that the synod at Schleitheim has been acted upon by the Holy Spirit, who ... brought the meeting into unity." This means that "the final authority in questions of biblical interpretation is the community of saints, informed and united by the Holy Spirit."⁷

To put this differently (and perhaps more speculatively), it is not so much that a community so gathered in the shaping of a nonsovereign shared life is right *about* the truth; it *is* "truth." To be *vereinigt* is how truth takes place in the world—indeed *vereinigung* is also used at the beginning of the preamble to signify the reconciling work of Christ. That is, *this is how* the relating and creative Spirit of God most authentically becomes a reality. Truth is not merely constitutive *to* community, nor is community subservient to truth; "truth," here, *is* relationship, it *is* community organized and shaped into sympoetic copresence.⁸ It is almost as Catherine Keller puts it, when she notes the ways truth is understood in Scripture is misunderstood when we approach it as an "absolute" claim, "nonrelative to anything else, *ab*solved of all interdependence, all conditions, all vulnerability, all passion, all change."⁹ Instead it is more like a "resolute" truth as faithfulness, a truth that must become a practice of interdependence, opening up toward "the most elemental truth of all—the delicate interdependence composing the living earth."¹⁰

This is a truth that in any case must be implemented "perseveringly," that must be "exercised," we read. It is not achieved once and for all but takes place in the iterative temporality of repetition. In this light we might also understand the remarkable (near) absence of apocalyptic motifs in this

---

⁵It thus approaches the perspective of Chantal Mouffe (who played a role in Chapter 2) when she writes that the political is essentially "a space of power, conflict and antagonism." See Mouffe, *On the Political*, 9.
⁶Snyder, *Life and Thought*, 166.
⁷Ibid., 167.
⁸As Snyder puts it, "Faith is not so much a matter of 'belief' or [even] 'trust' but rather, faith is even more a matter of practice." Ibid., 157.
⁹Catherine Keller, *On the Mystery: Discerning Divinity in Process* (Minneapolis: Fortress Press, 2007), 16.
¹⁰Keller, *Intercarnations*, 42.

preamble and postscript (and indeed in Schleitheim as a whole). It is limited to a citation from Titus. And even there, the author softens its imminent eschatological expectation. They render the Greek *en toi nun aioni* not as "in this age"—suggestive of an imminent expectation—but as "in this world [*in dieser Welt*]," suggestive of the task of making life amid the difficulties of reality as it is. Outside of this citation, the focus of the text overwhelmingly lies with that task. This is not to say that those present at the Schleitheim gathering might not, in a historical sense, have had lively apocalyptic expectations. But they do not let these short-circuit the task of making community real in the thick present.

Conclusion

Faithful life in catastrophic times cannot be merely individualistic. Nor indeed can it rest in simplistic hope that everything will be alright, that the forces of sovereignty, technological ingenuity, or apocalyptic intervention will turn up to save the day. Instead of hoping for a future, we are to begin where we are, in the thick present, to nurture a sympoetic interdependence. Life in times of crisis calls for community.

In conversation with Schleitheim, we have read of the sober realization that such community does not simply emerge of its own accord. Nor is it ever truly finished. It requires the interminable work of *making* community. This especially requires attention to its fundamental shape and principles: it is not only significant *that* we live together but also *how* we do so. Such questions are not to be put on hold in times of crisis—indeed perhaps such times especially require such communities of refuge, where freedom is a tangible reality.

One temptation particularly besets such community-making work: to shrink the extent of our solidarity to a narrow circle. It is certainly a very common tendency in times of crisis and catastrophe to do this, to widen the distance between us and the others, to seek a life that is made safe from what unfolds around it. In the Schleitheim text, this is embodied in its desire to clearly bind off the church from the outside world. For us, solidarities may instead become restricted to class, nation, or locale—in any case, this tendency is not strange to us and our time.

It is where this tendency is strongest that Schleitheim comes closest to tipping over into the logic of sovereignty it rejects elsewhere. This includes the prominence given to excommunication and, even more, in its sharp condemnation of the outside world. Here it harbors the haunting threat of community conceived as an organic whole, sharply bounded, acting with singular will, and demanding absolute conformity and loyalty—elements that together are deeply reminiscent of the kind of unitary authority of sovereignty. And indeed, in the few generations that followed Schleitheim, the development of Anabaptist congregations into bodies exacting total control over their congregants and demanding absolute obedience from them might point in a similar direction. If God only acts to provoke and invite human action, as I have argued throughout this book, there are no final guarantees against this tendency—it, too, must interminably be negotiated, resisted, and broken up.

This work of resistance finds an unlikely ally in the sheer messiness of creaturely existence. In spite of itself, the Schleitheim text gave witness to the way its own desire toward immunity and isolation was complicated. There appears to be some counteracting force working to undo the contours of dissociative identity. Schleitheim's attempts at a well-defined pure community are troubled at every step of the way, as ever further techniques and regulations are necessary, which, however, produce further ambiguities.

Something insists, a messiness or indeed creaturely relatedness reveals itself as impossible to decisively excise. In spite of the apparent intentions of Schleitheim's authors, this may yet be read as good news. Perhaps even God can be discerned in the way an insistent unruliness subverts and opens up our restricted solidarities into a wider belonging. Indeed, the text itself suggested a similar insight—when read against the grain, an insight certainly won below its immediate surface: that perhaps the distinction between the world outside the church, the "world" as a set of exploitative structures, wider creation, and those things already "united to Christ" was less unambiguous than anticipated.

With the narrowness of that inside-outside script nuanced, other strains of this text and the community it envisions began to appear: most notably, it became readable as seeking not just a different (divine) sovereignty to replace the worldly order but a *nonsovereign community*. In a world marked by crisis, catastrophe, and collapse, such a community forms a space for new beginnings, where a collaborative kind of freedom can become a tangible reality. But a nonsovereign community is also a community without guarantee, and its constitution, regulation, and shaping follows a logic not of finality but of repetition. The form of life it seeks is not inevitable and is never finally achieved.

The text is thus alive with a sense of the fragility and persistent incompleteness of such community: shared life must interminably be made, and remade, negotiated, cared for, regulated, and asserted. This is no less true for our situation today. Many of us may have come to see the realities in which we grew up (political, economic, ecclesial, or otherwise) as inevitable, normal, the way things always will be. But of course this is not the case, and perhaps a stronger sense of their fragility and non-inevitability will be necessary. Spaces of freedom and solidarity and shared good life in this world are never simply a given but require constant care and work to be made real—which also means they are constantly open to their renewal. Repetition, after all, is reinvention.

Schleitheim is further under no illusion that shaping such spaces will be the result of a broad societal consensus. This is perhaps another temptation in times of crisis: instead of narrowing our scope of solidarity, we may find ourselves expecting the broadening of societal agreement. Certainly, these are times to come together; we may hear ourselves saying—are we not all in the same boat? Yet Schleitheim is deeply aware that "we" are certainly not in the same boat. Indeed, what feels as business-as-usual to some will already be felt as catastrophic to others. Crisis and collapse will be differently felt by different groups of creatures, and Schleitheim time and again emphasizes the combative and antagonistic aspects of community-making under such conditions.

But it does not stay with this antagonism. Though the precise relation or delineation between the community and its others is a significant (and in spite of itself complicated) preoccupation of this text, it is ultimately less interested in the overt struggle with that outside world than in how a liberation from it enables the shared life of a community of equals. And so its individual articles each discuss a particular technique or practice by which such shared life is instituted, regulated, and shaped.

We began in Chapter 1 with questions around freedom. Baptism regulates one's entry into the church community, and for Schleitheim, it must be freely chosen. Yet this community seeks to embody not the modern freedom of sovereign individualism but the freedom to make a beginning; the freedom embodied in baptism is not the freedom to decide independently of others but ultimately to act interdependently with others as equal among equals. The beginning marked in baptism does not neatly cut apart before from after, outside from inside, or messy creaturely life (*zoe*) from abstracted renewed life in the resurrection (*kainotes zoes*). Nor indeed does it represent a unilateral action by God or by the human being. Instead it remains a renewal within a relational process of divine-human interaction. For that is how God invites newness: as the invitation toward collaborative renewal. Catastrophe and crisis may limit the freedom to do as one wishes, but shared life in such times does not simply call for the restoration of such a narrow understanding of freedom (nor indeed for a "decisive" response by a sovereign). Instead, Schleitheim seems remarkably aware, it needs especially the care for spaces in which freedom as collaborative self-organization can become a tangible reality.

This also includes the defense of such spaces. The ecclesio-political community, as we read in Chapter 2, must be capable of exerting force. The means Schleitheim suggests to do so—admonition and the ban—may be ambivalent, but they indicate something about the nature of the church: from the start, the text seems aware that shaping shared life is a fragile endeavor. The path its members walk is, it appears, unstable and slippery, and slipping and falling is always possible. Even though it is made up of baptized members who walk in the newness of life, the shared life of the church is constantly in need of shoring up, of repeated discipline and admonition. Yet its persistent unfinishedness does not mean that community, as it here becomes readable, is merely a transient or momentary experience. Quite the opposite. It is exactly its incompleteness in the moment (that is, the way it is *not* the holistic momentary experience of the fullness of community) that points forward into an existence in time. The stability of the community, such as it is, exists by the grace of this iterative motion exemplified here in discipline; it exists and persists by the grace of precisely the incompleteness of each individual iteration.

Such a temporality of repetition stands in sharp contrast to the temporalities of catastrophe and crisis, which appear similarly as decisive rupture and singular dislocation. Sovereignty responds to such partial or complete discontinuity with the (structurally similar) dream of a decisive response. But repetition does not take this over. Even amid great discontinuities, shared life and spaces for freedom and solidarity are never made (nor indeed made safe) in a single stroke. Even amid catastrophic loss, the solution is not that next time, we will win, and definitively so—instead, the response is that there is a next time, and one after that; that this loss, too, will show itself as incomplete and unfinished; not the end, not quite.

And even in such times, there is breaking of bread: creaturely and bodily copresence in the sharing of sustenance. This became the subject of Chapter 3. Even after baptism and discipline, Schleitheim finds that its unity and distinctness remain incomplete, in need of supplementary gathering. Yet even in so gathering around the breaking of bread, the thick copresence or bodily togetherness of this gathering does not tip over into the homogeneity of oneness—the body is an assemblage, exemplified also by the way the "loaf" it becomes is immediately broken, distributed, and dispersed. The community's distinct identity remains in question, and the text goes to some lengths to address ambiguities in membership caused by its previous two articles. Paradoxically, the fellowship gathers not in the presence of Christ but in His memory—that is, His *absence*. And it is this absence from which the call toward collaborative self-organization—that is, toward co*presence*—seems to emerge. God here appears as absence, an absence that seems to create the space and conditions for creaturely action and self-organization. This gathering takes place as a bodily sharing, but it does so with marked disinterest in physical *place*—an ambivalence also taken on in Chapter 4.

Chapter 4 discussed the community's relation to the outside, particularly Schleitheim's instruction that it should be separate from the world and its evil. As a response to collapse and catastrophe (evils indeed), this is perhaps not difficult to understand. Catastrophe rips apart relationship, and Schleitheim here seems to follow that pain into a separation that would insulate the nascent community from a loss that would be, or is, unbearable. Even if (we might add) such separation will also fail to keep the community safe from what is unfolding.

Yet the text goes further, suggesting the whole world *is* catastrophic—while also complicating itself, nuancing a vision of good and evil simplistically mapped onto church and outside world. On closer reading, we found a veritable landscape that is outside the church yet in some way inside God's embrace, an embrace wider and wilder than Christians perhaps tend to imagine. The "world" that must be rejected is, on more precise reading, only a small part of the universe: specifically those structures that bind creaturely freedom and set themselves up as false totalities. To shape community in times of catastrophe requires not cold isolation but the capacity to see this divine relationality and take our place among it, even among its rupture and collapse. This also means the capacity to join God in feeling and mourning the loss of so much *zoe*. A nonsovereign community does not except itself out of that mourning but takes shape in its midst—as a place of refuge: even amid evil, life amid creaturely belonging can be good. In catastrophe and collapse, *a* world is perhaps lost—but not *the* world, certainly not the universe, and a new beginning may yet, insistently, be possible.

As part of its self-organization, a community may entrust some tasks to specific persons. In Chapter 5, we saw how the text envisions pastors to be elected by the community itself, not (say) appointed by a higher ecclesial authority nor indeed imagined as chosen by God directly. It seems to envision the pastor less as a leader than as someone from the community's midst who tends the whole. They care for collective practices and represent the community to the outside world. This is a community that is not an organic *one*; community is an undertaking that does not merely happen or emerge by itself. Its assembly and collective action require work, resources, and organization. But those entrusted with the care for these things remain submerged in the community, and their role is mostly occasional, partial, and clearly delimited. The text does not instruct obedience to authoritarian figures—certainly a common response to crisis and catastrophe—but embodies care for organization and process. This is not only a question of democratic sensibilities, we might note: it also makes the community resilient in times when reliance on individual leadership figures would make it especially vulnerable to persecution.

The break with the logic of sovereignty runs through Schleitheim as a whole. It is discussed more directly as a political relation in Chapter 6. Schleitheim both recognizes and rejects what it calls the order of the "sword," which seems to refer to a kind of authority rooted in the capacity to distinguish between lives worthy of protection and those worthy of death. The text shows an acute sense of its ambivalence. The sword of sovereignty is defined both by its capacity for destruction and by its capacity to nurture and create spaces for human flourishing. In spite of its limited legitimacy, such a rule is ultimately incompatible with the type of order the church is called to embody. In emulation of Jesus, who rejects the position of political authority, the church is called to be a community where we can unlearn obedience and unlearn our imagination of God as a sovereign master. Yet the relation between the ecclesio-political community and the way the world around it is governed is underdetermined: different kinds of relationship between the sword and non-sword orders remain possible, giving rise to interminable negotiation.

God here appears as a force at home in such contradictions, one whose call or command appears wholly different to different collectivities: as sovereign lawgiver to some, as a nonsovereign Messiah to others. This also means God's relationality may be present (if ambivalently so) where the faithful least expect it. In times of crisis and catastrophe, we may here find ourselves encouraged—Chapter 4 notwithstanding—to build wide alliances. Sovereign structures may yet have a role to play in God's wish for this planet. The incompatibilities this produces are not finally resolved.

Finally, Chapter 7 discussed a more metaphysical aspect of Schleitheim's rejection of sovereignty that became apparent in its rejection of oath-swearing. In oath-swearing, God is called upon to guarantee a statement or promise through the distinction between blessing and curse (oath and perjury, truth and lie, inside and outside). Schleitheim reads it fundamentally as a claim of mastery, an attempt to bring the world under the dominion of one's words with divine guarantee. As such a practice, it grounds the sovereign dominion of some human beings over others. Schleitheim instead argues that the relation between words, things, God, and human beings structurally does not allow for such guarantees: the place of power remains empty; it is not in our capacity to fulfill what we swear. Instead of such guaranteed words, human community takes place in the logic of repetition, embodied in the closing lines: let your words be yes, *yes*, no, *no*.

God does not make Godself available for grounding relations of dominion of some creatures over others, instead appearing as one who calls into a particular way of being-with in time. In this way, the rejection of oath-swearing is not just one historical case of political nonparticipation but encapsulates the entirety of Schleitheim's project: a nonsovereign community of equals whose shared life takes shape in repeated practice and whose relation to the wider world is not fixed in dominion. In times of crisis and catastrophe, it may perhaps implore us to be wary of whatever and whoever promises certainty and guarantees; instead, to embrace the ambiguity of life amid unruly *zoe*. Indeed it is especially the experience of rupture in catastrophe and collapse that should make us wary of the proud confidence of sovereignty and of worldly structures of exploitation: they, too, cannot fulfill what they promise.

In Chapter 2, I cited Ernst Bloch's depiction of Christianity as either defined from a past, to which it strives to be loyal, or from a future, from which it expects the dissolution of what is for the sake of what may be. The enduring relevance of Schleitheim for our time, and for the crises and catastrophes that we may yet experience in the middle half of the twenty-first century, seems to me to consist of the way it resists both poles of this schema. It encourages us to build community in a way that neither merely harkens back to an origin nor merely expects a better future—but that begins, where it is, in a thick copresence.

CONCLUSION

In beginning again in catastrophic times, such community-making may yet find itself accompanied by the kind and encouraging voice from God, inviting into *sympoiesis* and renewal. But this voice will not be an overwhelming presence. It will not take place in the registers of sovereign rule nor indeed of apocalypse. Instead, we may learn to find it in the very forces of creaturely messiness that seem to undo and trouble the narrowing of our solidarities—in what opens up, widens, and sets loose renewed relationship to wider *zoe*. And it may point us to where another beginning remains possible—even now.

Appendix: The Schleitheim Confession

Preamble

BROTHERLY UNION [*vereinigung*] OF A NUMBER OF CHILDREN OF GOD CONCERNING SEVEN ARTICLES

May[1] joy, peace, and mercy from our Father through the union [*vereinigung*] of the blood of Christ Jesus, together with the gifts of the Spirit—who is sent from the Father for the strength and comfort and perseverance of all believers in all tribulation until the end, Amen—be to all lovers of God and children of light, who are scattered everywhere, where they are ordained [*verordnet*] by God our Father, where they are with one mind assembled together in one God and Father of us all: Grace and peace of heart be with you all, Amen.

Dear brothers and sisters in the Lord: first and supremely we are always concerned for your consolation and the assurance of your conscience, which was previously confused, so that you may not always remain foreigners to us and by right almost completely excluded but that you may turn again to the true implanted members of Christ, who have been armed through patience and knowledge of themselves, and have therefore again been united with us in the strength of a godly Christian spirit and commitment [*eifer*] for God.

It is also apparent with what cunning the devil has turned us aside[2] so that he might destroy and bring to an end the work of God which in mercy and grace has been partly begun in us. But Christ, the faithful Shepherd of our souls, Who has begun this in us, will certainly direct and teach it til the end, to His honor and our salvation [*heil*], Amen.

Dear brothers and sisters, we who have been assembled in the Lord at

---

[1] This translation primarily follows the translation provided by John C. Wenger. See Wenger, "Schleitheim."

It is supplemented and amended where appropriate, drawing on the later 1550 print version held by the Mennonite Historical Library at Goshen College and made available through the Schleitheimertal Museum: see Michael Sattler, *Brüderlich Vereinigung Ezlicher Kinder Gottes: Sieben Artikel Betreffend* (publisher not identified, 1550), https://www.e-rara.ch/zuz/content/titleinfo/17792168.

Other renderings consulted include that by John Howard Yoder and Heinold Fast; see Yoder, *Legacy*, 39–45; Sattler, "Brüderliche Vereinigung."

A comparison between different manuscripts and print versions (which differ minimally) is not the purpose of the present study.

[2] Fast translates "*hintergangen*," suggesting that the devil had not turned the authors away from the right path so much as snuck by them to turn away the others. See Sattler, "Brüderliche Vereinigung," 61.

Schleitheim on the Margin [*Schlaten am Randen*][3] make known in points and articles to all who love God that we have been united as concerns us to abide in the Lord as God's obedient children and sons and daughters, who are and shall [*sollen*] be separated from the world in everything, and—to God alone be praise and glory without the contradiction of any brothers—fully at peace.[4] In this we have perceived the oneness of our Father and of our common Christ, and their Spirit was with us. For the Lord is the Lord of peace and not of quarreling, as Paul points out. That you may understand in what articles this has been formulated you should observe and note [the following].

A great offense has been introduced by certain false brothers among us so that some have turned aside from the faith, while they intended to practice and observe the freedom of the Spirit and of Christ, but have missed the truth and (to their judgment) are given over to the lustfulness [*geylheyt*] and freedom [*freyheyt*] of the flesh. They think faith and love may do and permit everything, and nothing will harm them nor condemn them since they are believers.

Observe, you who are God's members in Christ Jesus, that faith in the Heavenly Father through Jesus Christ does not take such form. It does not produce and result in such things as these false brothers and sisters do and teach. Guard yourselves and be warned of such people, for they do not serve our Father but their father, the devil.

But you are not that way. For they that are Christ's have crucified their flesh with its lusts and desires. You understand me well and [know] the brothers whom we mean. Separate yourselves from them for they are wrong. Petition the Lord that they may have the knowledge which leads to repentance and [pray] for us that we may have stability to persist in the way which we have begun, for the honor of God and of Christ, His Son, Amen.

The articles which we discussed and on which we were united are these: (1) baptism; (2) ban; (3) breaking of bread; (4) separation from abominations; (5) shepherds in the community [*gemeyn*]; (6) sword; and (7) oath.

One

First observe concerning baptism: baptism shall be given to all those who have been taught [*gelernt seind*] repentance and amendment of life, and who believe truly [*in der warheit*] that their sins are taken away through Christ, and to all those who wish to walk in the resurrection of Jesus

---

[3]The town of Schleitheim is in a border territory of the Swiss confederation, so on the "border" or margin, as Wenger translates. It is, however, also (as Yoder also notes) located near a small mountain range named the *Randen*, which in turn seems to derive its name from its steep slopes framing a high plateau.

[4]Fast renders this a separate sentence: "God alone be praise and worship, that it took place without the contradiction of any brother and to complete contentedness." See Sattler, "Brüderliche Vereinigung," 61.

Christ, [and wish to be buried with Him in death][5] so that they may be resurrected with Him, and to all those who with this significance request it [baptism] of us and demand it through themselves [*durch sich selbs*]. This excludes all children's baptism, the highest and first abomination of the Pope. In this you have the ground and testimony of Scripture and the practice of the Apostles. Matthew 27, Mark 16, Acts 2, 8, 16, 19. This we wish to hold simply, yet firmly and with assurance.

Two

Second we are agreed [*vereiniget*][6] as follows on the ban: the ban shall be employed with all those who have given themselves to the Lord, to follow [*nachzuwandeln*] in His commandments, and with all those who are baptized into one body of Christ and who are called brothers or sisters, and yet who slip sometimes and fall into sin [*fallen in ein fal und sünd*],[7] being inadvertently overtaken. The same shall be admonished twice in secret and the third time openly disciplined or banned according to the command of Christ in front of the whole community [*gemeyn*]. Matthew 18. But this shall be done according to the regulation of the Spirit before the breaking of bread, so that we may break and eat one bread, with one mind and in one love, and may drink of one cup.

Three

Third, in the breaking of bread we have become one [*eynes worden*] and agreed: all those who wish to break one bread in remembrance of the broken body of Christ, and all who wish to drink of one drink in remembrance of the shed blood of Christ, shall be united [*vereiniget*] beforehand in one body of Christ, that is into the community [*gemeine*] of God whose Head is Christ, which is to say by baptism. For as Paul points out, we cannot at the same time partake of the Lord's table and the table of devils; we cannot at the same time drink the cup of the Lord and the cup of the devil. That is, all those who have fellowship with the dead works of darkness have no part in the light, and all who follow the devil and the world have no part with those who are called unto God out of the world. All who lie in evil have no part in the good.

Therefore it shall and must be [*sol und mus seyn*]: whoever has not been called by one God to one faith, to one baptism, to one Spirit, to one body, with all the children of God's

---

[5]Wenger adds this passage, which is removed in the print edition on which I am drawing. It is also included by Yoder and Fast.
[6]The word here and in similar instances below is *vereiniget* (or *vereynigt*), which means more than simple agreement but something like being united. It is the same word used in the title (*vereinigung*) rendered as "union." For the spiritual significance of this unification or agreement, see Excursus.
[7]The German of the print version is literally "into a falling and sin." Wenger, Yoder, and Fast translate "sin and error" (or v.v.) based on other manuscripts.

community, cannot be made into one loaf [*ein Brot*] with them,[8] as indeed must be done if one is to break bread in truth, according to the command of Christ.

Four

Fourth we are agreed on separation. [it] shall take place from the evil[9] and from the wickedness which the devil planted in the world, thus: simply that we shall not have fellowship with them and not run with them in the multitude of their abominations. This is the way it is: since all who have not stepped into the obedience of faith, and have not united [*vereynigt*] themselves with God so that they wish to do His will, are a great abomination before God, it is not possible for anything to grow or spring from them except abominable things. For there is nothing other in all creation than good and evil, faithful and unfaithful, darkness and light, world, and those [who have come] out of the world, God's temple and idols, Christ and Belial, and none can have part with the other.

To us then the command of the Lord is also clear when He calls upon us to be and become separate from the evil; thus He will be our God, and we shall be His sons and daughters.

He further admonishes us to go out from Babylon and the earthly Egypt that we may not become part of the pain and suffering which the Lord will bring upon them. From all this we should learn that everything that is not united with our God, and Christ is nothing other than an abomination that we should shun and flee from. By this is meant all popish and antipopish works[10] and church services, meetings and church attendance,[11] drinking houses, guarantees and commitments [of] unbelief,[12] and other things of

---

[8]Wenger translates this as "one bread," which has the advantage of sounding less odd. Since bread is an uncountable noun in English, however, this elides the connotation of a single thing, body, or unity, instead suggesting being of one kind or one material. "Loaf" is thus preferable, as Yoder also translates.

[9]Fast renders it "*von den Bösen*" (plural), so from the evil ones. See Sattler, "Brüderliche Vereinigung," 64.

[10]Snyder and Yoder both translate "repopish," taking the *wider* in *widerbepstlich* (Fast: "*widerpäpstlich*") as *wieder*, again, not *wider*, against. Yoder comments this is "supported by Zwingli's translation" and makes the point that "new Protestant churches are at some points copies of what was wrong with Catholicism," which he argues was widespread in Anabaptist circles at the time. See Snyder, *Life and Thought*, 263n16; Sattler, "Brüderliche Vereinigung," 64; Yoder, *Legacy*, 41, 41n61.

[11]Possibly the first of these three is not best rendered *Gottesdienste*, church service (as the print edition has it), but *Götzendienst*, idolatry, as some manuscripts suggest. See Yoder, *Legacy*, 41n62. Fast renders it all as popish and antipopish *Werke und Gottesdienste, Versammlungen, Kirchenbesuche*, which seems plausible, given that indeed not all gatherings are church services, and not all visits to a church are in the framework of a gathering or service (we might imagine individual prayers at a shrine or pilgrimages). Sattler, "Brüderliche Vereinigung," 64–5.

[12]In the print edition, this is rendered *Burgerschafften und verpflichtung des unglaubens*. *Bürgerschaft* means citizenship, which would suggest Schleitheim means participation in public political and legal life. This seems odd since such participation is treated at length in Article VI. Yoder notes this might in fact be (as it is in one manuscript) *Bürgschaft*, so a kind of "guarantee

that kind, which the world regards highly and yet are carried on in flat contradiction to the command of God in accordance with all the injustice which is in the world. From all these things we shall be separated and have no part with them for they are vain abomination, which will make us hated before our Christ Jesus, who has set us free from the servitude of the flesh [*entledigt hat von der dienstbarkeit des Fleisches*] and fitted us for the service of God through the Spirit which He has given us.

Therefore there will also unquestionably fall from us the unchristian, devilish weapons of violence—such as sword, armor and the like, and all their use [either] for friends or against enemies—by virtue of the word of Christ, resist not evil.

Five

Fifth we are agreed as follows on pastors in the community[13] of God: the pastor in the community of God shall, as Paul has prescribed, be one who out-and-out has a good report of those who are outside the faith. This office shall be to read, to admonish and teach, to warn, to discipline, to ban in the community, to lead out in prayer for the advancement of all the brothers and sisters, to begin to break the bread,[14] and in all things see to the care of the body of Christ, in order that it may be built up and improved and the mouth of the slanderer be stuffed.

This one moreover shall be supported of the church which has elected him, wherein he may be in need, so that he who serves the Gospel may live of the Gospel as the Lord has ordained. But if a pastor should do something requiring discipline, he shall not be dealt with except with two or three witnesses. And when they sin, they shall be disciplined before all in order that the others may fear.

But should it happen that this shepherd be displaced or through the cross led to the Lord [i.e. be martyred] another shall be ordained in place in the same hour so that

---

or security supporting a promise," which would mean this refers to "such matters as signing notes and mortgages and affidavits in less than good faith." Alternatively, it might refer to guilds or social clubs. Fast renders it broadly as *Bündnisse und Verträge des Unglaubens*, so "alliances and contracts of unbelief." *Bündnis*, however, can also refer to something stronger than an alliance, like a coalition, confederation, or pact. See Yoder, *Legacy*, 41n64; Sattler, "Brüderliche Vereinigung," 65.

Though the Fast/Yoder rendering thus seems plausible, their interpretation that it therefore refers to specifically *economic* contracts is less than clear; Wenger suggests "commitments [made in] unbelief" might well refer to such things as Sattler's own vow of celibacy. See Wenger, "Schleitheim," 249n28.

[13] Wenger translates "*gemein*" consistently as "church," but its meaning in early new High German is broader, referring to community or indeed common (*gemein*) life more generally. Snyder and Yoder render it variously as "church" or "congregation"; for Fast, it is always "*Gemeinde*."

[14] Wenger translates *anheben* as "to lift up" the bread, but in early new High German, its meaning is simply to begin. This word also appears in the preamble, where God has "begun" [*angehebt*] His work in the believers.

APPENDIX

God's little people and flock may not be destroyed.[15]

Six

Sixth we are agreed as follows concerning the sword: the sword is ordained of God [*ein Gottesordnung*] outside the perfection of Christ, which punishes and kills the wicked and guards and protects the good. In the Law the sword was ordained for the punishment of the wicked and for their death, and the same [sword] is [now] ordained to be used by the worldly magistrates.

In the perfection of Christ, however, only the ban is used for a warning and exclusion of the one who has sinned, without putting the flesh to death, merely the warning and the command to sin no more.

Now it will be asked by many who do not recognize [this as] the will of Christ whether a Christian may or should employ the sword against the wicked for the defense and protection of the good or for the sake of love.

Reply is unanimously revealed as follows: Christ teaches and commands us to learn of Him, for He is meek and lowly in heart, and so shall we find rest to our souls. Thus Christ says to the heathenish woman who was caught in adultery, not that one should stone her according to the law of His Father (and yet He says, as the Father has commanded me, thus I do), but in mercy and forgiveness and warning to sin no more, spoke, go and sin no more. Such [an attitude] we also ought to take completely according to the rule of the ban.

Secondly, it will be asked concerning the sword, whether a Christian shall pass judgment in worldly dispute and strife such as unbelievers have with one another. This is the united reply: Christ did not wish to decide or pass judgment between brothers in the case of the inheritance but refused to do so. Therefore we should do likewise.

Thirdly, it will be asked concerning the sword, shall one be a magistrate if one should be elected as such? The reply is as follows: they wished to make Christ king, but He fled and did not view it as the arrangement of His Father.[16] Thus shall we do as He did, and follow Him, and so shall we not walk in darkness. For He Himself says, He who wishes to come after me, let him deny himself and take up his cross and follow me. Also, He Himself forbids the authority of the sword saying, the worldly princes lord it over them, etc., but not so shall it be with you.

Further, Paul says, whom God did foreknow He also instructed to be conformed to the image of His Son, and so on. Also Peter says, Christ

---

[15]Yoder and Fast add: "but be preserved by warning and be consoled" (Yoder), "*sondern durch die Mahnung erhalten und getröstet wird*" (Fast). See Yoder, *Legacy*, 42; Sattler, "Brüderliche Vereinigung," 66.
[16]Fast renders it "*hat die Ordnung seines Vaters nicht berücksichtigt*," so something like "did not consider what his Father ordained."

has suffered, not ruled, and left us an example, that you should follow His steps.

Finally it will be observed that it is not appropriate for a Christian to serve as a magistrate because of these points: the government order [*regiment*] is according to the flesh, but the Christians' is according to the Spirit; their houses and dwelling are bodily in this world, but the Christians' are in heaven; their citizenship is in this world, but the Christians' citizenship is in heaven; the weapons of their conflict and war are carnal and against the flesh only, but the Christians' weapons are spiritual, against the fortification of the devil. The worldlings are armed with steel and iron, but the Christians are armed with the armor of God, with truth, justice, peace, faith, salvation, and the Word of God. In sum, as is the mind of Christ toward us, so shall the mind of the members of the body of Christ be through Him in all things, that there may be no split in the body through which it would be destroyed. For every kingdom divided against itself will be destroyed.

Now since Christ is as it is written of Him, His members must also be the same, that His body may remain whole and united to its own improvement and upbuilding.

Seven

Seventh we are agreed as follows concerning the oath: the oath is a confirmation among those who are quarreling or making promises. In the Law it is commanded to be performed in God's Name, but only in truth, not falsely. Christ, who teaches the perfection of the Law, prohibits all swearing to His [followers], whether true or false—neither by heaven, nor by the earth, nor by Jerusalem, nor by our head—and that for the reason which He shortly thereafter gives, for you are not able to make one hair white or black. So you see it is for this reason that all swearing is forbidden: we cannot fulfill [*erstatten*][17] that which we promise when we swear, for we cannot change [even] the very least thing on us.

Now there are some who do not give credence to the simple command of God but object with this question: well now, did not God swear to Abraham by Himself [*durch sich selbs*], since He was God (when He promised him that He would be with him and that He would be his God if he would keep His commandments), why then should I not also swear when I promise to someone? Reply: hear what the Scripture says: God, since He wished more abundantly to show unto the heirs the steadfastness of His counsel, inserted an oath that by two steadfast things (in which it is impossible for God to lie) we might have a strong consolation. Observe the meaning of this Scripture: what God forbids you to do, He has power to do, for everything is possible for Him. God swore an oath to Abraham, says the Scripture, so that He might show

---

[17] Fast: "*garantieren*," guarantee.

that His counsel is steadfast. That is, no one can withstand nor thwart His will; therefore He can keep His oath. But we can do nothing, as is said above by Christ, to keep or perform [our oaths]: therefore we shall swear nothing.

Then others further say as follows: it is not forbidden of God to swear in the New Testament, when it is actually commanded in the Old, but it is forbidden only to swear by heaven, earth, Jerusalem, and our head. Reply: hear the Scripture, He who swears by heaven swears by God's throne and by Him who sits on it. Observe: it is forbidden to swear by heaven, which is only the throne of God: how much more is it forbidden [to swear] by God Himself? You fools and blind, which is greater, the throne or the one sitting on it?

Further some say, because evil is now [in the world, and] because man needs God for [the establishment of] the truth, so did the apostles Peter and Paul also swear. Reply: Peter and Paul only testify of that which God promised to Abraham with the oath. They themselves promise nothing, as the example indicates clearly. Testifying and swearing are two different things. For when one swears one is in the first place promising future things, as Christ was promised to Abraham whom we a long time afterwards received. But when one testifies, one is testifying about the present, whether it is good or evil, as Simeon spoke to Mary about Christ and testified, behold this [child] is set for the fall and rising of many in Israel, and for a sign which shall be spoken against.

Christ also taught us along the same line when He said, let your speech be yes, yes; and no, no; for whatsoever is more than these comes of evil. He says, your speech or word shall be yes and no. One cannot understand this to mean that he would have permitted the opinion [that swearing is in order].[18] Christ is simply yes and no, and all those who seek Him simply will understand His Word. Amen.

Postscript

Dear brothers and sisters in the Lord: hese are the articles of certain brothers who had heretofore been in error and who had failed to understand the true reason [*den waren verstand*], so that many weaker consciences were confused, causing the Name of God to be greatly slandered. Therefore there has been a great need for us to become of one mind in the Lord, which has come to pass. To God be praise and glory!

---

[18]The German is not immediately clear here, literally reading something like "which the people [*man*] would [*wölle*] not understand so he permitted the opinion." Fast's rendering seems most plausible to me: "*was man nicht so verstehen kann, als ob er den Eid zugelassen habe*" ("which one cannot take to mean that he would have permitted the oath").

Wenger retains the mystery of the original, translating: "[however] when one does not wish to understand, he remains closed to the meaning." Yoder renders it "so that no one might understand that He had permitted it." See Sattler, "Brüderliche Vereinigung," 70; Wenger, "Schleitheim," 252; Yoder, *Legacy*, 44.

Now since you have so well understood the will of God which has been made known by [durch] us, it will be necessary for you to achieve perseveringly, without interruption [harriglich unabgewelzt vollnbringen], the known will of God. For you know well what the servant who sinned knowingly is due as his recompense.

Everything which you have unwittingly done and confessed as unjust doing is forgiven you through the faithful prayer which is offered by us in our meeting for all our shortcomings and guilt. [This state is yours] through the gracious forgiveness of God and through the blood of Jesus Christ. Amen.

Keep watch on all who do not walk according to the simplicity of the divine truth which is stated in this letter from us in our meeting, so that everyone among us will be governed by the rule of the ban and henceforth the entry of false brothers and sisters among us may be prevented.

Separate from you that which is evil and the Lord will be your God, and you will be His sons and daughters. Dear brothers, keep in mind what Paul admonishes his Titus. He says thus, the grace of God has appeared, bringing salvation to all, training us to renounce impiety and worldly passions, and in the present world to live lives that are self-controlled, upright, and godly, while we wait for the blessed hope and the manifestation of the glory of our great God and Savior, Jesus Christ. He it is who gave himself for us that he might redeem us from all iniquity [Ungerechtigkeit] and purify for himself a people of his own who are zealous [eiffrig] for good deeds.

Think on this and exercise yourselves therein and the God of peace will be with you.

May the Name of God be hallowed eternally and highly praised, Amen. May the Lord give you His peace, Amen.

The Acts of Schleitheim on the Margin, on Matthias' [Day], Anno MDXXVII.

BIBLIOGRAPHY

Agamben, Giorgio. *The Highest Poverty: Monastic Rules and Form-of-Life*. Stanford: Stanford University Press, 2013.
Agamben, Giorgio. *Homo Sacer: Sovereign Power and Bare Life*. Stanford: Stanford University Press, 1998.
Agamben, Giorgio. *The Sacrament of Language: An Archaeology of the Oath*. Stanford: Stanford University Press, 2010.
Alizart, Mark. *The Climate Coup*. Cambridge: Polity Press, 2021.
Arendt, Hannah. *Between Past and Future: Six Exercises in Political Thought*. New York: Viking Press, 1961.
Arendt, Hannah. *The Human Condition*. Chicago: University of Chicago Press, 2018.
Arendt, Hannah. *On Revolution*. London: Penguin Classic, 2006.
Arendt, Hannah. *The Origins of Totalitarianism*. San Diego: Harvest Books, 1973.
Armour, Ellen T., and Susan M. St. Ville. "Judith Butler—in Theory." In *Bodily Citations: Religion and Judith Butler*, edited by Ellen T. Armour and Susan M. St. Ville, 1–14. New York: Columbia University Press, 2006.
Bender, Harold. "The Anabaptist Vision." *American Society of Church History* 13 (1944): 3–24.
Benjamin, Walter. *The Arcades Project*. Edited by Rolf Tiedemann. Cambridge, MA: Harvard University Press, 2002.
Benjamin, Walter. *Illuminations: Essays and Reflections*. Edited by Hannah Arendt. New York: Schocken Books, 2007.
Benveniste, Émile. *Dictionary of Indo-European Concepts and Society*. Chicago: Hau Books, 2016.
Betz, Johannes. "Eucharistie." In *Herders Theologisches Taschenlexikon*, edited by Karl Rahner, 2:226–41. Freiburg: Herder, 1972.
Biesecker-Mast, Gerald. *Separation and the Sword in Anabaptist Persuasion*. Telford: Cascadia, 2006.
Bloch, Ernst. *Thomas Münzer Als Theologe Der Revolution*. Frankfurt am Main: Suhrkamp, 1976.
Burgess, John P. "Baptism." In *The Cambridge Dictionary of Christian Theology*, edited by Ian A. McFarland, David A. S. Fergusson, Karen Kilby, and Iain R. Torrance, 52–4. Cambridge: Cambridge University Press, 2011.
Burkholder, John Richard. "Historic Nonresistance." In *Mennonite Peace Theology: A Panorama of Types*, edited by John Richard Burkholder and Barbara Nelson Gingerich, 11–18. Elkhart: AMBS/IMS, 2024.
Butler, Judith. *The Force of Nonviolence: An Ethico-Political Bind*. London: Verso, 2020.
Butler, Judith. *Undoing Gender*. London: Routledge, 2004.

Caputo, John D. *The Insistence of God: A Theology of Perhaps*. Bloomington: Indiana University Press, 2013.

Caputo, John D. *Radical Hermeneutics: Repetition, Deconstruction, and the Hermeneutic Project*. Bloomington: Indiana University Press, 1987.

Catlin, Jonathon. "Toward an Interdisciplinary Conceptual History of Catastrophe." *EuropeNow*, 2022. https://www.europenowjournal.org/2022/01/30/toward-an-interdisciplinary-conceptual-history-of-catastrophe/ (accessed June 13, 2025).

Coogan, Michael D., Marc Z. Brettler, Carol A. Newsom, and Pheme Perkins, eds. *The New Oxford Annotated Bible: New Revised Standard Version with the Apocrypha: An Ecumenical Study Bible*. Fully revised fourth edition. Oxford: Oxford University Press, 2010.

Dickinson, Colby, and Adam Kotsko. *Agamben's Coming Philosophy: Finding a New Use for Theology*. London: Rowman & Littlefield, 2015.

Driedger, Michael. "Anabaptists and the Early Modern State: A Long-Term View." In *A Companion to Anabaptism and Spiritualism, 1521–1700*, edited by John D. Roth and James M. Stayer, 507–44. Leiden: Brill, 2007.

Finger, Thomas N. *A Contemporary Anabaptist Theology: Biblical, Historical, Constructive*. Downers Grove: InterVarsity Press, 2004.

Foucault, Michel. *The Government of the Living: Lectures at the Collège de France, 1979–1980*. New York: Palgrave Macmillan, 2014.

Foucault, Michel. *The History of Sexuality: Volume 1, an Introduction*. New York: Pantheon, 1978.

Goossen, Rachel Waltner. "'Defanging the Beast': Mennonite Responses to John Howard Yoder's Sexual Abuse." *Mennonite Quarterly Review* 89 (January 2015): 7–80.

Gregory, Brad S. "The Radical Reformation." In *The Oxford History of the Reformation*, edited by Peter Marshall, 144–90. Oxford: Oxford University Press, 2022.

greig, jason. "No Exceptions: Baptism beyond Exclusion." *Vision: A Journal for Church and Theology* 25, no. 2 (2024): 82–90.

Haraway, Donna. *Staying with the Trouble: Making Kin in the Chthulucene*. Durham: Duke University Press, 2016.

Hardt, Michael, and Antonio Negri. *Assembly*. Oxford: Oxford University Press, 2017.

Hauerwas, Stanley. *The Hauerwas Reader*, edited by John Berkman and Michael Cartwright. Durham: Duke University Press, 2001.

Heinzekehr, Justin. *The Absent Christ: An Anabaptist Theology of the Empty Tomb*. Telford: Cascadia, 2019.

Hoogstraten, Marius van. "The Anabaptist Moment: Improper Beginnings, Ecclesiopolitical Decisions, and a Nonviolent Sovereignty." *Mennonite Quarterly Review* 95 (October 2021): 495–512.

Hoogstraten, Marius van. "Das Reich Gottes Als Ver- Und Entortung: Mennonitisches Denken in Der Krise." In *Die Reich-Gottes-Botschaft in Theologie Und Politik: Jahrbuch Friedenstheologie 2023*, edited by Matthias-W. Engelke, Stefan Federbusch, Gottfried Orth, Michael Schober, and Stefan Silber, 19–30. Norderstedt: Oekumenisches Institut für Friedenstheologie, 2023.

Hoogstraten, Marius van. "Doperse Biomacht: Balthasar Hubmaier, de Tucht En de Ban." *Doopsgezinde Bijdragen* 48 (2022): 13–30.

Hoogstraten, Marius van. *Theopoetics and Religious Difference: The Unruliness of the Interreligious. A Dialogue with Richard Kearney, John D. Caputo, and Catherine Keller*. Tübingen: Mohr Siebeck, 2020.

Hoogstraten, Marius van. "Unlearning Obedience: The Ecclesiopolitical Critique of the 'Sword' in the Schleitheim Articles." *Conrad Grebel Review* 41, no. 2 (2025): 115–36.

Hoogstraten, Marius van. "Without Sovereign Guarantee: Reading Schleitheim on the Oath with Giorgio Agamben." *Mennonite Quarterly Review* 97 (2023): 367–82.

Hubmaier, Balthasar. "A Simple Instruction." In *Balthasar Hubmaier: Theologian of Anabaptism*, edited by H. Wayne Pipkin and John H. Yoder, 314–38. Classics of the Radical Reformation. Walden: Plough, 2019.

Hubmaier, Balthasar. "On Fraternal Admonition." In *Balthasar Hubmaier: Theologian of Anabaptism*, edited by H. Wayne Pipkin and John H. Yoder, 372–85. Classics of the Radical Reformation. Walden: Plough, 2019.

Hubmaier, Balthasar. "On the Christian Ban." In *Balthasar Hubmaier: Theologian of Anabaptism*, edited by H. Wayne Pipkin and John H. Yoder, 409–25. Classics of the Radical Reformation. Walden: Plough, 2019.

IPCC. "*Summary for Policymakers.*" In Climate Change 2023: Synthesis Report. Contribution of Working Groups I, II and III to the Sixth Assessment Report of the Intergovernmental Panel on Climate Change, edited by Hoesung Lee and José Romero, 1–34. Geneva: IPCC, 2023.

Kearney, Richard. *Anatheism: Returning to God after God*. New York: Columbia University Press, 2011.

Kearney, Richard. *Postnationalist Ireland: Politics, Culture, Philosophy*. London: Routledge, 1997.

Keller, Catherine. *Apocalypse Now and Then: A Feminist Guide to the End of the World*. Boston: Beacon Press, 1996.

Keller, Catherine. *Cloud of the Impossible: Negative Theology and Planetary Entanglement*. New York: Columbia University Press, 2015.

Keller, Catherine. *Face of the Deep: A Theology of Becoming*. London: Routledge, 2003.

Keller, Catherine. *Intercarnations*. New York: Fordham University Press, 2017.

Keller, Catherine. *On the Mystery: Discerning Divinity in Process*. Minneapolis: Fortress Press, 2007.

Keller, Catherine. *Political Theology of the Earth: Our Planetary Emergency and the Struggle for a New Public*. New York: Columbia University Press, 2018.

King, Richard. *Orientalism and Religion: Post-Colonial Theory, India and the Mystic East*. London: Routledge, 1999.

Koontz, Gayle Gerber. "Ecclesiology, Authority, and Ministry: An Anabaptist-Mennonite Perspective." In *The Heart of the Matter: Pastoral Ministry in Anabaptist Perspective*, edited by Erick Sawatzky, 60–73. Telford: Cascadia, 2004.

Kotsko, Adam. "What Happened to Giorgio Agamben?" *Slate*, 2022. https://slate.com/human-interest/2022/02/giorgio-agamben-covid-holocaust-comparison-right-wing-protest.html (accessed June 13, 2025).

Latour, Bruno, and Dipesh Chakrabarty. "Conflicts of Planetary Proportion—a Conversation." *Journal of the Philosophy of History* 14, no. 3 (2020): 419–54.

Lefort, Claude. *Democracy and Political Theory*. Cambridge: Polity Press, 1988.

Leu, Urs B., and Christian Scheidegger, eds. *Das Schleitheimer Bekenntnis 1527*. Zug: Achius, 2004.

Malm, Andreas. *How to Blow up a Pipeline: Learning to Fight in a World on Fire*. London: Verso, 2021.

Marchart, Oliver. *Post-Foundational Political Thought: Political Difference in Nancy, Lefort, Badiou and Laclau*. Edinburgh: Edinburgh University Press, 2007.

Marshall, Peter, ed. *The Oxford History of the Reformation*. Oxford: Oxford University Press, 2022.

Mbembe, Achille. "Necropolitics." In *Biopolitics: A Reader*, edited by Timothy Campbell and Adam Sitze, 161–92. Durham: Duke University Press, 2013.

Mennonite Church Canada, and Mennonite Church U.S.A. *Confession of Faith in a Mennonite Perspective*, 1995. https://www.mennoniteusa.org/wp-content/uploads/2024/02/Confession-of-Faith-In-a-Mennonite-Perspective.pdf (accessed June 13, 2025).

Mouffe, Chantal. *On the Political*. New York: Routledge, 2005.

Müller, Tadzio. *Zwischen Friedlicher Sabotage Und Kollaps. Wie Ich Lernte, Die Zukunft Wieder Zu Lieben*. Wien: Mandelbaum, 2024.

Murray, Stuart. *Biblical Interpretation in the Anabaptist Tradition*. Thunder Bay: Pandora Press, 2000.

Myers, Ched, ed. *Watershed Discipleship: Reinhabiting Bioregional Faith and Practice*. Eugene: Cascade, 2016.

Neiman, Susan. *Evil in Modern Thought: An Alternative History of Philosophy*. Princeton: Princeton University Press, 2015.

O'Connell, Mark. "Why Silicon Valley Billionaires Are Prepping for the Apocalypse in New Zealand." *The Guardian*, February 15, 2018. https://www.theguardian.com/news/2018/feb/15/why-silicon-valley-billionaires-are-prepping-for-the-apocalypse-in-new-zealand (accessed June 13, 2025).

Ollenburger, Ben C. "The Hermeneutics of Obedience: A Study of Anabaptist Hermeneutics." *Direction* 6, no. 2 (1977): 19–31.

Packull, Werner O. *Mysticism and the Early South German-Austrian Anabaptist Movement, 1525–1531*. Scottsdale: Herald Press, 1977.

Penner, Kimberly L. "Mennonite Peace Theology and Violence against Women." *Conrad Grebel Review* 35, no. 3 (2017): 280–92.

Pitts, Jamie. "Baptism, Postliberal and Anabaptist Theologies, and the Ambiguity of Christian Practice." *Mennonite Quarterly Review* 90, no. 3 (July 2016): 323–44.

Pries, Edmund. *Anabaptist Oath Refusal: Basel, Bern, and Strasbourg, 1525–1538*. Thunder Bay: Pandora Press, 2023.

Prodi, Paolo. "Der Eid in Der Europäischen Verfassungsgeschichte: Zur Einführung." In *Glaube Und Eid*, edited by Paolo Prodi and Elisabeth Müller-Luckner, VII–XXIX. Munich: R. Oldenbourg, 1993.

Roberts, Laura Schmidt, Paul Martens, and Myron A. Penner, eds. *Recovering from the Anabaptist Vision: New Essays in Anabaptist Identity and Theological Method*. London: T&T Clark, 2020.

Rosner, David J. "Introductory Essay: Catastrophe and the Limits of Understanding." In *Catastrophe and Philosophy*, edited by David J. Rosner, xi–xxiii. Lanham: Lexington, 2018.

Roth, John D., ed. *Letters of the Amish Division: A Sourcebook*. Goshen: Mennonite Historical Society, 1993.

Roth, John D. "The Church 'Without Spot or Wrinkle' in Anabaptist Experience." In *Without Spot or Wrinkle: Reflecting Theologically on the Nature of the Church*, edited by Karl Koop and Mary H. Schertz, 7–25. Eugene: Wipf, 2015.

Roth, John D., and James M. Stayer, eds. *A Companion to Anabaptism and Spiritualism*. Leiden: Brill, 2007.

Said, Edward W. *Beginnings: Intention and Method*. New York: Columbia University Press, 1985.

Sattler, Michael. *Brüderlich Vereinigung Ezlicher Kinder Gottes: Sieben Artikel Betreffend*. publisher not identified, 1550. https://www.e-rara.ch/zuz/content/titleinfo/17792168 (accessed June 13, 2025).

Sattler, Michael. "Brüderliche Vereinigung Etlicher Kinder Gottes." In *Der Linke Flügel Der Reformation*, edited by Heinold Fast, 60–71. Bremen: Carl Schünemann, 1962.

Scarsella, Hilary Jerome, and Stephanie Krehbiel. "Sexual Violence: Christian Theological Legacies." *Religion Compass* 13 (2019): 1–13.

Schlachta, Astrid von. *Täufer: Von Der Reformation Ins 21. Jahrhundert*. Tübingen: Narr Francke Attempto, 2020.

Schmitt, Carl. *Political Theology: Four Chapters on the Concept of Sovereignty*. Chicago: University of Chicago Press, 2005.

Schmitt, Carl. *The Concept of the Political*. Chicago: University of Chicago Press, 2007.

Silving, Helen. "The Oath: I." *Yale Law Journal* 68, no. 7 (1959): 1329–90.

Snyder, C. Arnold. *Anabaptist History and Theology*. Kitchener: Pandora Press, 1995.

Snyder, C. Arnold. "The Birth and Evolution of Swiss Anabaptism (1520–1530)." *Mennonite Quarterly Review* 80, no. 3 (October 2006): 501–645.

Snyder, C. Arnold. "The Influence of the Schleitheim Articles on the Anabaptist Movement: An Historical Evaluation." *Mennonite Quarterly Review* 63, no. 3 (October 1989): 323–44.

Snyder, C. Arnold. *The Life and Thought of Michael Sattler*. Scottdale: Herald Press, 1984.

Snyder, C. Arnold. "The Schleitheim Articles in Light of the Revolution of the Common Man: Continuation or Departure?" *The Sixteenth Century Journal* 16, no. 4 (1985): 419–30.

Soelle, Dorothee. *Beyond Mere Obedience*. Cleveland: Pilgrim Press, 1982.

Steenwyk, Maki Ashe van. *The Unkingdom of God: Embracing the Subversive Power of Repentance*. Downers Grove: InterVarsity Press, 2013.

Stevens, Raphael, and Pablo Servigne. *How Everything Can Collapse: A Manual for Our Times*. Cambridge: Polity Press, 2020.

Strolovitch, Dara Z. *When Bad Things Happen to Privileged People: Race, Gender, and What Makes a Crisis in America*. Chicago: University of Chicago Press, 2024.

Strolovitch, Dara Z., and Chaya Y. Crowder. "Respectability, Anti-Respectability, and Intersectionally Responsible Representation." *PS: Political Science & Politics* 51, no. 2 (2018): 340–4.
Strübind, Andrea. *Eifriger Als Zwingli: Die Frühe Täuferbewegung in Der Schweiz.* Berlin: Duncker & Humblot, 2003.
Villegas, Isaac Samuel. "The Ecclesial Ethics of John Howard Yoder's Abuse." *Modern Theology* 37, no. 1 (January 2021): 191–214.
Wenger, John C. "The Schleitheim Confession of Faith." *Mennonite Quarterly Review* 19, no. 4 (1945): 243–53.
West, Traci C. *Wounds of the Spirit: Black Women, Violence, and Resistance Ethics.* New York: New York University Press, 1999.
Yoder, John H., ed. *The Legacy of Michael Sattler.* Classics of the Radical Reformation. Walden: Plough, 2019.

INDEX

abomination 13, 18, 63, 66, 72–5, 98
absence 10, 48, 50, 55–9, 61, 88, 90, 126, 136
action 20–3, 28, 34, 38, 81, 91, 102, 107, 116, 122, 134–7
Adorno, Theodor 70–1
Agamben, Giorgio 101–2, 105, 119, 121–3
Alizart, Mark 2
ambiguity 9, 10, 14–17, 20, 26, 28–9, 38–41, 45–6, 47, 52–5, 62, 72–3, 75, 79, 100, 108–9, 113, 120, 124, 125–6, 138
ambivalence 10, 11, 48, 59, 60, 97, 100, 102, 105, 109, 135–8
anabaptists 3–8, 13–15, 19, 24, 27, 29, 32–5, 42, 50, 54, 57, 59, 63, 64, 69, 77, 85, 87, 93–5, 109–11, 113, 115–18, 128–9, 133
anatheism 27
antagonism 7, 9, 11, 52, 64, 78, 87, 94, 99, 107, 129–30, 135
anthropocentrism 60
apocalypse 2, 4, 7, 42–3, 46, 66, 69, 130, 131, 133, 139
Arendt, Hannah 10, 14, 21–4, 28, 37, 60–1, 70, 71, 100–1, 106, 107
assemblage 62, 136
assembly 11, 39–40, 46, 47, 50, 56, 59, 88–90, 96, 127, 129, 137
assertion 2, 9, 15, 19, 31, 32, 34–46, 51, 53–4, 61, 90, 97, 104–5, 109, 117, 119, 122–3, 125, 134
authority 3, 5, 6, 10, 11, 13, 35, 39, 56, 81–91, 93–112, 115, 117, 118, 130, 133, 137

ban 10, 31–46, 54, 82, 85, 97, 104–5, 135

baptism 6, 8, 9–10, 13–29, 34–6, 40, 45, 47, 49–51, 54, 73, 77, 83, 104, 116, 117, 120, 135–6
  infant 6, 13, 16, 18, 27, 54
becoming 2, 11, 24, 37, 43, 48, 56
beginning 1, 4, 8, 10, 13–29, 31, 34–6, 42, 43, 64, 80, 84, 87, 134–5, 137, 139
  beginning-again 24–8, 77
  freedom as 20–4
  and origin 25, 28, 43
belief 8, 19, 125, 130
  see also Creed
belonging 1, 6, 8, 9, 15, 17, 53, 59–61, 75, 76, 79, 80, 98, 115, 117, 134, 137
Bender, Harold 15, 17
benedictine 7, 33, 84, 105
Benjamin, Walter 70
Benveniste, Émile 114, 121
Betz, Johannes 55
Bible 5, 85, 95
  Schleitheim's use of 18–19, 34, 49–52, 67, 83–4, 97–8, 103, 118–19
Biesecker-Mast, Gerald see Mast, Gerald
biopower 34, 101
bios see Zoe
Bloch, Ernst 42, 138
body
  bodily copresence 47–61, 136
  of Christ 19, 32, 47–61, 82–6, 88, 98, 136
  collective body 8, 9, 36–7, 38, 39, 41, 47, 52, 61, 75–6, 114, 115, 129
borders 9, 14–16, 27–8, 35, 40–1, 54–55, 64–5, 75, 79, 94, 99, 110, 119
  policing 9, 15, 53–5, 62

INDEX

bread, breaking of 10, 32, 33, 39, 47–61, 82, 84–5, 87, 88, 136
Burgess, John 13, 26
Burkholder, John Richard 93
Butler, Judith 44, 71

call 10, 55–9, 90–1
capacity 21–9, 32, 34, 35, 42, 61, 79, 88, 97, 99–105, 108, 111, 118, 120, 122–3, 137, 138
Caputo, John D. 37, 43
care 2, 10, 60, 82–7, 90, 104, 134–5, 137
catastrophe 2, 6–7, 68–71, 133–9
Catlin, Jonathon 68, 70
children 18, 27, 41
choice 6, 8, 14, 16–17, 20, 24, 27, 28, 77, 85
Christ *see* Jesus
Christ, perfection of 93, 96–7, 107, 109, 111, 118
climate 1, 65, 69
collaboration 2, 11, 20, 25, 56, 61, 94, 104, 108, 134–6
  divine-human 3, 10, 90
collapse 1, 64–5, 68–72, 77–8, 80, 134–8
collapsology 69
colonialism 4, 65, 68, 71, 101
communion 19, 32–3, 39, 47–61
  see also breaking of bread
confession 8, 108, 125
Confession of Faith in a Mennonite Perspective 95
conformism 14, 16, 31, 32, 40, 88, 91, 107, 133
contingency 9, 36, 37, 43, 61; 78
control 5, 14–17, 26, 31, 59–61, 78, 81, 89, 116, 121, 122, 124, 133
creed 8, 125 *see also* belief
crisis *see* catastrophe, collapse
curse 114, 122, 123, 138
cut 10, 15–17, 20, 26, 27, 29, 38, 135

death 22, 26, 34–6, 68, 71, 94, 96, 100, 101, 105, 108, 111, 123, 137
  of Christ 19–20
  of God 26

decision 10, 14–17, 20, 23–5, 69, 85, 88–9, 102, 105
democracy 1, 11, 14–15, 57–58, 81–3, 89–90, 102, 103, 106, 123, 137
devil 49–50, 54, 63, 66, 67, 72, 74, 79, 98, 99, 106–7, 128
disambiguation 46, 47, 53, 59, 62
discipline 8, 10, 11, 14, 18–19, 26, 31–46, 47, 51, 54, 61, 68, 76, 81–7, 105, 125, 135–6
distinctness 47, 52–3, 59, 62, 136
dominion 11, 17, 80, 114, 122–5, 138
Driedger, Michael 117
dualism 7, 40, 41, 49, 53–5, 58–9, 66–7, 72–5, 87, 108
Durch sich selbs 17, 20

ecclesio-political 8–11, 19, 36–8, 42–3, 58, 93–4, 126, 130
economy 1, 4–6, 8, 15, 60–1, 67, 69, 71–3, 76, 86, 116, 126, 134
empire 4, 5, 66, 70, 77, 104
emulation 94, 98, 103, 111, 137
equality 10, 21–4, 31, 89–90, 100, 102, 106, 108, 135, 138
ethics 8, 19, 94
evil 7, 10, 32, 49, 54, 63, 66–7, 69–70, 72–9, 107–9, 129, 136–7
ex nihilo 25, 29
ex profundis 25
exception 1, 17, 23–4, 28, 60, 101, 103
exclusion 31–2, 35, 40, 53, 54, 62, 64, 85, 105
excommunication 8, 10, 31–46, 47, 85, 104–5, 133, *see also* ban
expectation 7, 8, 32, 36, 42–3, 50–1, 131
exploitation 4, 60, 77–8, 80, 98, 104, 106, 126, 134, 138

faith 2, 5, 7–8, 13, 18, 22–4, 28, 37, 42–3, 46, 47, 50–1, 60, 66–7, 82, 87, 95, 98, 104, 110, 125, 128, 130
Fast, Heinold 20, 67
finality 41, 105, 134
Finger, Thomas 13, 16, 50
Foucault, Michel 34, 101

fragility 10, 24, 36, 37, 42–3, 45–6, 53, 85–6, 90, 107, 126, 134–5
freedom 5, 8, 10, 11, 14–17, 20–4, 26–9, 31–2, 38, 46, 60–1, 66, 76–80, 89, 100, 104, 106–7, 128, 133–7
future 2, 10, 25, 42, 45, 70–1, 78, 118, 125, 133, 138

god 1, 11, 20, 23–7, 29, 37, 48, 56, 66, 74–5, 79, 89–90, 104, 107–8, 114, 118–19, 126, 130, 134–9
   as sovereign 23, 27, 89, 94–6, 103–4, 108, 111, 113
god's temple 74–5, 79
gods 114
Goossen, Rachel Waltner 95
government 98, 99, 102, 111, 117
Gregory, Brad S. 6
greig, jason 16
ground 9, 57, 123
guarantee 1, 11, 31, 36–7, 42–3, 45, 67, 90, 104–5, 113–26, 134, 138

Haraway, Donna 2, 42
Hardt, Michael and Antonio Negri 11, 88–91, 102
Hauerwas, Stanley 64, 75
Heinzekehr, Justin 56
Holy Roman Empire 5
homogeneity 40, 75, 79, 88, 91, 136
hope 1–7, 22–3, 81, 129, 133
Hubmaier, Balthasar 32–4, 38–40, 48, 50, 63

imagination 11, 103, 107–8, 111, 137
immunity 10, 71, 79, 134
incompatibility 17, 94, 97, 98–9, 106–11, 119, 137
incompleteness 25, 29, 36, 47, 51–2, 55, 58, 61, 125, 134, 136
independence 10, 17, 21, 59, 61
individualism 10, 14, 16, 20, 128, 133, 135
inside/outside 9, 15, 19, 27, 35, 40–1, 51, 57, 62, 79, 102, 123, 134–5, 137–8
insistence 10, 37, 46–7, 53
instability 43, 108–9

interdependence 1–2, 10–11, 14, 17, 21, 25–8, 61, 69, 123, 130, 133, 135
Intergovernmental Panel on Climate Change 1
invitation 20, 22, 24, 27, 36, 43, 46, 56, 58, 89, 104, 135

Jesus 13, 18, 19, 23, 28, 34, 40, 50, 56–7, 67, 77, 84, 95, 97–8, 102–4, 109, 117, 121, 125, 129, 137
   as nonsovereign 11, 103–7, 111, 138

Kearney, Richard 26–7, 65
Keller, Catherine 1, 25–6, 37, 42, 44, 71, 103, 130
King, Richard 65
kingdom 4, 102
   of god 104, 117
   two-Kingdom theology 94, 111
Klee, Paul 70
Koontz, Gayle Gerber 82, 86–7
Kotsko, Adam 102, 123

language 68, 114, 122–4, 126
Latour, Bruno, and Dipesh Chakrabarty 80
Law 95–6, 98–9, 101, 103, 106, 110–11, 115, 138
   Mosaic Law 96, 97, 99, 101, 103, 109, 118
leadership 7, 10–11, 31, 53, 81–92, 137
Lefort, Claude 9, 57–8
Leu, Urs B., and Christian Scheidegge 6
liberalism 15, 17
liberation 66–7, 78, 87, 89, 135
loss 5, 7, 10, 29, 71, 77, 79, 136–7
loyalty 42, 53, 114–17, 120, 133

magistrates 96–8, 108–10, 118
Malm, Andreas 2
Marchart, Oliver 9, 52
Martens, Paul 3, 95
Mast, Gerald 64, 72, 78, 108–9
Mbembe, Achille 101
membership 6, 8–9, 15, 31, 34, 40–1, 136
mennonite(s) 3, 7, 13, 15–16, 33, 95
messiness *see* ambiguity

INDEX

metaphysics 36, 42–3, 45, 49, 53, 55–6, 58, 66, 73, 87, 104, 116, 118, 138
miracle 22–3, 28, 103
modern 1, 10, 14–17, 20, 28, 34, 52, 57–60, 71, 84, 94–6, 99–103, 106, 115, 135
modernity 2, 4, 14, 21, 34, 48, 60, 70–1, 101, 115
Mouffe, Chantal 9, 36, 43, 52, 130
Müller, Tadzio 69–70
Münster 7
Müntzer, Thomas 5, 33
Murray, Stuart 95
Myers, Ched 60

natality 22, 25–6
nature 29, 36, 38, 60, 72, 104
Negri, Antonio *see* Hardt, Michael and Antonio Negri
Neiman, Susan 69–71
New Zealand 66
Newness 22–9, 64, 135
nonhuman beings 17, 59–60, 73
nonresistance 31, 93
nonsovereignty 3, 10–11, 31–2, 40, 45–6, 58–61, 65, 72, 79, 82, 88–91, 93–4, 96–8, 102–8, 111, 113–14, 117, 124, 130, 134, 137–8
nonviolence 7, 95, 106, 110

O'Connell, Mark 66
oath 8, 11, 113–31, 138
  in history 114–18, 122–4
  promissory and assertory 119
obedience 66–7, 77, 93–6, 103–5, 108, 110, 111, 113, 115, 117, 124, 126, 134, 137
Old Testament 78, 96, 100, 118
Ollenburger, Ben C. 95
oneness 10, 39–40, 51, 88, 127, 136
order 9, 11, 16, 54, 58, 61, 67–71, 79, 86, 94, 96–111, 115–17, 123, 134, 137–8
outside *see* inside/outside

pacifism 67, 93, 99
  strong 95, 104
  weak 104 *see also* nonviolence
Packull, Werner O. 6

participation 20, 27, 50, 54, 56, 67, 76, 116–18, 125, 128, 138
pastors 5, 8, 10, 18, 81–91, 137
patriarchy 31, 86
Paul 48–50, 67, 82, 84, 119, 127
Peasants' War 5–7, 9, 33, 69, 79, 81, 89, 99, 109, 127
Penner, Kimberly L. 95
Penner, Myron A. 3, 95
Pitts, Jamie 19, 27–8
place 1, 48, 59–61
planet 1, 11, 59, 66, 79–80, 111
plurality 32, 40, 46, 57, 61, 91, 107
political, the 9, 52, 60, 89, 101, 106, 123, 130
Pope 18, 67, 76, 100
possibility 9, 24, 36–7, 39, 44, 53, 71, 108–9, 114, 120–1, 129
power, 5, 7, 20, 23, 34–8, 58, 67, 69, 78, 85, 89–90, 94, 97–108, 111, 115–16, 123, 126, 130
  distinct from violence 106
  place of (lefort) 57–8, 89
practice 2, 8–10, 13, 15–16, 19, 31–2, 36, 41–6, 48–9, 51–2, 54, 57, 59, 62, 73, 76, 82, 86–9, 100, 105, 110–11, 113–19, 124–6, 130, 135, 137–8
prayer 37, 82–7, 129
presence 10, 22–3, 33, 42, 47–62, 75, 85, 88, 90, 127, 136, 139
Prodi, Paolo 115–16
protest 64, 78, 80
provocation 27, 56, 90, 103
punishment 34, 41, 77, 96–7, 100, 105
purity 31, 39–41, 46, 55, 62, 129

reading 3, 11, 80, 85
recollection 32, 42–5
reformation 3–7, 48–9, 58, 71, 128
  radical 3–7
refuge 63–80, 104, 133, 137
reinvention 44–6, 55, 78, 110, 134
relatedness 8–9, 15, 17, 26, 59, 61, 77, 134
relationship 2, 14, 20, 26, 28, 34, 37, 39–40, 48, 59, 63, 65, 69, 71, 73, 75, 77, 80, 89, 91, 97, 99,

102, 103, 107–11, 124–6, 130, 137, 139
remembrance 48, 50, 51, 55–8
repetition 10, 11, 25, 31–46, 47, 52, 55, 105, 114, 124–6, 130, 134, 136, 138
representation 57–8, 82, 85, 87–8, 90, 137
re-presentation *see* representation
respectability 87
resurrection 8, 17, 19–28, 86, 135
 as *kainotes zoes* 26, 135
revolution 5–6, 42, 89, 96, 99, 106
Roberts, Laura Schmidt 3, 95
Rosner, David J. 68
Roth, John D. 3, 33–4
rupture 10, 69–70, 79, 126, 136–8

sacred 5, 48, 59, 114–15, 117
safety 1–2, 10, 26, 31, 39–40, 46, 63–5, 77, 105, 126, 133, 136
Said, Edward W. 25
sanction 10, 32, 34, 40–1, 44, 85, 96–7, 99, 101–5
Sattler, Michael 7–8, 33, 48, 84, 94
Scarsella, Hilary Jerome, and Stephanie Krehbiel 95
Schlachta, Astrid von 3–5
Schleitheim (place) 6
Schmitt, Carl 23, 52, 101, 103, 105
self-governance *see* self-organization
self-organization 11, 19, 21–5, 28, 37–8, 56–61, 77, 82, 88–91, 104, 135–7
separation 10, 14–16, 41, 53, 59, 60, 62, 63–80, 108–10, 113, 116, 136
separatism 7, 11, 60, 71–2, 75, 77–80, 93, 109, 113
Servigne, Pablo and Raphael Stevens 69–71
Silving, Helen 115–16, 119
Sin 8, 17–20, 24, 32–5, 38–41, 46, 84, 95, 97, 129
Snyder, C. Arnold 3–8, 13, 33, 53, 81, 84, 95, 99, 109, 116, 128, 130
Soelle, Dorothee 95
solidarity 69, 72, 79, 119, 133–6
sovereignty 10–11, 21, 23, 27–8, 57, 59–61, 72, 88–90, 94, 100–8, 111, 113, 116–20, 123–6, 133–4, 136–8
spirit 32–3, 50–1, 60, 67, 84, 95, 98, 106, 110, 127–8, 130
stability 6, 10, 42–5, 52, 54, 69, 126, 136
state 9, 15, 32, 34, 67, 69, 76, 93–111, 115–16
Stayer, James 3
Steenwyk, Maki Ashe van 104
Stevens, Raphael *see* Servigne, Pablo and Raphael Stevens
Strolovitch, Dara Z. 69, 87
Strübind, Andrea 6–7
struggle 5, 35–6, 38, 52, 55, 58, 78, 89, 116, 135
supplement 9–11, 47, 51–2, 56, 62, 69, 78, 90, 98–9, 109–10, 127, 129, 136
Switzerland 3, 5–7, 11, 33, 48, 115
Sword 11, 34, 67, 93–111, 123–4, 137–8
sympoiesis 2, 28, 38, 42, 48, 56–8, 60, 61, 94, 130, 133, 139

task 2, 10, 19, 28, 35–7, 43, 46, 79, 82–90, 94, 104, 108, 121, 131, 137
teaching 18–20, 34, 76, 84–5, 119
 "taught" 8, 17, 20, 22–4, 29, 85
temporality 7, 10, 32, 36, 41–6, 52, 105, 126, 130, 136
time 2, 8, 10, 17, 32, 35–6, 41–6, 57, 68–9, 124, 126, 136, 138
torah *see* law
totalitarianism 46, 58, 60, 71
tragic 9, 29, 35, 41, 45–6, 54, 73–74
troubling 40, 41, 54, 64, 73–5, 79, 97, 134, 139
truth 3, 11, 19, 36, 43, 57, 68, 75, 85, 98, 110, 114–15, 119–26, 129–30, 138

unfinishedness 2–3, 9–10, 38, 41, 43, 135–6
unity *see* oneness

Vereinigung 32, 40, 88, 128–30
Vereynigung see Vereinigung
Villegas, Isaac Samuel 95
virtuosity 21–2, 100

weakness 36–8, 104, 122–3, 128
Wenger, John C. 20, 33
West, Traci C. 95
women 7, 81, 95
work 10, 25, 29, 36–7, 40–1, 46, 49, 51, 73, 78, 83–90, 98, 104, 106, 111, 130, 133–4, 137
world 1, 4, 7, 10, 14–17, 21–3, 28–9, 34, 36, 38, 40–2, 48–54, 59–61, 63–80, 82, 87, 90–1, 95, 96, 98, 106–10, 113–26, 127, 129–31, 133–8
worship 33, 49–50, 68, 85

Yoder, John H. 94–5, 99, 127
  as perpetrator of sexual violence 94–5

Zoe/Bios 26, 28, 79, 86, 126, 135, 137–9
Zwingli, Huldrich 4–6, 48, 50